# FREED TO BE ME: A SERVANT BY DESIGN

# FREED to Be *Me*:
## A Servant by Design

Adv. Chr. Res.

### Dr. Robert S. Maris, Ph.D.
#### with Anna Maris Kirkes, MFA

Copyright © 2014 Transpersonal Technologies, L.L.C.
All rights reserved.

# FREED TO BE ME: A SERVANT BY DESIGN

## DR. ROBERT S. MARIS, PH.D. WITH ANNA MARIS KIRKES, MFA

Copyright © 2014 Transpersonal Technologies, L.L.C.
All rights reserved.
Design/Creative Direction by: Sarah E. Duet
Illustration by: Katie J. Winningham

Paperback Edition ISBN: 978-0-9905074-2-0
E-book Edition ISBN: 978-0-9905074-3-7

*Freed to Be Me: A Servant by Design* is largely based upon Dr. Taibi Kahler's *Process Communication Model®* and adapted by Dr. Maris into the *Process Spiritual Model™*. (Original Process Communication Model® Copyright © 1982-1995 by Kahler Communications, Inc.) No part of *Freed to Be Me: A Servant by Design* may be printed or reproduced by any means—electronic, mechanical, recording, or photographic—or portrayed, translated, or included in any information storage and retrieval system without permission in writing from the publisher. All graphics within this work are the trademark property of Transpersonal Technologies, L.L.C.

Scripture quotations are taken from THE HOLY BIBLE, NEW INTERNATIONAL VERSION®, NIV® Copyright © 1973, 1978, 1984, 2011 by Biblica, Inc.® Used by permission. All rights reserved worldwide. Other Scripture quotations are taken from the Holy Bible, New Living Translation, copyright ©1996, 2004, 2007 by Tyndale House Foundation. Used by permission of Tyndale House Publishers, Inc., Carol Stream, Illinois 60188. All rights reserved. Scripture quotations from THE MESSAGE. Copyright © by Eugene H. Peterson 1993, 1994, 1995, 1996, 2000, 2001, 2002. Used by permission of Tyndale House Publishers, Inc. Scripture taken from the NEW AMERICAN STANDARD BIBLE®, Copyright © 1960, 1962, 1963, 1968, 1971, 1972, 1973, 1975, 1977, 1995 by The Lockman Foundation. Used by permission.

Want to learn more?
Transpersonal Technologies, L.L.C. provides a number of online personality inventories designed to help individuals explore, understand, and appreciate their own unique designs more fully. To learn more about the inventories available or to take the *Freed to Be Me: A Servant By Design*™ *Profile*, visit us at:

www.servantsbydesign.com

Also on the web:
Facebook: Servants by Design
Twitter: servantbydesign

## TO LAURA

Whose grace and unconditional love
give us the courage to want to become
the best versions of ourselves

# Table of Contents

01 | THE ROLE OF THE SERVANT
02 | THE PROCESS SPIRITUAL MODEL™
03 | CHARACTER STRENGTHS (PART I)
04 | CHARACTER STRENGTHS (PART II)
05 | PERSONALITY STRUCTURE
06 | PERCEPTIONS
07 | PSYCHOLOGICAL NEEDS
08 | PHASING: REWIRING
09 | DISTRESS: THE GREAT DISTORTION
10 | REDEEMED DESIGNS
11 | MANY MEMBERS, ONE BODY

APPENDICES
A | THE GOOD NEWS
B | PCM® KEY TERMS

# Foreword

You, our reader, are a precious and unique creation of God. So am I. So is each and every individual you encounter. Yet all too frequently you receive the message—whether directly or indirectly—that who you are is not quite good enough. You "should" be thinner, stronger, taller, shorter, richer, smarter, kinder, more patient, more intellectual, more nurturing, more fun, more serious, more spiritual....and the list goes on. We decided to write *Freed to Be Me: A Servant by Design* to add a voice of hope to this conversation about "who you are" by highlighting *who God is*.

You are a glorious being made to reflect God's image. In the eyes of the One who made you, you are loved and accepted just as you are. You have intentionally been given certain gifts and not others, and God has given you a purpose, a calling, and a mission to fulfill. You can lay down the heavy burden of pretending, feeling guilty, performing to prove you are lovable, competent, valuable, or attempting to earn safety, a sense of belonging, and acceptance. You can have the "life abundant" that Jesus promised. It is our prayer for you that as you embrace God's design for you, His delight in you, and the good work for which He has equipped and called you, you can take up the easy yoke of freedom—the freedom to be exactly who God created you to be—His Beloved Servant, by Design!

By His grace and to His Glory become fully yourself,
**Robert Maris and Anna Maris Kirkes**

## 01 | The Role of the Servant

*Oh yes, you shaped me first inside, then out;*
*you formed me in my mother's womb.*
*I thank you, High God—you're breathtaking!*
*Body and soul, I am marvelously made!*
*I worship in adoration—what a creation!*
*You know me inside and out,*
*you know every bone in my body;*
*you know exactly how I was made, bit by bit,*
*how I was sculpted from nothing into something.*
*Like an open book, you watched me grow*
*from conception to birth;*
*all the stages of my life*
*were spread out before you,*
*the days of my life all prepared*
*before I'd even lived one day.*[1]

To be known is perhaps our greatest desire and our greatest fear. How could someone see who we truly are—confronting the cracks in our souls, the wounds we carry in our hearts, the selfishness that at times rears its head, the self-doubt that lies deceptively dormant—and yet still love us? To be known fully and to still be loved—that is *true* freedom, a redemptive release from a perpetual prison of pretending, perfectionism, and despair.

---

[1] Psalm 139:13-16, The Message.

What if the One who created you, who knows exactly how you were made, offers you this kind of freedom? He who knows you inside and out "is living among [us]. He will take delight in you with gladness. With His love, He will calm all your fears. He will rejoice over you with joyful songs."[2] Can your heart comprehend this Good News? God **delights in you!** This God who knows all your hiding places and secret shames, who is present in your greatest failures and victories—this God declares you to be "marvelously made!" He sees and knows who you have been and who you are. But He also knows who you have been created to be; He knows who you *already* are—redeemed for His glory, adopted into His family, empowered by His Spirit, and created for His good purposes.

On one level, this is a book about personality—about exploring who you are and who you have been created to be. But ultimately, this book is only one chapter that fits into the much, much larger story of God's masterful creation and ultimate redemption of humankind. Thus to understand who you truly are in the larger story, we must begin by looking to the main character of the story of humanity—God Himself.

## Claiming our Roles as His Image-Bearers

Our first introduction to men and women in the scope of creation occurs in Chapter 1 of the book of Genesis (a word literally meaning "beginnings" or "origins"). Regarding God's creation of humankind, the Genesis author uses these descriptive words: "God spoke: 'Let us make human beings in our image, make them reflecting our nature.'"[3] From the very beginning of the Creation story, we as humans are defined as Image-Bearers—beings intentionally created as mirrors to reflect God's character. This capacity and calling to reflect God's image is at the core of who we are, central to our identities, crucial to our purpose. This identity, woven into the very fabric of our human nature, resonates with a longing and awareness deep in the core of our design. We were created to bear, reflect, and share God's glory with one another. The calling to be Image-Bearers of Jehovah God continues into

---

[2] Zephaniah 3:17, New Living Translation.
[3] Genesis 1:26-28, The Message.

the New Testament for first century followers of Jesus Christ, as Paul instructs the church at Ephesus to "put on the new self, created to be like God in true righteousness and holiness" and to "be imitators of God, therefore, as dearly loved children, and live a life of love."[4]

This was not just a calling for the ancient Israelites. It was not only for first-century followers of Jesus. The calling and privilege of bearing God's image extends to us, now, in this present moment.

## EMBRACING OUR ROLES AS HIS GRATEFUL SERVANTS

Our purpose within the Creator's grand design calls us to reflect His image, His character, and His qualities as His unique creation. Yet this calling to bear God's image inspires and sparks a corresponding change in lifestyle—*who we are* is intricately and intimately tied to *what we do*. By claiming our identity as Image Bearers, we are freed to embrace our corresponding roles as Servants of the Living God.

Our roles as servants in God's kingdom are as integral and ancient as our identities as Image-Bearers. In the Garden, God gave Adam a charge as His servant over creation: "Be fruitful and multiply. Fill the earth and govern it. Reign over the fish…the birds…and the small animals that scurry over the ground."[5] As an Image-Bearer, Adam was invited by God to be uniquely involved in overseeing creation—participating in its sustainment and care over time. He was directed to serve God in specific ways, with particular functions.

Later followers of Jesus—including Paul, Peter, James, and Jude—identified themselves as servants of God as well. In his letters to several early churches, the apostle Paul tapped into the greater meaning of what it means to serve God with whole heart and mind and soul by identifying himself as a "bondservant" of Christ. Paul's use of the word *bondservant* powerfully resonated with the culture that he directly addressed, referencing a particular position and way of life found within ancient society. By utilizing the word "bondservant" to describe his devotion to Christ, Paul gives incredible insight into how we can fully embrace our God-

---

[4] Ephesians 4:23; 5:1, New International Version.
[5] Genesis 1:28, New Living Translation.

given roles as servants.

In ancient Hebrew culture, selling oneself as a servant to a fellow Israelite was sometimes the only viable option for individuals who saw no other way to survive. Becoming an indebted servant gave a means to provide for one's family and maintain property and land with the possibility of better days ahead.[6] This kind of indebted servant mortgaged his property and worked for six years with the understanding that at the end of that time, he would be released from the master having paid his debt. The Torah makes a special provision, however, for servants who wanted to voluntarily continue their servitude—bondservants:

> "But if the servant declares, 'I love my master and my wife and my children and do not want to go free,' then his master must take him before the judges. He shall take him to the door or the doorpost and pierce his ear with an awl. Then he will be his servant for life."[7]

This shift from servant to bondservant marked a radical choice of lifestyle—one who was working to pay a debt for a limited period of time literally dedicated his life to the master. It was an intentional, free choice. A choice to stay. In this case, a covenant was cut—a solemn, binding agreement made between master and servant before the elders in which the servant's ear was pierced with an awl as a sign of his or her obedience for a lifetime. This bondservant was then responsible for responding to the master's call at any and every time. In effect, he gave up his individual will and right to a life apart from the master. In return, the master promised to abundantly meet the needs of his bondservant, providing shelter, food, clothing, protection, a sense of home, and meaningful work. This bondservant was *grafted into* the master's family and invited into the master's heritage. The bondservant's position was one of honor, of value, of the master's priceless trust.

What does this idea of a bondservant have to do with us? We too have an incalculable debt to be paid. Like the farmer who has stacked up too much debt to repay even over a lifetime of service, our very lives, our eternal souls, are at

---

[6] Bondservant, Slave. In *Today's Bible* [website]. From Smith, W. (1884). Slave. In *Smith's Bible Dictionary*. Retrieved from http://www.biblereferenceguide.com/keywords/bondservant.html
[7] Exodus 21:5-6, New International Version.

stake as the price for sin against a holy God. No amount of hard work, good faith effort, or time will cancel our debt of sin. The wages of this sin, as Paul says to the church at Rome, is death.[8]

Enter upon this hopeless state of humanity a good, compassionate, and merciful Master. Rather than angrily holding our debt over our heads, or wrenching payment for our sins through brutal, endless servitude or suffering, or simply washing His hands of the whole matter and looking away, God invites us to become His bondservants. He extends a *relational* invitation to join Him in the work of His kingdom…a place where beautiful things are being made from the dust, where the lame walk and the blind see, where swords and spears are beaten into plowshares and pruning hooks.[9] In return for the surrender of our lives to Him, He promises to care for us as His own children. We are not servants relegated to a back entrance or treated with cold unfamiliarity. God adopts us into His family as His own sons and daughters, forever sheltered under the light of His love and care with all the freedoms of the children of the Master. He does not promise us prosperity or a life void of difficulty. But He promises us Himself—a relationship with the Living God that floods our lives with purpose, meaning, and love.

How then do we go about reflecting God's image? What does it look like to gratefully embrace servanthood? And how does all of this relate to a discussion on personality?

## As Image Bearers…

### *We do so uniquely.*

Though we as human beings share the divine calling to bear God's image, we fulfill this purpose in distinctive and unique ways according to our particular personalities, strengths, weaknesses, and stories. Far from being a haphazard collection of atoms, the sum of random experiences, or the product of behavioral reinforcement, you have been individually endowed by a good Creator with a *unique design*. Actually believing this truth—the glorious reality that you are uniquely, specifically, lovingly designed

---

[8] Romans 3:23, New International Version.
[9] See Micah 4:3.

*with purpose, on purpose*—transforms everything about the way you live. Living into this unique design revolutionizes your view of yourself, opening up new avenues of freedom and acceptance of self and others. Many of us spend a great deal of precious energy running after a vague image of who we *should* be and end up feeling unfulfilled, frustrated, and unknown. When you better understand and claim who **you** were created to be, you can begin to wholeheartedly live into the fullness of that design and join with King David in gratefully proclaiming: "Body and soul, I am marvelously made!" Rather than trying to become someone other than yourself, you are free to gratefully live into who you *already are*.

## *We do so imperfectly.*

How do we reconcile this idea that we are created in God's image and called to reflect His character with the stark reality of our marred, imperfect lives? Jesus alone has perfectly reflected the character of God, unstained by sin. "He [Jesus] is the image of the invisible God, the firstborn over all creation…For God was pleased to have all his fullness dwell in him."[10] The authors of Scripture unflinchingly and unapologetically portray the rest of the characters within God's story in the midst of major weaknesses, glaring failures, significant doubt, and deep woundedness.

So what's one to conclude from this list of motley characters? Certainly we can say with increasing confidence that God is gracious and patient with people who offer less than stellar performances…over and over again. But might we also venture to say that God is interested in more than just work, more than accomplishment, more than checking off a list of tasks? This by no means downplays God's fiercely passionate and steadfast commitment to the work of an unimaginable redemption—not just of humankind but also of creation in its entirety, right down to the groaning earth. But His use of human beings in the midst of our imperfections highlights His desire for relationship with us.

In addition to this grand restoration (or perhaps as part of it), God is in the business of shaping character and investing in relationships with people—messy, stubborn, ill-qualified,

---

[10] Colossians 1:15, 19, New International Version.

inefficient, incomplete people who must be renovated from the inside out. Infinitely valuable individuals who, at the core of their humanity, still bear a divine image no matter how blurred, broken, or buried. Theologian Dallas Willard spoke eloquently to both the ruin and glory of the human soul:

> "G.K. Chesterton somewhere says that the hardest thing to accept in the Christian religion is the great value it places upon the individual soul. Still older Christian writers used to say that God has hidden the majesty of the human soul from us to prevent our being ruined by vanity. This explains why even in its ruined condition a human being is regarded by God as something immensely worth saving. Sin does not make it worthless, but only lost. And in its lostness it is still capable of great strength, dignity and heartbreaking beauty and goodness."[11]

For all the distortions and twisting of the initial image present in ourselves and in our world, we can discern the tracings (however faint) of a reflection smudged by sin but divine in nature. We see something infinite and beautiful in the gaze of a child. We glimpse supernatural compassion in a woman like Mother Teresa who reflected a divine empathy. We respect a commitment to justice in others that echoes God's heart as an advocate of the helpless. With grace-empowered eyes, we can see glimpses of our God given roles as Image-Bearers in the "ordinary" people around us.

## *We do so by grace and through the Spirit.*

We depend upon God's grace and power to make His image increasingly clear in us. On our own, we are powerless to "fix" ourselves and heal our own wounds. Nor can we attempt to fix each other without actually deepening the wounds we are trying to heal. This would be as impossible and damaging as collecting shards of a broken mirror and willing them to come back together. We depend upon the *Spirit* as the source of our discernment and empowerment; we also trust the Author of life to redeem every aspect of our story. As Paul encourages the believers in Rome,

> "This resurrection life you received from God is not a timid, grave-tending life. It's adventurously expectant,

---
[11] Willard, Dallas. (2002). *Renovation of the Heart* (pp. 46). Colorado Springs, CO: NavPress.

greeting God with a childlike 'What's next, Papa?' God's Spirit touches our spirits and confirms who we really are. We know who he is, and we know who we are: Father and children."[12] As we learn to dwell in this kind of Spirit-filled, Spirit-identified life, we are freed to live into and serve out of our unique designs with joyous, trusting abandonment. By grace and through the Spirit, we are adventurously expectant.

*We do so in community.*

    Theologians have scratched their heads for years over the mystery of the Trinity—a God who is three in one, all separate yet unified. However, this mysterious Trinity does reveal a crucial aspect of God's unchanging character: God is inherently relational. In a divine, mysterious, supernatural way, He is and has ever been in relationship with Himself. God has also persistently pursued relationship with us as human beings, from walking in the Garden with Adam and Eve, to seeking them even after they chose disobedience and separation, to providing Christ His Son as a perfect sacrifice paving the way back to intimacy and connection with Him. History rings out with an epic, passionate, relational pursuit of God for His people. Thus if we are to reflect God's image, we cannot do it alone. We can only fully reflect God's image in the context of relationships and as members of a community.

    In his honest work, *Blue Like Jazz*, Donald Miller talks about a conversation with his pastor Rick in which Rick strongly urges Don to move from a lifestyle of isolation and self-reflection to one of community. "I should have people around bugging me and getting under my skin because without people I could not grow—I could not grow in God, and I could not grow as a human," Miller states after trying out this sometimes uncomfortable idea of living communally, in dependence on and connection to others. "We are born into families, [Rick] said, and we are needy at first as children because God wants us together, living among one another…you are a human, and you need other people in your life in order to be healthy."[13]

    In community, our unique designs interact with those of our brothers and sisters to provide a fuller, richer reflection of

---

[12] Romans 8:14-16, The Message.
[13] Miller, Donald. (2003). *Blue Like Jazz* (pp.173). Nashville, TN: Thomas Nelson, Inc.

God's character—His patience, provision, justice, grace, forgiveness, and more. The book *TrueFaced* describes this God-reflecting community in this way: "This community expects and anticipates imperfection. Yes we honor others in the community of saints, but we also face the reality of each other's sin. We applaud vulnerability and view godliness as something much more than the presence of good behavior and the absence of bad behavior...no one feels a need to hide, for no one's parading his or her own righteousness. Everyone feels safe to be real and alive."[14] Living alongside and in community with others is God's design for us as individuals bearing His image and serving His kingdom. We will explore how this aspect of our unique designs expresses itself in relationships later in this book as we consider what it means to be the Body of Christ.

We are Image-Bearers of the Creator of the Universe. But we are also servants of the Living God, invited into relationship with Him as a loving Master and part of His plan for redemption.

## As Grateful Servants...

*We serve with joy and gratitude.*

Enthusiastic, generous service overflows from the individual who is confidently grateful for his or her secure place in God's family and unique purpose in His work. The bondservant serves joyfully not only because he or she experiences the Master's gracious provisions for tangible needs, but also because serving the Master means an invitation into a bigger, more meaningful life story. Paul encourages the church at Ephesus and future members of the larger Church of God with these words regarding service:

> "FOR WE ARE GOD'S HANDIWORK,
> CREATED IN CHRIST JESUS TO DO GOOD WORKS,
> WHICH GOD PREPARED IN ADVANCE FOR US TO DO."[15]

This offers me incredible comfort, to know that God uniquely crafted me for good, meaningful work in His kingdom. Yet before Paul mentions these "good works

---

[14] Thrall, B., McNicol, B., & Lynch, J.S. (2004). *TrueFaced* (pp. 108). Colorado Springs, CO: NavPress.
[15] Ephesians 2:10, New International Version.

prepared in advance," he situates us in relation to who we are and who God is. We are God's handiwork, designed and molded with the detailed care of a Master Craftsman. As Architect of our designs, He knows we will best fulfill our purposes when we serve out of an acknowledgement and celebration of His handiwork in our unique designs. When we boldly live into and joyously serve from our unique designs, we come alive in powerful, Kingdom-building, soul-expanding kinds of ways. Irenaeus, a second-century follower of Jesus, describes the fulfillment of our purpose in this way: "The glory of God is the human being *fully alive*, and the life of the human consists in beholding God."[16]

## *We do so willingly.*

The position of bondservant is one of considerable honor. The bondservant is entrusted with matters central to the Master's heart. In actuality, the bondservant *himself* is central to God's heart. Soak in Jesus' words to His dearest friends, the disciples (and to us who too are His disciples):

> "I no longer call you servants, because a servant does not know his master's business. Instead, I have called you friends, for everything that I learned from my Father I have made known to you. You did not choose me, but I chose you and appointed you so that you might go and bear fruit—fruit that will last."[17]

As servants of God, we serve "not reluctantly or under compulsion,"[18] but rather with the joyous expectancy of those who understand they are radically loved, with the confident humility of those whose lives have been and are continually being transformed, with the willingness of the ransomed and redeemed.

## *We do so purposefully.*

Imagine a lump of clay determined to make itself into a pot. Without an axis on which to turn, without the strong, guiding hands of the Potter, the clay is helpless to form itself. As the Psalmist says, "For it is He who made us, and not we

---

[16] Irenaeus in *Against the Heresies of Gnosticism*. Qtd by Manning, Brennan (2000). *Ruthless Trust: The Ragamuffin's Path To God* (pp. 48). New York, NY: Harper Collins.
[17] John 15:15-16, New International Version.
[18] 2 Corinthians 9:7, New International Version.

ourselves."[19] No amount of will or potential can change this inanimate object from nothing to something. The process demands an intelligent Creator, a center from which to take shape. "For it is God who works in you to will and to act according to His good purpose."[20] This "good purpose" is intricately tied to a beautifully shaped, *intentional* design. The same Potter who initiated this transformation from nothing to something with the skillful shaping of an Artist—this same Potter must have a vision in mind for this clay-turned-craft. Though He starts with a lump of clay, He intends to make a flower vase, or a coffee mug, or a set of dinner plates, or a mask. This ceramic has a function—purposeful function—that stems from an intentional, effective design.

Throughout this book, we will look at the Potter's design in our individual personalities as powerful indicators of what we were made to do. For example, as you get a clearer picture in Chapter 4 of your greatest Strengths, you will notice certain professions, activities, and ways of being in the world will either allow you to express and act out of this functional design or perhaps limit you. If you're made like a coffee mug, it follows that holding coffee just might be your thing!

## *We do so with others.*

> "Two are better than one, because they have a good return for their labor: if either of them falls down, one can help the other up."
> "Though one may be overpowered, two can defend themselves. A cord of three strands is not quickly broken."[21]

We need one another in order to live out our unique designs. Throughout the spread of the early Church, individuals joined under the unity of Christ to form partnerships and greater communities. In sending His disciples away from Jerusalem and out into the larger world, Jesus sent them two by two in order that they might support one another. The apostle Paul often took along traveling companions on his missionary journeys, including Barnabas, John Mark, and Silas. Paul then wrote letters to partners in

---

[19] Psalm 100:3, New American Standard Version.
[20] Philippians 2:13, New International Version.
[21] Ecclesiastes 4:9-10, 12, New International Version.

churches whom he relied upon to sustain the growing body of believers in their communities. Paul's friends Priscilla and Aquila were a husband and wife team who served together as effective partners in early Church ministry.

What can we draw from these examples? We are not seeking a formula for how to build churches or do ministries, but rather affirming that we are called to work *together* in building the Kingdom of God. And we need the abundance of gifts, strengths, and even weaknesses that each individual brings in order to truly and lovingly serve God, each other, and the world. It is in our differences that we work out the living, breathing reality of God. We will talk more in depth about how we serve together as what Christ calls His Body, the Church, in Chapter 11.

## *We serve and co-labor with God and experience His Presence.*

Serving God is always a matter of a love relationship with Him, not a list of "to-do's." He does not demand work from us like an employer dictating to his employees. In their study on *Experiencing God*, authors Henry Blackaby and Claude King explain that as we serve God, we come to know and love Him more. Blackaby and King assert, "God is always at work around you."[22] God invites us to serve with Him—to join Him in the places where He is already at work—as a way to allow us to experience, know, and love Him more. When we are involved in God's work with Him, we feel His presence among us. We might sense His mercy or His justice compelling and strengthening us as we work. We depend upon His power and His direction to sustain us. Far from servants who get their hands dirty while the master sits comfortably at a distance, we join God where He is already working, hands in the dirt, stooping down in His gentleness and strength to make His people great.[23]

## *We do so expecting eternal reward.*

Jesus indicated that serving Him faithfully and willingly results in eternal reward. This is different than performing works to earn your salvation or to try to get God to like you

---

[22] Blackaby, Henry T. & King, Claude V. (1990). *Experiencing God: Knowing and Doing the Will of God* [Workbook]. Nashville, TN: Lifeway Christian Resources.
[23] See Psalm 18:35.

more. Remember, serving alongside God is a matter of relationship—an invitation to know and love Him better. When you accept Jesus's redeeming work on the cross, you are fully justified, fully saved, fully covered by the blood and righteousness of Christ. But we do have a choice whether or not to be faithful in the service to which God has called us. Jesus told this story to His disciples about the reward for faithful service:

> "Again, it will be like a man going on a journey, who called his servants and entrusted his wealth to them. To one he gave five bags of gold, to another two bags, and to another one bag, each according to his ability. Then he went on his journey. The man who had received five bags of gold went at once and put his money to work and gained five bags more. So also, the one with two bags of gold gained two more. But the man who had received one bag went off, dug a hole in the ground and hid his master's money.
> After a long time the master of those servants returned and settled accounts with them. The man who had received five bags of gold brought the other five. 'Master,' he said, 'you entrusted me with five bags of gold. See, I have gained five more.'
> His master replied, 'Well done, good and faithful servant! You have been faithful with a few things; I will put you in charge of many things. Come and share your master's happiness!'"[24]

In Jesus's parable, each servant was entrusted with a certain amount of money, representing literal financial wealth or even the wealth of talent, gifts, or circumstances. Each of the three servants had the opportunity to serve God with what he had been given or to hoard these gifts for himself. The Master commended the first two servants who served faithfully and boldly, declaring, "Well done, good and faithful servant!" Then the Master promised that these servants would receive more chances for service and more responsibilities in the kingdom of God as a result of their faithfulness.[25]

---

[24] Matthew 25: 14-30, New Living Translation.
[25] Interestingly, the servant who had been given only one bag of money buried it in the ground out of fear of the Master, believing that if he lost any of what he had been given he would be punished. It is the man's decision to hoard out of mistrust that keeps him from the eternal reward and the encouraging proclamation, "Well done, good and faithful servant."

We have been made to reflect God's image to ourselves and to each other. We have been called and given the gift of serving God as our good and loving Master. As you grow in understanding and appreciating God's unique intention in creating you, may you know the joy of living as His Servant by Design.

# 02 | *The Process Spiritual Model*™

Throughout the course of this book, you will gain a framework for understanding and appreciating individual personality gifting and the ways in which these unique, God-given qualities give color and life to our relationships, ministries, and the Kingdom of God. This God-intentioned design includes our perceptions and experiences of others, of ourselves and of God—and how these perceptions shape how we interact with the world. It is important to state that this framework is not exclusive truth or the *right* way to think about personality, relationships, and the like. It is simply *one* way of cultivating a deeper sense of identity and purpose that has proven beneficial, eye-opening, and freeing for many individuals, churches, organizations, etc. across the world.[26]

## PROCESS COMMUNICATION® AND PROCESS SPIRITUAL™ MODELS

The *Process Spiritual Model*™ is based upon Dr. Taibi Kahler's original *Process Communication Model*® [27] as interpreted through a Christian worldview.[28] At its core, the *Process Spiritual Model*™ seeks to place your understanding of personality in the larger context of seeing God at work

---

[26] For more information about how PCM® and PSM™ have been used both nationally and internationally, consult the foreword.
[27] Kahler, T. (1979). *Process Communications Model*™ *(In Brief)*. Little Rock, AR: Taibi Kahler Associates, Inc.; adapted by permission.
[28] Maris, R. (1996). *Your Great Design*. Little Rock, AR: Transpersonal Technologies, L.L.C..; Maris, R. and Richardson, J. (2002). *Servants by Design Profile*. Little Rock, AR: Transpersonal Technologies, L.L.C.; From Kahler, T. (1979). *Process Communications Model*™ *(In Brief)*. Little Rock, AR: Taibi Kahler Associates, Inc.; adapted by permission.

within your unique design and your life. As you become increasingly aware of who He has intended you to be, your desire and freedom to serve Him with joyous abandon flourishes. On an interpersonal level, the common language about similarities and differences introduced in the *PCM*® and *PSM*™[29] can lead to clearer, more successful communication in your relationships, resulting in deeper intimacy and a greater appreciation for your spouse, children, friends, or colleagues. On an individual level, an increased understanding of how you have been specially gifted and created will lead you to a richer sense of personal worth and gratitude. It is our hope and prayer that in looking at life through the particular framework laid out in this book, you might gain bigger eyes, a deeper appreciation for your gifts as well as the strengths of others, and an increasingly vibrant hope that you are made with purpose, on purpose.

## *Elements of Your Design*

Through a theoretical, research based lens, the *Process Communication Model*® and the subsequent *Process Spiritual Model*™ seek in part simply to categorize those characteristics and qualities that are present in all individuals and tend to cluster together in predictable patterns. In Dr. Kahler's original work on *PCM*®, he was able to identify and describe six distinct **Personality Types**.[30] Kahler noted four different but interconnected aspects of these Personality Types to explore in greater depth:

**1) *Character Strengths*** —Dr. Kahler's original research identified three key Character Strengths for each Personality Type.[31] These Character Strengths are at the core of who we are, how we define ourselves, what we are "good at," and how we are most likely perceived by others.

**2) *Perceptions*** —Dr. Kahler labeled each Personality Type's primary mode of viewing the world as one's Perception.[32] Our Perception refers to the God-given lens through which we experience life, distinctly shaping how we see ourselves,

---

[29] PCM®- Process Communication Model; PSM™- Process Spiritual Model.
[30] From Kahler, T. (1979). *Process Communications Model*™ *(In Brief)*. Little Rock, AR: Taibi Kahler Associates, Inc.; adapted by permission.
[31] From Kahler, T. (1988, 1992, 2000, 2004). *The Mastery of Management*. Little Rock, AR: Taibi Kahler Associates, Inc.
[32] From Kahler, T. (1988, 1992, 2000, 2004). *The Mastery of Management*. Little Rock, AR: Taibi Kahler Associates, Inc.

others, God, and the world around us.

**3) Psychological Needs**[33]—Dr. Kahler discovered that each of the six Personality Types has particular Psychological Needs, which must be met in order for an individual to function in a healthy way.[34] Considering Kahler's concept of Psychological Needs through the lens of the *Process Spiritual Model*™, we will look at how God has designed us to be uniquely energized and motivated, allowing us to participate in healthy work, ministry, and relationships. We will also consider how desiring these Psychological Needs can open new doors of dependence and trust in God to provide for these Needs.

**4) Distress**—Dr. Kahler postulated that when we do not receive our Psychological Needs in healthy ways, we fall into predictable patterns of attempting (often unconsciously) to meet these needs in unhealthy ways.[35] Kahler identified observable behavioral "clues," or **Drivers**,[36] that indicate a potential descent into misbehavior and negative emotions known as the **Distress Sequence**.[37] In the *Process Spiritual Model*™, we will uncover and explore the **Deceptions**[38] that precede these Driver behaviors. These **Deceptions**—lies or falsehoods occurring at the level of the heart—indicate that we are believing a lie about our worth, security, and safety. When we believe and orient our lives around these Deceptions, we depend upon ourselves by distorting our greatest strengths rather than relying on God to meet our needs.

## More than a "Type"

For teaching purposes, we will initially view the six Personality Types as separate from one another, exploring each Type as a one-dimensional "stereoType" or caricature. However, the six "pure" Personality Types that Dr. Kahler identified do not exist in isolation; instead, they are more like

---

[33] From Kahler, T. (1988, 1992, 2000, 2004). *The Mastery of Management*. Little Rock, AR: Taibi Kahler Associates, Inc.
[34] From Kahler, T. (1996, 2012). *The Process Communication Model® Seminar—Seminar One: Core Topics*. (pp. 49). Little Rock, AR: Kahler Communications, Inc.
[35] From Kahler, T. (1996, 2012). *The Process Communication Model® Seminar—Seminar One: Core Topics*. (pp. 57). Little Rock, AR: Kahler Communications, Inc.
[36] From Kahler, T. (1988, 1992, 2000, 2004). *The Mastery of Management*. Little Rock, AR: Taibi Kahler Associates, Inc.; Kahler, T. (1996, 2012). *The Process Communication Model® Seminar—Seminar One: Core Topics*. Little Rock, AR: Kahler Communications, Inc.
[37] From Kahler, T. (1996, 2012). *The Process Communication Model® Seminar—Seminar One: Core Topics*. (pp. 57). Little Rock, AR: Kahler Communications, Inc.
[38] From Maris, R. (1996). *Your Great Design*. Little Rock, AR: Transpersonal Technologies, L.L.C.

different facets of a complete and complex personality. Dr. Kahler discovered that, in reality, we are each a distinct combination of all six Personality Types, arranged like floors in a building or "Personality Condominium."[39]

In the *Process Communication Model*®, the particular stacking and arrangement of these six Personality Types is known as one's **Personality Structure.** [40] In the *Process Spiritual Model*™ and throughout the remainder of this book, we will refer to Kahler's six Personality Types as "**personality floors**," emphasizing that your personality is a complex combination of *all six floors* which comprise your unique, God-given Personality Structure.

As we look further into the characteristics of each personality floor, you might identify with some qualities of one personality floor but not find every aspect of that floor to be true of you. Some of your personality qualities might even feel contradictory to one another and lead to internal conflict. Perhaps you have trouble reconciling your deep emotions with your commitment to logical, rational thought. These kinds of apparent paradoxes are possible, because you are not one single personality floor but rather a uniquely designed combination of all six. This unique combination and arrangement of the individual floors of your personality into a more complete and integrated Personality Structure will be discussed fully in Chapter 5: Personality Structure.

By noticing and talking about the patterns in our personalities, we have better tools with which to understand one another and ourselves. We are by no means suggesting a cookie cutter approach to people or personality by denying individual differences or attempting to reduce the complexity of what it means to be human into a single label. This kind of "pigeon-holing" can be dangerous, overlooking the nuances of each individual personality and missing out on the uniqueness of our design. Rather, we seek to cultivate an awe at how diversely gifted and equipped each individual is while at the same time pointing out instances of overlap, of similarity, and of consistent, observable behavior.

---

[39] From Kahler, T. (1982, 1996). *Process Communication Management Seminar.* Little Rock, AR: Taibi Kahler Associates, Inc.
[40] From Kahler, T. (1982, 1996). *Process Communication Management Seminar.* Little Rock, AR: Taibi Kahler Associates, Inc.

## Looking Ahead

Using the framework of the *Process Spiritual Model*™, we can notice and predict how these characteristics and patterns in our personalities play out in our daily lives and interactions. Recognizing your particular Perception (Chapter 6) provides clues for communication and relationships—what will feel natural, what will require greater effort, and what you can do to avoid certain pitfalls or relational deadlocks. Drawing conclusions about your Psychological Needs (Chapter 7) and Character Strengths (Chapters 3 and 4) within this framework can give you valuable information about what ignites you, leading to renewed clarity on where to invest your energy and revealing the kinds of service and occupations in which you will be the most fulfilled and effective.

Identifying the design of your individual personality allows you to predict what needs you might feel more keenly and offer some ideas about why these needs surface when they do (Chapters 7 and 8). Recognizing what motivates you and what drains you can enable you to choose healthy ways to find inspiration and energy for full life and service. And when operating outside of your unique design, an awareness of the particular Deception to which you are vulnerable and your patterns of Distress can help you recognize your descent into unhealthy beliefs and behaviors, empowering you to choose to believe the truth about who you are (Chapter 9).

As you unveil truths about your unique design, it is our hope that the truth indeed sets you free. Information alone will not change your heart or transform your actions; only the power of God's spirit and His grace at work in your life has the capability to do that. But as grace and truth mysteriously marry and mingle, deeper understanding and clearer perceptions can lead to intentional choices that move you ever closer to hope, to freedom, to truly loving yourself and others. These instances of choice happen moment-to-moment in the cadence of a familiar conflict; these choices ultimately add up over days, months, and years to reorient, revolutionize, and redefine the direction of your life.

For example, you might apply a newfound knowledge of your unique Character Strengths by accepting what you had formerly devalued in yourself and boldly offering this Strength as a service. This would be an external sign of internal growth—a deepening acceptance of who you are stripped of unhealthy pretense, expectation, or façades. In your relationships, application of this material often looks like changing relational patterns or assumptions. As you grow in awareness of yourself and others, you can begin to identify miscommunications *as they happen*. On a day-to-day, sometimes moment by moment basis, you can choose differently in the midst of conflict by intentionally shifting or broadening your particular perspective (Perception). [41] Opening your eyes to the ways others might see and talk about the world reinforces your ability to appreciate, delight in, and even depend on the wide array of Character Strengths and perspectives available. You might be able to see your spouse through new eyes or find a renewed approach to relate to the child who has always evaded you.

## SEEING GOD THROUGH NEW EYES

Yet the most revolutionary change that could occur in your life as a result of understanding how you have been uniquely designed is a shift in toxic or distorted views about who God is and how He sees you. Perhaps recognizing that you do not have to be perfect opens you up to seeing that God receives you even in your imperfections. Or accepting that you have lived most of your life to please and appease others frees you to see a similar pattern in your interactions with your Heavenly Father.

Applying these kinds of major shifts in belief and behavior requires boldness and grace supplied by God's Spirit. Changing habitual patterns, beliefs, or ingrained responses in order to walk in the direction of deeper connection to God and others is both an act of obedience and an ongoing process of quiet transformation (see Chapter 10). Such cultivation of the soul requires a patient and painful pruning deep down at the root level. By better understanding the ways in which you habitually view yourself, God, and the world, you will identify some of the **basic beliefs** underlying

---

[41] Dr. Kahler emphasizes not only the importance of shifting Perceptions in order to ensure effective communication but also shifting one's "Channel of Communication." From Kahler, T. (1996, 2012). *The Process Communication Model® Seminar—Seminar One: Core Topics*. (pp.33). Little Rock, AR: Kahler Communications, Inc.

your thoughts, emotions, and actions.

THIS IS WHERE REAL CHANGE BEGINS—
AT THE LEVEL OF THE HEART.

King Solomon, the wisest man in recorded history, encourages the readers of Proverbs to "above all else, guard your heart, for it is the wellspring of life."[42] And Jesus made the same connection between this well-guarded heart and the overflow of its contents into our lives: "The good man brings good things out of the good stored up in his heart, and the evil man brings evil things out of the evil stored up in his heart. For the mouth speaks what the heart is full of."[43]

Many authors concerned with spiritual transformation point to the need to change the heart. We hope to add to the discussion by helping you identify what is in your heart, unveiling the heart's contents and processes partially as the product of your unique design. We also hope to illuminate ways in which that heart needs refining and redefining. A deeper understanding of the beliefs stored in our hearts, then, seems essential to making external changes actual, living realities. We desperately need the waters of God's grace to trickle through the deepest cracks and corners of our hearts and heal us at our very core. Then we're free to live out a great and glorious design. Then we are free to laugh, delight, and marvel at the differences amongst people that can be transformed from battlegrounds of miscommunication to gardens of intimacy and relationship. This is what happens when personality theory becomes living, breathing, applicable, grace-and-truth-soaked reality—you can finally live into your destiny as a Servant by Design.

---

[42] Proverbs 4:23, New International Version.
[43] Luke 6:45, New International Version.

# 03 | *Character Strengths (Part I)*

Have you ever tried to peel an apple with a spoon?
Scramble an egg with a straw?
Chop a steak with a spatula?
Any luck?
Without the proper tool, employed for its original intent and purpose, completing a simple task in the kitchen becomes trickier than solving a Rubik's cube. Sometimes it becomes downright impossible. But stick that spatula into a mess of eggs, and you can easily whip up breakfast. When the spatula is recognized for what it has been made to do, the tool can be utilized for the strength of its design.

And so it is, on an infinitely deeper and more complex level, with people. Stick a quiet, big-picture, introspective person in front of a crowd expecting a stand-up comedian, and other than a handful of awkward silences, very little will happen. Place this same big-picture person in a situation requiring vision, imagination, and out of the box thinking, and ideas like Einstein's theory of relativity happen. Asking Einstein to ignore his strengths and instead be someone else is a little like asking a spoon to peel an apple.

In this chapter, we will further explore the six personality floors. For ease of introduction, we will first introduce these six personality floors in their "pure" forms as discovered by Dr. Kahler in his original research, as caricatures of the six **Personality Types**.[44]

---

[44] From Kahler, T. (1979). Process Communications Model™ (In Brief). Little Rock, AR: Taibi Kahler Associates, Inc.; adapted by permission.

Yet we must always keep in mind that we are "fearfully and wonderfully made" complex beings, rather than one-dimensional characters. Each individual's personality is a complex combination of all six personality floors, arranged in any of 720 different orders.[45] We will look more in depth at how these six floors of your personality and their specific arrangement comprise your individual **Personality Structure** in Chapter 5.[46] Right now, let's introduce these six personality floors one at a time.

Dr. Kahler's original research identified three key **Character Strengths** for each Personality Type or personality floor.[47] You will likely identify with some of these strengths more strongly than others. You might not initially recognize these Character Strengths as purposeful and individual aspects of your design, because they are so central to who you are that they seem like a "given." But the more you observe and interact with others, the more you might notice differences in what "comes naturally" for each individual.

Not everyone readily shows compassion. Not everyone adapts to unforeseen challenges. Not everyone approaches problems through an analytical and sequential trail of logic. Not everyone willingly dedicates himself or herself to meaningful causes with the same level of commitment. Not everyone has a sense of humor or lives in the present, bringing joy and light to the darkest of situations. And not everyone can see beyond the immediate and superficial to the deeper, more ethereal, or eternal.

Let's begin our introduction with a personality snapshot to flesh out the Character Strengths of each personality floor—adapted from Dr. Kahler's six Personality Types[48]—in tangible, everyday situations. In the following stories, you'll meet six different individuals who exhibit the innate gifts God has built into each personality floor.

---

[45] From Kahler, T. (1996, 2012). The Process Communication Model® Seminar—Seminar One: Core Topics. (pp. 16). Little Rock, AR: Kahler Communications, Inc.
[46] From Kahler, T. (1982). *Process Communication Management Seminar*. Little Rock, AR: Kahler Communications, Inc.; adapted by permission.
[47] From Kahler, T. (1988, 1992, 2000, 2004). The Mastery of Management. Little Rock, AR: Kahler Communications, Inc.; adapted by permission.
[48] From Maris, R. (1996). *Your Great Design*. Little Rock, AR: Transpersonal Technologies, L.L.C. Adapted from Dr. Kahler's six Personality Types (Achiever (Thinker), Harmonizer (Harmonizer), Dreamer (Imaginer), Persister (Persister), Energizer (Rebel) and Catalyzer (Promoter)) ; From Kahler, T. (1988, 1992, 2000, 2004). *The Mastery of Management*. Little Rock, AR: Kahler Communications, Inc.

## Harmonizer Character Strengths—

SENSITIVE, WARM, COMPASSIONATE

*Elise mends a broken heart:*

"She won't talk to anyone. Be prepared for a lot of intimidating silences."

"But don't make her mad; her temper is infamous."

"Meaner than a snake. Cooks like an angel though."

"Well, you're a better person than me if you can put up with her for a whole summer. Are you sure you still want to stay there? You can change your mind, you know."

Elise couldn't deny that she was nervous. According to her mother, there was a reason they had not been in contact with her father's oldest sister since Elise was just a toddler. Her aunt Viola, nine years her father's senior, had inherited the old family cabin and surrounding acres the year after Elise was born. The blowout between Aunt Viola and Elise's father had happened the next winter, and since then, there had been no contact. Only caustic references or a general avoidance of Viola's existence. That is, until Elise had asked her parents if she could spend the summer after she graduated high school with her Aunt Viola. Certain that Viola would refuse, her parents had agreed. All three of them had been more than a little shocked when Viola telegraphically responded: "What day does she arrive?"

With one hand resting on the steering wheel, Elise reached her free hand across the truck bench to touch the tea cozy she had spent weeks designing and sewing for this strange and intimidating aunt. She felt the paisley patterned fabric and marveled at its softness, hopeful that her aunt would feel all the meaning behind the gift. Elise could hear her own words echoing in that last conversation with her father before she'd left the house for the summer long visit.

"Maybe she's just lonely, Dad. She's been by herself for so many years. Maybe she needs someone to talk to. Maybe I can help."

"What she needs is a new heart," her father had retorted with a clenched jaw. "To replace the stubborn one she has."

What she needs, Elise felt, is some love.

Elise glanced at the crumpled directions in her lap one more time. With a quick jerk of her wheel, she almost missed the final left turn onto the wooded and overgrown path that must have once been considered a driveway. Weaving the old pickup around potholes and branches, Elise finally saw the cabin through the clearing, bathed in streaks of sunlight that filtered through the trees. She took a deep breath.

Elise's pretext for visiting her aunt: to learn family recipes and study under her aunt's genius in the kitchen in preparation for the possibility of culinary school in the next few years.

Her unofficial but deeper desire: to heal the rift between her aunt and the rest of her family. With characteristic empathy and deep emotional intuition, Elise sensed how the broken relationship with the older sister who had once been his best friend ate away at her father slowly. She sensed the way the bitterness covered his deep hurt like a scab and could empathize with his unspoken, unacknowledged longing for peace. She felt his hurt as if it were her own. And though she had never admitted it to her father, Elise had always secretly worried about her Aunt Viola's heart just as fervently.

Aunt Viola sat on the front porch with hands folded and resting in her lap, rocking back and forth like a metronome.

"Aunt Viola!" Elise exclaimed with her characteristic expressiveness. Shutting her truck door, she approached her aunt with a warmth and openness that invited Viola to feel immediately at ease. "I'm so glad to see you. And so grateful you've let me come for the summer," Elise's voice and manner radiated kindness, and she spoke with an expectant eagerness.

"Well," Aunt Viola replied with a voice that sounded gravelly from disuse. The corner of her mouth rose ever so slightly at the sincerity of this niece she barely knew. The moment of ensuing silence would have been awkward for Elise, but her focus was on how her aunt might be feeling.

"Don't just stand there," Viola shifted uncomfortably in her rocking chair. "Come on in out of the heat."

Elise's face lit up as she remembered the tea cozy in the car. "Oh! I have something for you!" Elise raced back to the car and delicately pulled out the tea cozy, running back to the front porch.

"Dad mentioned that you love to drink tea," Elise

extended the tea cozy to Viola, who took it with barely controlled emotion. Viola fingered the handiwork with slightly watery eyes. It had been at least a decade since anyone had fashioned something with such tender care, just for her. In fact, it had been years since anyone had shown any personal interest in her at all or even been brave enough to venture up the driveway. And Elise looked so much like her father that Viola could feel the searing pain of recognition running up and down her throat.

"I thought we might drink some tea together this summer," Elise said with sensitivity, reading Viola's expression. She reached out and touched Viola's shoulder carefully. "I'd love to hear your stories. Especially of you and Dad growing up."

Viola sniffed and tried to substitute her forming tears with stoic sternness, but she was completely taken aback and rendered defenseless by Elise's demonstrative, affectionate nature. Funny that Viola felt immediately more seen, more understood, more cared for by this eighteen-year-old niece than she had by anyone in a long, long time. "Your father is a renegade," she responded gruffly. "Always was."

Elise put herself in her aunt's shoes for a moment, imagined what it must be like to feel utterly alone and disconnected from the family that had once been so dear. Aunt Viola must be aching for someone to listen, to understand. Whatever had happened between Viola and her father years ago, Elise was sure it must be hurting Aunt Viola to carry that wound angry and alone.

"Hungry?" Viola finally managed.

<><><>

"You know, Aunt Viola, I was nervous about coming here this summer," Elise said later at the dinner table. "But I can't think of anywhere else I would rather be than here with you."

Viola was again caught off guard by Elise's emotional transparency, her willingness to share her feelings with such depth and intimacy. Somehow Elise's openness unconsciously invited Viola to unlock the steel gate of her own emotions—a gate that had previously been not only shut but firmly padlocked with the resolve to never open again.

Viola started to speak and then found she couldn't quite get out words without accompanying tears. Elise sensed Viola's struggle and said nothing. After another long moment of silence, Elise gently placed her hand upon Viola's own and squeezed it tenderly.

"I've always wanted to get to know you," Elise said simply.

Viola said nothing and withdrew her hand, avoiding Elise's gaze. Elise took the hint and continued eating her meal. A few moments later, however, Elise felt Viola grab her hand and give a weak but significant squeeze.

## *Harmonizers: An Overview*

Guided by their sensitive hearts, Harmonizers exude warmth and compassion wherever they go. With their uncanny ability to sense the needs of others, they are uniquely gifted to build others up and encourage in personally nurturing and empathetic ways. They experience life through highly tuned and sensitive emotions, perceptive of the slight shifts of mood in a friend or the emotional atmosphere of a room. Their emotional expressiveness and genuine understanding invite others to share their feelings freely with a sense of safety, care, or acceptance.

Harmonizers care deeply about *who* people are rather than just what they do. With their sensitivity to, and respect for, each individual's needs, they are particularly effective arbitrators, seeing past surface-level problems and dealing with the hurt feelings that often lie below. This desire for harmony spurred Elise to be a mediator in her family, believing that even a decade long grudge could be healed with proper care.

Harmonizers also highly value and excel in intimate relationships. They desire to know others and to be known and will take risks of emotional investment and vulnerability to build intimacy. For Elise, entering into Aunt Viola's loneliness for the possibility of relationship and restoration seemed infinitely worthwhile.

They make others feel at ease because of their genuine care and warmth. Harmonizers also pay attention to their environment, focusing on creating an atmosphere of physical and emotional comfort. Candles, textures, warm colors, appealing smells can all be a part of a Harmonizer's nest. In conversations, a Harmonizer is likely to encourage and give ample amounts of positive feedback.

Harmonizers like to meet tangible as well as emotional needs in order to show their care for another. They might bake meals for a grieving family, offer to babysit for a single mother, or bring flowers to someone who is ill. Elise made a personalized tea cozy to bring to her aunt in order to show her affection. Whatever the Harmonizer does, it blossoms from a tender and empathetic heart.

Remember again that we are each a combination of all six personality floors. Thus someone with a strong Harmonizer floor who also possesses a strong Dreamer floor (which we will explore later) might appear more introverted, yet their presence will still quietly invite others to feel understood and loved.

## Achiever Character Strengths—

LOGICAL, RESPONSIBLE, ORGANIZED

*Dane does what's needed:*

It had been almost nine years since the levees had broken and the water had changed everything. Water—both life-giving and life- taking. The citizens of the city of New Orleans and other Gulf Coast communities understood that reality with painful clarity after Hurricane Katrina.

The members of Crescent Grove Church in Slidell had watched the water rise and rise and rise, whether from their rooftops, in shelters in Northern Louisiana, or televised in the living rooms of family members states away. For those who returned, the eleven-foot high water line stained across the 152 year old church served as a tangible reminder—a dividing line between the old reality and the current one. Even after all this time, the new reality was still an adjustment.

Dane Tipton was serving his nineteenth year as an elder at Crescent Grove Church in that August of Katrina. Known for his practicality and competence with planning and finances, Dane also acted as the church's financial manager. Dane and his wife Sarah had taken nine feet of water in their home, salvaging only a few photo albums and trinkets from the upstairs bedroom.

Though they were not wealthy, Dane had set aside a

considerable amount in savings throughout the years as an emergency fund. His children had always teased him about his management (or over-management, his daughter liked to say) of money, but Dane felt the need to be prepared even for circumstances of high consequence and low probability.

"Now that the kids are out of the house, it doesn't make sense to have three extra bedrooms," Dane told Sarah unemotionally a few weeks after the flooding. "I've calculated what we would save annually if we moved into a one or two bedroom house. Financially, it's logical to sell this land and move into one of these four neighborhoods. And, if we do that rather than staying here, we will have 37% more of our own money to pour into rebuilding the church and other relief efforts throughout the city."

For Crescent Grove Church, Dane Tipton had always been a dependable resource. But in the months immediately following Katrina, his clear head and attention to details were absolutely indispensable.

A week after most of the church's staff made their way back into the city, Dane approached the church's secretary, Leila, carrying a thick binder.

"I recently compiled a spreadsheet of our listed members with home addresses and all available contacts," Dane reported matter-of-factly. "I noticed a few months ago that our directory had not been updated this year or last, so I've been working on this project for a while. But now I've added some extra details that should be beneficial in coordinating relief efforts, such as what resources members have mentioned contributing, extra skills such as carpentry that will come in handy and such." He handed her the binder, which was neatly organized with colored alphabetical tabs.

"This is…perfect," Leila managed. She flipped through the pages with appreciation. "We've been meaning to compile something like this, but it takes so much time. And I've been nearly distraught about how to get in touch with a lot of our members."

At a meeting two weeks later of the available elders and staff, Dane presented a well thought out, sequential plan for both managing the church's own rebuilding project and also plugging returning members into relief efforts throughout the city.

"I think it would make sense for our church to partner with

the following organization," Dane suggested. "If we join efforts, we are more likely to make significant progress in several areas at once rather than becoming stagnant in one area. Whatever progress we make will have to be slow and methodical, but we can start moving forward."

The pastor, who looked equally hopeful and exhausted, nodded his head. "Owen, perhaps you could be in charge of making that connection?"

Fellow elder Owen Yarborough agreed. But it was Dane Tipton who took the responsibility of following through with the organization for the next weeks and even months, making consistent calls and ironing out details to coordinate efforts. And now, almost nine years later, Dane was still following through when much of the world seemed to have forgotten about the work still to be done.

"Another team coming in this week, Dane?" Sarah studied her husband's lined face as she passed the jambalaya to their oldest son, Jacob.

Dane stood up to refill all the water glasses. "Yes. 24 people from a church group in Oklahoma. And then a youth group from near Tallahassee arrives next Thursday."

"You still coordinating all of that through the church, Dad?" Jacob asked. He had been in graduate school in North Carolina when Katrina happened and had only made it home a few times since then. "I can't believe how much there still is to be done."

"There's always more work to be done, Jake. Just when one phase of recovery is finished, another step begins. Like a lot of things in life, it requires a good deal of long term planning," Dane handed Jacob his replenished glass and sat down.

Jacob's face showed concern. "You've barely slowed down for nine years now, Dad."

Dane sipped his water before answering, his pencil resting behind his ear in readiness for jotting down any immediate thoughts or calculations. "If we want to see certain goals reached, then we have to plug away at the details in between."

"Your father," Sarah mentioned admiringly between bites of jambalaya, "has taken on a great deal of responsibility—in the church and elsewhere. But he's kept such a clear head all along."

"Someone had to," Dane said.

"I've certainly felt cared for," Sarah looked at Dane in simple acknowledgement. "Even when everything around felt uncertain and out of control, I had confidence that your father was doing everything he could—and more—to take care of us."

"There are some circumstances I obviously don't have control over, and I leave those details to God's care and competence," Dane remarked with a peace he could not have claimed even five years ago. "Because He continues to show me that He is more than capable. But the things that I do have control over…those I am responsible to care for as best as I can. Like your mother, and you, and our church, and our city."

Jacob studied his father, who had always been a picture of stability. Even in the midst of chaos. He felt slightly at a loss as to how to acknowledge such consistency and hard work, especially to someone like his father who rarely engaged in emotional outbursts. Dane met his eyes then, and Jacob wondered whether his father read in them what Jake could not form into words. After a pause, Jacob finally raised an eyebrow.

"Pass the jambalaya?"

## *Achievers: An Overview*

Achievers are gifted with competent minds and the ability to think logically and analytically. As they move through the world, Achievers naturally tend to collect information, sort facts, categorize data, and identify solutions. With an eye for details, Achievers anticipate what needs to be done and take logical action. They set and move toward specific goals in a stepwise fashion. From his Achiever personality floor, Dane took what looked like the overwhelmingly impossible task of rebuilding post-hurricane and logically broke it down into detailed, manageable steps. Achievers are not afraid to set high standards for themselves and call others to the same expectations through their consistent examples.

Achievers are faithful and methodical stewards of time and money. As part of what he viewed as stewardship and provision, Dane had set aside finances in order to be prepared for the unexpected. Responsible and fair, Achievers can prioritize effectively and allocate their resources to what they consider most important. Their honesty can border on bluntness, but typically they are simply "stating the facts." Because they see the long term, Achievers often put off immediate gratification for an optimal final outcome. When others have lost interest or become distracted, Achievers plug away at the nitty-gritty to see a worthwhile project to completion.

When looking at a problem to solve, Achievers objectively gather relevant data and unemotionally compute the most logical solution. They are clear thinkers and are not swayed by opinions or feelings but instead reach logical conclusions via facts and analysis. Dissatisfied with anything less than excellence, Achievers continue to investigate a problem until the best possible solution is reached. Achievers tend to view life through a "cause and effect" lens. They use sequential thinking skills both to articulate steps that need to be taken and predict logical outcomes. Achievers use phrases such as, "Does it make sense?" or "If…then."

In relationships as in work or ministry, Achievers tend to be stable, consistent, and responsible. They invite those they love to feel secure and cared about through their provision, planning, and reliability. In a world of apparent confusion and chaos, Achievers have the ability to stick with the facts, focus on what's important, and discipline themselves to achieve worthwhile goals.

## PERSISTER CHARACTER STRENGTHS—

OBSERVANT, DEDICATED, CONSCIENTIOUS

*Geoffrey, tried and true:*

Something wasn't right.

Cross over, loop through, pull down, cross under, loop, loop, tug right left right.

Geoffrey had been doing the same Windsor knot in his tie for the past 42 years. He didn't even need the mirror anymore, but he liked to watch his fingers deftly weaving in and out. The shirt might change—from white to an occasional blue, from short sleeves to long sleeves as he deemed appropriate for the weather —but the tie remained constant.

Of course not everyone wore ties to work these days. But Geoffrey believed the tie was important. It spoke of professionalism, of commitment, of his dedication to the explicit cause of his work. A dedication that had not faded like the distinguished silver of his hair but had deepened throughout the years.

Geoffrey's eyebrows furrowed together in a concentrated frown as he shook his head almost imperceptibly. He couldn't put his finger on it. No matter how many times Geoffrey picked apart his latest legal case at the office, he couldn't forsake his concern that there was injustice hidden within the cracks, lurking in a corner that he had yet to overturn.

"Geoff?"

The furrows deepened even further and then released as he noticed his wife's reflection in the bedroom mirror. Her petite body was framed in the doorway; her expressive face looked tired but lovely.

Alexandra gave him a lopsided smile and walked with cautious, deliberate steps toward the bed. Geoffrey was immediately at her side as her hands blindly reached behind her to find the solid surface of the bed. With painstaking attention, Geoffrey observed pain flicker across her face as he supported her weight until she sank into the mattress.

"Old girl's not as spry as she used to be," Alexandra quipped with the slightest edge of weariness tingeing her usual ease and amusement.

Geoffrey's eyes did a quick scan to make sure his wife of 48 years was comfortably seated.

"You shouldn't be coming up and down the stairs so often," he stated.

Alexandra shrugged and brushed a strand of silver hair from her face. "I don't like being stuck downstairs," she replied. "All alone." And with a familiar wink of her left eye that had captured his heart 48 years, two months, and eight days ago, she added wryly, "While you're up here staring at your tie trying to solve the injustices and problems of the world as usual."

"That's why we installed the intercom," Geoffrey braced his hands against his knees and sat next to Alexandra. He didn't exactly feel spry these days either. "I wanted you to have the intercom so I could get to you quickly."

Alexandra studied her husband's lined face with as much

tenderness as concern. In all the ups and downs of their life together, Geoffrey had steadily provided all she had ever asked for...and much that she had not even anticipated needing. Since her battle with rheumatoid arthritis had intensified the past spring, Geoffrey had busied himself with making the house as navigable as possible for her. He read articles, talked to acquaintances, and made his way through every room in the house with a critically observant eye and a notepad. "We shouldn't have so many chairs in this room. You might fall." He foresaw every potential danger or threat. Geoff had always been more gifted with ideas than with tools or any sort of home repair, so he hired the best quality carpenters to add extra railings for her protection.

And all the while he had continued his career as a defense attorney, particularly advocating for those he saw as underprivileged or taken advantage of in cases against corporations that he considered unethical and exploitive.

"You're a good man, Geoff," Alexandra wiggled his tie and then put a wizened hand on his cheek. She met the eyes of this husband who had proven over and over again that he could be counted upon, that he was a man of honesty and virtue and solid values. He lived by his principles in an era where many were trading theirs in for what was convenient. "Always have been. You've taken good care of me."

Geoff's eyes wandered to the picture on the mahogany dressing table of him, Alexandra, and their three children with a vibrant ocean sunset in the background. That must have been over ten years ago now. He had done his best to provide and care for his family. Even as an undergraduate studying to become a lawyer, he had committed to being an upstanding and honest husband and father with the same steadfastness as his calling to fight against injustice in courts of law.

"Something isn't right with the proceedings of this trial, Lexi," Geoffrey sighed and straightened his tie. "After all these years, I still believe in integrity in the courtroom. And I don't trust this latest witness; there's something off about his character."

"I'd trust your assessment of that," Alexandra said. "You're usually right on target. If you think this guy is up to no good, he probably is."

Geoffrey nodded. He had often been recognized for his

discernment—knowing when something was right and when it wasn't, having a talent for evaluating whether an idea or a person was in line with God's will and character or not.

"Better head up there," he cleared his throat. He started to stand up and gave the bed a good once-over. "And we ought to get a new mattress. Better quality. This one's too soft; it's too hard to get in and out of."

Alexandra laughed softly. "Whatever you say." She knew better than to argue with that look of determination.

## Persisters: An Overview

Persisters are dedicated, conscientious, and observant. Geoffrey was consistently dedicated to his core system of values, which included fighting against injustice in a court of law as well as being an honorable and protective husband and father. Though every Persister will not have the same belief system, he or she will be driven, regardless, by an internal set of standards that manifests in deep, steadfast conviction. Whether or not you agree with what a Persister believes, it is hard not to respect and admire the consistency of belief and character, the alignment of conviction and action that penetrate his or her life.

Persisters have a strong sense of morality, character, dependability, and tradition. Like Geoffrey, they are often committed to issues of justice. Even in the face of difficulty, monotony, or persecution, the Persister is able to firmly stand—without wavering—behind the principles in which he or she believes. If necessary, Persisters have the fortitude and resolve to sacrifice their very lives for the sake of a cause or belief they deem worthy.

Persisters are also able to give firm opinions, beliefs, and evaluations. Equipped with a natural and unfaltering sense of discernment, Persisters are not easily swayed or charmed. They are keen observers of life and of people, simultaneously taking information in and forming an evaluative judgment of what they observe. "This doesn't line up with what I believe," a Persister might say within a few minutes or even a matter of seconds of hearing a sermon on the radio or reading the back cover of a book. Geoffrey used his keen observational skills in an effort to protect his wife in her growing illness, walking through the house like a highly trained assessor. He spotted every potential threat and anticipated danger, taking firm steps to assure Alexandra's safety. Their loyalty, integrity, and steadfastness make Persisters dependable, stable partners, friends, or colleagues.

## DREAMER CHARACTER STRENGTHS—

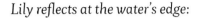

CALM, REFLECTIVE, IMAGINATIVE

*Lily reflects at the water's edge:*

The wooden bench hid quietly beneath an overgrowth of verdant green vines and a carpet of clover. This bench—the one tucked along the south bank of the pond near the weeping willow—occupied most of her summer hours. Since the time when she was toddling on unsteady legs, Lily would gravitate toward this one bench at her grandfather's pond. Even as a young child, she would sit still for hours and let her gray eyes wander across the water thoughtfully. The bench had been a safe place to flee, to reflect, to simply *be* during the year her parents' marriage was visibly falling apart. After Pappaw Tilly had died three years ago, the quiet guesthouse with the view of the weeping willow had become Lily's haven, the nest in which she happened to settle. The tranquility of the land, the natural wildlife surrounding the water, and the solitude of the simple, cozy cabin ideally complemented Lily's reflective nature and introspective tendencies.

And somewhere in the quietness of those countless evenings by the water, Lily's soul had acquired a depth and serenity much like the glassy surface of that pond. Regardless of hardship or chaos around her, Lily was centered, fairly unflappable, deeply at peace. She didn't feel the same anxiety or the same desperate need for answers as those around her. In fact, she liked to live in the questions. The limits or boundaries of the mind that left others stuck only multiplied Lily's contemplation and intrigue. In the vast and open field of her imagination, reflections, and ideas, there was no time crunch or need to come up with a product. There was only boundless, open space and a patient willingness to let ideas come and go, to run away, to bloom slowly, or to appear suddenly like a hot air balloon on a summer day. And that's what she did on this overgrown bench as a freelance writer and poet, as morning grew into afternoon and faded into twilight without much notice from Lily.

Her dearest friend Angela often marveled at Lily's perpetual state of calm. The two had bonded over a mutual aversion to gym class at Wildwood Middle School and remained close for the past 12 years. It had taken awhile before Lily was comfortable enough to share her near constant stream of thoughts and musings with Angela. Over ten years ago on this very bench, Lily had sat quietly next to Angela while her friend devoured the last few pages of Lily's first novel.

"*I don't know anyone else who thinks about life like you do, Lily,*" Angela had said with wide, appreciative eyes. "*You just…see things differently. And your imagination!*" Angela tapped the manuscript with her index finger rapidly. "*You create this whole other world! How do you think this stuff up?*"

Lily had shrugged humbly. She had always seen the world through that imaginative lens. There had been numerous occasions when her quiet and contented presence had calmed Angela in the midst of a panic or comforted Lily's grandfather in the final months of his life.

Lily's face was serene as she sat motionless, almost forgetting about the pen in her hand. The quick flash of a red-winged blackbird across the pond caused Lily to blink and return to her present surroundings. A half-finished poem, along with several possibly unconnected metaphors, analogies, and images, sat in her lap. With an unhurried and reflective air, Lily brushed a strand of hair out of her eyes. She was remembering a conversation at church last Sunday.

Angela, Lily, and a group of men and women in their mid to late 20s were gathered around the coffee station near the sanctuary entrance. As usual, Angela stood in the thick of things and talked with exaggerated hand gestures. Lily positioned herself slightly at the edge of the group, feeling comfortable being a part of the conversation without needing to speak often or even be noticed. She sipped her coffee thoughtfully as Angela continued speaking.

"*If we just had a venue,*" Angela was saying, punctuating her thought with the opening of her hand. "*A place for these kids to go that was productive and not destructive, you know what I mean?"*

"But the church doesn't have enough money to build a community center. I wish we had that kind of space here, but we just don't." Ian was an accountant and always the voice of logic. Lily mused on how in the world he kept up with so many numbers.

"It's all about the programs these days anyway. Those kids want something to do, some sort of game or sport or entertainment. It has to be exciting or new or stimulating to draw and keep any kind of attendance with teens," another voice chimed in.

Lily noticed the seeds of a thought beginning to form as she listened.

"What do you think, Lily?" Angela could see Lily pondering but knew she wouldn't volunteer the information on her own.

Lily characteristically wanted to let the various possibilities swimming around in her head marinate and soak, hesitating to speak or share until she had thought and considered deeply. *"I need a little more time to process,"* Lily replied.

Angela nodded. "Let me know if anything comes up that you want to share. I'll be eager to hear it."

And now on this bench the thought came to her.

*What if she were to…*

*And she so happened to have…*

*Of course, it was completely unlike anything else the church had tried.*

Lily smiled. It was worth a try. Lily stood and made her way around the pond, climbing the slight hill on the north side of the pond until she reached the plateau. Her eyes, lit up in the throes of the idea, swept across the abandoned garden plot that had been her grandfather's joy.

What if she were to donate this plot for the church's use? What if these kids from inner city Birmingham, the ones their church had been trying to reach for months without success, could hop in a church shuttle and spend time in the country? It would be unlike anything they had ever done. And it wouldn't cost more than some seeds. What if they learned to garden, to nurture something and watch it grow, and transform before their eyes? Couldn't the power of that metaphor, the lived experience of change and growth and new life, open one's eyes in a way that a hundred sermons or programs or church events might not?

It might just be crazy enough to work. And thankfully Angela was not only enthusiastic about ministry but detail oriented and good at putting plans into action. Angela would doubtless ask Lily again soon if she'd had any ideas, and Lily would be happy to dream with her.

The garden sat in all its tangled disarray. To the average eye it looked like a mess that had been neglected for far too long, needing tilling and weeding and who knows what else. To Lily, it looked like a space for imagination to run wild and dream up unusual solutions.

## *Dreamers: An Overview*

Dreamers are calm, reflective, and imaginative. With their innovative minds, Dreamers contemplate life and ideas at a level that others often do not reach, though they rarely experience the need to share these ideas with others. Lily felt safe enough in her friendship with Angela to occasionally vocalize the constant musings and "What if's?", but the majority of a Dreamer's thoughts remain unspoken.

For the Dreamer, these ideas and reflections do not have to become realities in order to be valuable. They love to imagine possibilities and unusual solutions to problems. Whereas other personality floors may get caught up in details, policies, and concrete realities, Dreamers operate in the realm of abstraction, metaphor, and analogy. This kind of abstract thinking is part of what allows them to see beyond the tangible and imagine a different reality that others might not see. In a situation where it seems all the possibilities have been exhausted, Lily offers a different perspective unbound by the same limitations that keep others going in mental circles. Dreamers are willing and able to think outside of the box.

Because they are not tied to the tangible, Dreamers offer a patient appreciation for the process or journey of life. They have a sense that life is "happening" to them. Others often depend upon the Dreamer's serene outlook and calm presence to bring a sense of peace to their busy or anxiety-filled lives. Lily's friend Angela, for example, looked to Lily for calm in the midst of daily realities as well as crises. The Dreamer's unique gift is to see what cannot be easily or readily seen and reflect it back to the world through a lens of peace and serenity.

Dreamers find simple contentment when working on mundane tasks that allow them time for reflection. They are generally skilled at working with their hands. Dreamers follow clear directions and are dependable servants in even the most unglamorous of tasks. In relationships, Dreamers experience intimacy through proximity and working alongside others, serving those they love with simple, deep loyalty.

## Catalyzer Character Strengths—

ADAPTABLE, PERSUASIVE, AND CHARMING

*Kristin faces a challenge head-on:*

"Well, your credentials are certainly impressive," the fifty-something, balding man ran his handkerchief over his thick eyebrows to wipe away the beads of sweat. "Sorry," his look was rueful. "It's brutal here in the summertime. Sure you're ready to move to Atlanta?"

"Absolutely," Kristin Macy nodded her head without hesitation. "I'm ready today."

Mr. Tony Michaels, co-director of the MADIA (Make a Difference in Atlanta) Community Center for inner city youth, looked at Kristin with a mixture of scrutiny and admiration. Kristin returned his gaze with confidence. This job as co-director of an inner city community center targeting at risk adolescents was right up her alley.

Removing his glasses, Mr. Michaels leaned forward in the office chair, which seemed 15 years past its prime. He sighed slowly. "I'll be frank with you, Ms. Macy, this is no easy program. I've lasted here for nine years, and that's about nine years longer than any of my other co-directors. The situation, the resources…it's desperate."

Kristin continued to meet his gaze but said nothing, waiting for the right moment to articulate her position clearly. She was dressed sharply in a dark red ladies suit, recognizing that especially in these situations it was important to present oneself as competent and successful.

"Like I said earlier, your credentials are impressive," Mr.

Michaels continued twirling his glasses in one hand. "But I wonder if, no offense meant, you have what it takes here, Ms. Macy."

There was an appropriate pause before Kristin leaned forward in her seat, her eyes alive with excitement. "Mr. Michaels, you don't know me. But the bottom line is: I'm qualified for this job. And not only am I qualified, but I am confident this is the exact place I want to be. I specialize at coming in to struggling programs, working with limited resources, and bringing about significant change in a fairly short period of time. Notice on my résumé," Kristin reached across the desk and ran her finger along the numerous bullets as she continued speaking, "that I haven't stayed any one place particularly long. I address this right off the bat to be up front with you. By nature, I am an initiator. But I'm not a maintainer. I will do what I can to change this program and set you up to where it can continue to run smoothly and to grow in the years to come."

Mr. Michaels swallowed slowly. There was a charisma that radiated from Kristin Macy, declaring a confidence that was founded and inspirational rather than arrogant. He *wanted* to believe her.

"Well," he started slowly. "We certainly need a change. But I hope you're ready for a challenge."

Kristin smiled charmingly. "Mr. Michaels, I thrive on a challenge. You'll see."

<><><>

"Evening, Ms. Macy," Kristin's 84 year old neighbor called from her front porch. Kristin was wrestling a few grocery bags out of her trunk in the dusky humidity of an Atlanta September night.

"Good evening, Ms. Gloria. Tell that grandson of yours again that I'll pay him to tune up this junker," Kristin replied and gave an indicating glance to her car, a 2014 Audi Cabriolet.

Ms. Gloria laughed. "You're awful bold to have a car like that 'round here, Ms. Macy. But yes indeed, I talked to him. His eyes lit up like a Christmas tree."

"Good," Kristin replied, shutting her trunk and re-gathering her grocery sacks. "A lot of rip-off mechanics around here. Tell him I'll pay him well. Have a good night, Ms. Gloria."

Kristin had been in the neighborhood for four months now. She laughed just remembering the look on Mr. Michaels' face when she had revealed the neighborhood to which she'd be moving.

"Ms. Macy, do you know anything about that part of Atlanta?" He had almost choked on his coffee.

"Sure," Kristin replied confidently. "But I'm not going to move here to do inner city work and live out in some ridiculous suburb. I'll be just fine."

"It's risky," he had insisted. "It's more than risky."

Kristin had nodded. "Yes. But I'm not one to avoid a risk when I see an opportunity to make a difference. And the only way I'll get to know people, the only way I'll see where we need to take chances and make changes, is if I live where I work. God called me here to make a difference. So that's where I'll be, Mr. Michaels."

There had been no arguing with her. And certainly as a single, Caucasian woman in her late thirties, Kristin Macy had made quite the impression in her neighborhood. But her fearlessness, her direct style of communication, and her genuine investment in doing everything in her power to better the community were quickly earning her a place of respect that was almost unheard of for "outsiders" in this neighborhood.

In some ways, she was a woman of paradoxes. Kristin drove a fast and expensive car (and had already replaced several rounds of slashed tires) and always dressed sharply, because she loved nice things. But she was more than willing to live in a tiny shotgun house if it meant being available to what God might put before her. And while she fully understood the risks she was taking in this unusual lifestyle, Kristin infinitely preferred the adventure of living boldly and fully to any semblance of safety.

Things had certainly not been easy. Kristin found herself constantly having to negotiate and adapt to less than ideal situations—a basement in the community center that unexpectedly flooded, several major donors to the center who pulled out on their giving at the last moment, low attendance numbers to some of the after school programs she had put in place. But because she was confident in God's call and power, Kristin found these situations stimulating at some level. It made the day to day varied and exciting; it demanded the best of her and she always, somehow, landed on her feet. Even in the rare instances where she couldn't make things gel, she never took it personally. She had never been one to "cry over spilt milk."

Mr. Michaels' eyeballs had almost popped out when Kristin had somehow rallied the finances for the back-to-school community picnic and field day at the last moment. With skillful persuasion and charm, Kristin had used what little resources she had to regain some lost donors and to make new connections. It was hard for anyone to say no to the grand vision Kristin painted, her motivating words, and the Spartan example of the life she was leading. And though Kristin would eventually pack up and leave her little shotgun house for a new adventure before organizing her third back-to-school picnic, the community would not be the same in her wake.

## *Catalyzers: An Overview*

A catalyst is something that "precedes or precipitates an event." True to their name, Catalyzers move through life on the lookout for chances to take action or seize an opportunity, thriving on stimulation, excitement, and action. Rather than living a "safe" or "easy" life, Kristin chose to continually move into situations where she would encounter challenges, be asked to take risks, and have to draw upon considerable adaptability.

With their charisma and confidence, many Catalyzers are natural leaders. Catalyzers have an uncanny ability to make things happen, to inspire, to motivate and to lead others in forward motion. When Catalyzers sink their teeth into a project that has potential, they are persuasive and adept at bringing others to seeing things from their points of view.

Rather than being deterred or discouraged by obstacles, Catalyzers sense an adventure at hand and often respond with decisive action and bold risks. Thus Mr. Michaels' warnings to Kristin likely served the opposite function from what he intended; rather than being driven away in fear, Kristin was drawn to the seemingly unsolvable problems of the community center in which she wanted to invest. Catalyzers thrive on that sort of challenge and bring others on board simply by being who they are.

Once in a position of initiating or leading, Catalyzers have the ability to be firm and direct in their communication. They will delegate tasks that require more maintenance or detail orientation to others more suited for the task. Once Kristin had made bold changes, she was ready to move on to a new challenge and leave maintenance to someone else more qualified.

Catalyzers also have an innate ability to "network." Due to their charm and adaptability, they are at ease in a crowd of strangers and can find common ground with almost anyone. Thus Kristin could move into a neighborhood where she externally did not belong and manage to find common ground with her neighbors, earning their respect. Through well-honed intuitions, Catalyzers then have the ability to challenge and inspire others to do their best. In their relationships, they invite others to join in the adventure. Because they are constantly on the lookout for opportunities, they stay mentally aware of what and who can be used later as potential resources for the Kingdom of God.

## ENERGIZER CHARACTER STRENGTHS—

SPONTANEOUS, CREATIVE, PLAYFUL

*Riley reaches a rebel:*

Most days he still felt like a seven-year-old little boy trapped in a twenty-nine-year-old body.

It wasn't a bad thing, really. Looking around, Riley saw a lot of people his age missing out on the humor in life because they were too busy trying to be adults. If there was one thing he could do well, it was laugh at himself and refuse to take himself too seriously at any given moment—all the while appreciating that God too must have a sense of humor.

It was hard not to see the humor in situations when you worked with kids, Riley thought. Kept you from going crazy when they were out of control. Like right now, for instance. This was just ironic.

"I hate this stupid place," Cassidy finally met Riley's persistent gaze. The thirteen-year-old kid folded his thin arms across his chest as his voice grew louder. "I hate it. And I hate you for making me stay!"

Riley kept staring. It was like looking at himself in a mirror, fifteen years ago. The same oppositional nature, the strong reactions, the need to blame anyone and everyone but himself. Riley himself had been in and out of the same juvenile delinquency programs as Cassidy all throughout his adolescence. He too had tried to run away—countless times—from the same summer camp where he now volunteered. Riley knew the underlying shame poorly hidden beneath Cassidy's defiant and sullen exterior. And Riley knew the freedom from it all—the cycles of rebellion and unforgiveness and self-hatred redeemed. There was life—full and joyful life—and Riley wanted Cassidy to live it, to experience it for himself!

For a moment, Riley felt himself in a corner. Camp rules said one thing about how to deal with runaways. His experience said another; more rules would only give Cassidy more incentive to rebel. Sometimes, Riley thought, one had to think outside of the box. A little creativity never hurt.

"You and me at the dock in half an hour," Riley said. The left side of his mouth rose in the slightest lopsided grin. "And be ready to get wet."

<><><>

Cassidy's eyes were wide as he looked at the orange and yellow kayak and the tiny hole that was supposed to hold him inside. It looked flimsy. It looked small in the wide, flowing river. It looked like an absolute blast!

"Here you go, man," Riley tossed Cassidy a purple life vest.

"No way; I'm not wearing that."

Riley looked up from strapping on his own life vest and put on his most serious face. "It's either that or death." A little extreme maybe, but then again, Riley was prone to extremes.

Cassidy looked ready to put up a fight but decided against it. He snapped the plastic buckles shakily…one, two, three, four.

"You look great in purple," Riley teased. "It's your color."

Cassidy grunted and began muttering under his breath.

"What's that? Life vest on too tight? I can't hear you," Riley's outward tone was playful even as he was constantly brainstorming. How could he creatively reach this kid?

"The good news is," Riley continued talking as Cassidy

crossed his arms across his chest again, "that my vest is purple too."

Riley could only make out a few of Cassidy's words—most of which were unrepeatable.

"Yeah, you're right," Riley said, finishing the last of his preparations before hopping into the back seat of the kayak. "Mine's not purple. It's more of a lavender, wouldn't you say?"

Cassidy, who had been more than a little terrified by the entire process of getting into the kayak, could only react against everything Riley said. "No."

Riley began to paddle. "Dude, haven't you heard? Girls love lavender."

Muffled laughter escaped from Cassidy in the front seat before he could stop it.

"Whatever," Cassidy retorted with a smile hidden from Riley's view.

"I'm just saying," Riley was tapping into every creative, playful bone in his body. "Chicks dig it. That's why I wear the lavender."

Cassidy said nothing but continued to smirk.

"Hey, you uh, want to help a brother out here? Maybe paddle a bit?" Riley joked after several moments of silence. He hit his paddle against the water to splash Cassidy from behind.

Cassidy's eyes were staring eagerly at the approaching whitewater rapids splashing forebodingly near the upcoming curve of the river. He had never been on a river. Never been in a kayak. And certainly never navigated any sort of rapids. This was awesome.

"What do we do about...those?"

Riley peered around Cassidy's head. "The rapids?"

"Yeah," Cassidy managed to turn his head around enough to catch Riley's eyes.

"We go get 'em," Riley winked. "Glad you've got that purple vest on now, huh?"

<><><>

After four hours of navigating the rapids, finding a bank to disembark, and a spontaneous dunking war in the river (which Riley lost a few times on purpose), Cassidy could hardly remember why he had wanted to run away in the first place. He and Riley sat side by side on a half-rotted log, looking out over the flowing river and soaking in the noises of summer—cicadas, bullfrogs, the humidity that almost seemed to have a sound of its own.

"I had a lot of fun with you today, man," Riley looked at Cassidy with a genuine smile. Riley had a way about him, an unapologetic type of self-expression that looked and felt like freedom. Cassidy longed for that freedom. "The rapids were awesome."

Cassidy just nodded and shuffled his feet in the sand.

"I'm a screw up," he finally blurted out.

Riley, who never reacted to anything halfway, widened his eyes in surprise. "No way. You're not a screw up. " He had been trying to get to this point with Cassidy all summer, and now the moment was finally here.

"How do you know?" Cassidy retorted.

"Because, Cassidy," Riley shifted to face him more fully. "We are way more alike than you may know."

"Us? No way," Cassidy replied. "You're…energetic. And happy." A slight pause. "I'm not happy."

"I'm not always happy," Riley said, unafraid to express himself transparently. "And you're not always *un*happy! Think about today. You lived in the moment. You enjoyed yourself; we went on an adventure! I mean, we were totally alive today, Cassidy. Did you feel it?"

Cassidy bit his lip and hesitated for a moment. Finally he sat up straighter and looked at Riley. "Yeah. Yeah I did."

"Cass, I believe you can live that fully every day without doing the things you're doing. It won't be all roses; things will still feel awful at times. But that's part of it too, you know? The whole spectrum of joy and pain."

"Really?"

"Yeah," Riley patted Cassidy on the back like an older brother. "I've lived it. I'm still living it. It's a day to day kind of thing."

Cassidy nodded slowly.

"For now," Riley grinned his lopsided grin again. "I say we take one more swim in the river before we have to head back. Because I demand a dunking rematch."

"You're on," Cassidy said with an unexpected smile.

## Energizers: An Overview

With their innate spontaneity, creativity, and playfulness, Energizers exude an enjoyment of life that is inspirational and contagious. Their ability to find humor in any situation makes life not only bearable but also bright and filled with an unquenchable energy. Being "out of the box" is a lifelong pursuit for an Energizer, who will be quick to express uniqueness and individuality with admirable freedom and intensity. Riley modeled this kind of personal freedom and expression for Cassidy by being transparent about his own feelings, struggles, and history. Energizers respond with strong, immediate reactions: "I love it," "I hate it," "It's my favorite," "I can't stand it."

Many Energizers tend to be musically or artistically inclined and will often "try on" different hobbies, art forms, physical activities, fashion "looks," etc. just for the sake of new experience. They never do anything halfway but throw themselves into whatever is at hand with their whole selves. Others are swept up in the Energizer's vibrant, colorful world to experience what abundant, full life could look like. Energizers can even take the mundane or boring tasks of life and turn them into fun through their playful enthusiasm and energy.

Energizers thrive in group settings where they can entertain, be stimulated, and push or react against the surrounding people or ideas. Their ability to question and think creatively makes them excellent resources in a brainstorming or problem solving session, where an Energizer will often suggest an off the wall direction that no one else sees or take issue with an assumption that others tenaciously embrace. Rather than simply following the protocol for kids who attempted to run away, Riley took a completely different approach and involved Cassidy in fun and exploration.

Life with an Energizer is never boring; they will do whatever it takes to introduce new excitement, stimulation, or humor into a dull or ordinary situation. This ability to make the "now" memorable and to embrace the present reflects the freedom and joy found within the Spirit.

## Table 1: Character Strengths

| Personality Floor | Character Strengths |
|---|---|
| Harmonizer | Warm, compassionate, sensitive |
| Achiever | Logical, responsible, organized |
| Persister | Dedicated, observant, conscientious |
| Dreamer | Calm, reflective, imaginative |
| Catalyzer | Adaptable, persuasive, charming |
| Energizer | Spontaneous, creative, playful |

With permission from Kahler, T. (1988, 1992, 2000, 2004). *The Mastery of Management*. Little Rock, AR: Kahler Communications, Inc.

We've explored examples of how the Character Strengths associated with each personality floor might function in a variety of situations. In the next chapter, we'll look specifically at how these six personality floors affect our roles in the workplace, give direction to our ministries, and are present in our spiritual heritage.

# 04 | *Character Strengths (Part II)*

Solomon advised his hearers to "apply their hearts to instruction, and their ears to words of knowledge;"[49] in other words, make what you know real by allowing it to transform you from the inside out! Submitted to God's grace and truth, a deeper understanding of our different Character Strengths and abilities can lead to practical and revealing predictions about the kinds of work we will find energizing, the ways we might engage in relationships, and greater awareness about how these Character Strengths might be offered in service to building the Kingdom of God.

Put in another light, such an awareness can also lead us to identify what we are *not* gifted to do and clarify where we may be fruitlessly spending energy trying to be who we aren't. God may call us in specific situations of faith to do something for which we are not naturally gifted; but generally speaking, we work best when we work naturally out of our God-crafted designs.

> THE KNOWLEDGE OF WHAT WE'RE NOT UNIQUELY DESIGNED TO DO CAN BE JUST AS FREEING AS RECOGNIZING THE AREAS IN WHICH WE ARE GIFTED.

## HARMONIZERS: THE NATURAL NURTURER

Harmonizers excel in professions or careers where they are able to give individual attention and care. They feel fulfilled in caretaker positions. This could look like becoming a

---

[49] Proverbs 23:12, New International Version.

neonatal nurse and nurturing infants or taking a job in geriatrics tending to the physical and emotional needs of the elderly. Because teaching involves significant emotional investment, some Harmonizers might be drawn to teaching as a profession—particularly in settings that allow for more one on one interaction, such as nurturing or mentoring a child through tutoring or managing a smaller special needs class.

Harmonizers will do well in an environment where they feel personally cared about and supported. They will spend themselves in an effort to care for others, but will likely become progressively less engaged when the focus is on deadlines and productivity rather than caring for the individual. While they will bloom beautifully in jobs that require personal interactions (such as human resources or customer service), Harmonizers without significant strength in other floors of their personalities will wither when asked to operate either in isolation or in an atmosphere of personal competition.

Because of their natural gift of intuition, Harmonizers are likely to notice needs that others do not. Within churches, they are the ones who consistently visit elderly members of the congregation, volunteer in the nursery, or perhaps participate in a benevolence ministry. They might notice when another member stops attending and make a concerned and loving phone call. Their warmth invites others in, and therefore they are integral in helping newcomers plug into meaningful relationships. Their authentic empathy makes them powerful companions for the orphans and the widows, the impoverished, the grief-stricken or ill, or anyone who feels alone and needs support. When his disciples tried to "shoo away" the children crowding around Jesus, Jesus affirmed each child's infinite value, seeing these children for their inherent worth rather than for their ability to "contribute." Harmonizers live out the command to "be devoted to one another in brotherly love"[50] and to "live at peace with everyone…as far as it depends on them."[51] As vessels of God's abundant love and His remarkably compassionate heart, Harmonizers infuse those around them with a sense of infinite value and of belonging to an eternal family.

---

[50] Romans 12:10, New International Version.
[51] Romans 12:18, New International Version.

## "The Ones Jesus Loved"—the Apostle John and Mary, sister of Lazarus

The apostle John could have chosen any number of aliases in his Gospel account of Jesus' life, death, and resurrection. He might have mentioned himself as John, a fisherman from Galilee. Jesus gave John and his brother James the nicknames "sons of thunder," indicating the presence of powerful emotions. In John's Gospel account, it would have been typical to introduce himself as John, the son of Zebedee and the brother of James. Yet John refers to himself in his Gospel as "the one whom Jesus loved." As someone with a great deal of energy in his Harmonizer floor, John defined his identity in relationship to others and particularly situated himself under the umbrella of Jesus' love and affection for him. John's Gospel is the only one that includes the death of Lazarus and Jesus' powerful emotional response to the loss of his friend. Jesus' prayer for Himself, His disciples, and the believers to come recorded in John 14-17 is a caring, emotional, relational cry from Son to Father. Jesus asks of the Father that those who believe "may be one, Father, just as you are in me and I am in you. May they also be in us so that the world may believe that you have sent me."[52] The focus of Jesus' prayer is on intimacy, relationship, and wholeness in connection to one another.

John's first epistle focuses heavily upon the love of God and our identity as His children. "How great is the love the Father has lavished on us, that we should be called children of God! And that is what we are!"[53] John identifies compassion and resulting action as significant indicators that one truly knows and follows God. "If anyone has material possessions and sees his brother in need but has no pity on him, how can the love of God be in him? Dear children, let us not love with words or tongue but with actions and in truth."[54] Harmonizers are ready to quickly spend themselves—their money, time, affection, and love—in order to nurture and take care of others. They are moved by a compassion that originates deep within their tender hearts and moves them to take action to meet obvious needs and even to *anticipate* those needs out of a natural empathy.

---

[52] John 17:21, New International Version.
[53] 1 John 3:1, New International Version.
[54] 1 John 3:17-18, New International Version.

Mary, sister of Martha and Lazarus, also exhibits significant energy in her Harmonizer floor. In an utterly impractical act of adoration for the Lord, Mary pours fine, expensive perfume on Jesus' head. The fragrance of her act of worship angers the disciples, who immediately begin to calculate more logical uses for the perfume and criticize her emotional expression as worthless when compared to "all the good" that could be done with the money. Jesus, however, calls this demonstration "a beautiful thing." Jesus shows his love and appreciation for Mary's vulnerable and humble act of love, accepting the Harmonizer's valuable gifts of emotional transparency, intimacy, and self-giving. Harmonizers are also deeply aware of their senses, and Mary's act of worship embodies an awareness of the whole self in worship—engaging her body, mind, and soul. Mary "pours herself out" like exquisite perfume, and Jesus finds it moving, personal, and meaningful.

## Achievers: The Responsible Problem-Solver

Because of their analytical and fact-oriented mindsets, Achievers gravitate toward professions that deal heavily with facts, data, and numbers. Their competence with numbers and detailed calculations fits well with professions such as financial planners or certified public accountants. Achievers are constantly seeking out new information, so an occupation involving research of some sort—where they can immerse themselves in collecting and categorizing new data—appeals to them. Fields such as engineering that require logical problem solving abilities and practical application might offer Achievers a fulfilling challenge. Any job that entails in-depth, detailed analysis, such as a corporate analyst, demands an Achiever's eye for details and ability to objectively filter data to reach logical conclusions. An individual with a strong Achiever personality floor will likely work best in a situation where he or she is able to self-manage, rather than working with a team or under a great deal of direct supervision. Achievers are also competent to lead others, particularly through their own examples of hard work and excellence.

Achievers have powerful minds, and their intellects are needed in bringing God's kingdom. On multiple occasions, the religious leaders of the day attempted to ensnare Jesus in meticulous traps of the intricacies of Jewish law. Time and time again, Jesus outsmarted these leaders with logic, not only evading their traps but also clearly pointing out the wrong focus of the heart behind their questions. In the Kingdom, Achievers are also living examples of Paul's call to the Colossians to work ethically and reliably. "Whatever you do, work at it with all your heart, as working for the Lord, not for men, since you know that you will receive an inheritance from the Lord as a reward. It is the Lord Christ you are serving."[55] They bring invaluable focus and order to chaos, completing tasks with commendable follow through and responsibility. In this way, Achievers have the privilege to reflect the faithfulness and thoroughness that are infinitely true of God's character—"being confident of this, that He who began a good work in you will carry it on to completion until the day of Christ Jesus."[56]

## A Task of Epic Proportions—Nehemiah

God has revealed Himself in Scripture as a God of order and details. One has only to browse through the end of Exodus and the book of Leviticus with all the intricate instructions for offering sacrifices, the precise requirements for festivals, and the meticulous building measurements for the temple to recognize God's concern with specificity. As the chosen people of God, Israel is to be "set apart" by thorough adherence to numerous rules. But with negligent, rebellious, and forgetful hearts, Israel began to blur the details of following her God that had been carefully and clearly laid out for her good. The people's irresponsibility eventually resulted in the destruction of the beloved Jerusalem by foreign invaders and a forced exile from the land that had been promised to them.

In the month of Kislev in the twentieth year of King Artaxerxes, God called a hard-working, detail-oriented man named Nehemiah to oversee the overwhelming, arduous task of rebuilding the wall surrounding Jerusalem. The wall had been destroyed, and the battered community thrown into utter disarray with only a remnant surviving the nation's exile. Nehemiah, who was faithfully serving as a capable cupbearer

---

[55] Colossians 3:23-24, New International Version.
[56] Philippians 1:6, New International Version.

for the King of Persia, learned of the devastation in Jerusalem and responded with both grief and a sense of personal responsibility to restore peace and order. With carefully thought out plans and a logical, eager plea, Nehemiah gained the permission of King Artaxerxes to return to his homeland and orchestrate the rebuilding of the wall. With precision and authority, Nehemiah organized, delegated, and intelligently solved problems:

> Even before leaving Persia, Nehemiah anticipated details of his journey back to Judah and logically prepared—requesting letters of protection for his journey from governors of the Trans-Euphrates as well as a letter to Asaph to provide timber for the upcoming task of rebuilding.[57]
> He systematically and sequentially inspected the walls around Jerusalem before rallying others to help.[58]
> Nehemiah knew and organized each group's work on various sections of the wall (and felt the need to record, in detail, each worker's name and specific task).[59]
> When opposition became a threat to the wall's success and the people's safety, Nehemiah logically reorganized his workers to continue the task of rebuilding as well as to handle the opposition effectively.[60]

From his initial request to the king to the addition of the last stone to the wall, Nehemiah carried out the work systematically and effectively with clear leadership. By God's design, Nehemiah and his fellow Israelites accomplished a task in 52 days that could have taken years without careful organization and a sense of responsibility.[61] Yet Nehemiah maintains a humble attitude regarding his ability, recognizing without qualms that "this work had been done with the help of our God."[62] Even after his task of building the wall was completed, Nehemiah returned to Jerusalem and followed through on his responsibility to God and his people.

---

[57] Nehemiah 2:7-8.
[58] Nehemiah 2:13-16.
[59] See Nehemiah. 3.
[60] Nehemiah 4:15-21.
[61] Nehemiah 6:15.
[62] Nehemiah 6:16, New International Version.

## PERSISTERS: THE DEDICATED ADVOCATE

How might a Persister affect the world with his or her remarkable strength of character and conviction? Martin Luther King, Jr. utilized his inherent belief in right and wrong and the values of equality and justice for all to dedicate his life to the civil rights movement. In addition to being dedicated as a loyal and faithful husband, Geoffrey from our story in the previous chapter stood as an advocate for the disadvantaged in the court of law. Persisters might also be found in quality control and assessment jobs, using their critically observant eyes to weed out anything that does not meet a certain standard. Whatever a Persister ends up advocating, it is likely to involve an issue, cause, or ideal in which he or she believes deeply. They are also fiercely loyal to friends, family, and those they respect. Because of their dedication and commitment, they often rise to positions of leadership.

Persisters, with their ability to see beyond the immediate to the eternal, are a beautiful reflection of self-sacrifice in the Kingdom of God. Jesus embodied the epitome of this selfless sacrifice with His death on the cross, remaining obedient to the will of the Father and to His purpose amidst the deepest personal suffering. Physical comfort, insecurity, and man's approval are nothing to a Persister compared to the honor and worth of standing as an advocate for a worthy cause. Their discerning minds and critical eyes can be invaluable in preserving and upholding truth and integrity—of doctrine, of operation, and of personal character.

Paul spent countless hours fighting against toxic doctrines promoted by false teachers in the early church. He lost popularity, sleep, and any kind of easy life. But there was no question for him about whether the cause and person of Jesus Christ were worth giving up anything and everything. "For to me, to live is Christ," Paul declared, "and to die is gain."[63] A Persister's commitment to righteousness, justice, and truth is a powerful, living example of a life that is set apart.

---

[63] Philippians 1:21, New International Version.

## Character Redirected—Paul of Tarsus

The year is around 35 AD in the vibrant, buzzing chaos of Jerusalem. The death and resurrection of Jesus of Nazareth still reverberates down the streets, echoing in the hearts and lives of Jesus' disciples, friends, and enemies. With words of forgiveness on his lips, Stephen—"a man of God's grace and power"—breathed his last under the harsh pummel of stones and insults. Tried for blasphemy against God and Moses, Stephen defended himself before the Jewish Supreme Court —the Sanhedrin—affirming this Jesus of Nazareth as the predicted Messiah and earning a death sentence. Following Stephen's martyrdom, the author of the Acts of the Apostles records "on that day a great persecution broke out against the church at Jerusalem."[64]

At the apex of this sweeping persecution was a highly trained and respectable student of the law named Saul of Tarsus—a man who was "advancing in Judaism beyond many Jews of [his] own age and was extremely zealous for the traditions of [his] fathers."[65] Like many Pharisaic Jews of his day, Saul viewed these new followers of "the Way" as heretics and potential threats to the religious system of the Jewish tradition. With deep conviction and fierce passion, Saul went on a crusade against these followers of Jesus. "Going from house to house, he dragged off men and women and put them in prison."[66] In the face of a threat to what Saul believed and valued, there was no halfway response—only a dogged, wholehearted perseverance to fight against what he believed to be untrue. There was no limit to what Saul would do for his beliefs. Saul admits later: "In my obsession against them [these new Christians], I even went to foreign cities to persecute them."[67]

The year is now 62 AD. The strength and passion of this reformed Pharisee named Saul have not changed, but his beliefs have. After a transformative encounter with the risen Jesus of Nazareth on the road to Damascus, Saul's entire identity and life purpose are revolutionized. Now called Paul, he endures the greatest physical, emotional, and financial hardships imaginable for the sake of this Jesus and His

---

[64] Acts 8:1, New International Version.
[65] Galatians 1:14, New International Version.
[66] Acts 8:3, New International Version.
[67] Acts 26:11, New International Version.

followers whom he once persecuted so passionately. The same conviction, belief, and steadfast commitment that defined Saul before his encounter with Jesus has now been claimed for the Kingdom of God and redirected into the spreading of the true Gospel message. For the sake of his belief in Jesus, Paul has been flogged, thrown in prison, beaten, shipwrecked, insulted, stoned, and spent countless nights hungry, cold, and naked.

As a strong, steadfast Persister, Paul continually pays the ultimate sacrifice for the cause of Christ. "I have been crucified with Christ," Paul confidently states, "and I no longer live, but Christ lives in me."[68] Once Paul believed the security of his position rested in his ability to be righteous, to fully and purely follow the law, to be morally superior. But with the new eyes of Christ, Paul boldly claims a new belief: "not having a righteousness of [his] own that comes from the law, but that which is through faith in Christ—the righteousness that comes from God and is by faith."[69]

## DREAMERS: THE CALM REFLECTOR

Dreamers find fulfillment and peace in working on tasks others might find menial or mundane. They are generally skilled in working with their hands. Thus, jobs requiring manual labor or repetitive action like construction, carpentry, or bricklaying might appeal to the Dreamer. Jesus himself was a carpenter before the beginning of his healing and teaching ministry, and numerous times in the Gospels, Jesus isolates himself from the disciples and crowds to spend meditative time alone, speaking to the Father. Dreamers also thrive when they are given clear direction and then left alone to complete the task in solitude. This kind of solitary occupation gives a Dreamer the mental space for reflection they constantly desire. Since they value solitude, have rich imaginations, and deal in an internal world of abstractions, symbolism, and metaphors, some Dreamers tend to gravitate toward writing or poetry.

As seen in the likes of the prophet Daniel or Jesus' mother, Mary, Dreamers exhibit remarkable capability for

---

[68] Galatians 2:20, New International Version.
[69] Philippians 3:9, New International Version.

service and surrender in the Kingdom. Because they are not as tied to daily, observable reality as the other five personality floors, Dreamers often grasp and live in light of a bigger picture. Abstract, spiritual concepts such as eternity, the Trinity, and "time as an illusion" fit with the Dreamer's sense that there is infinitely more to reality than what we can perceive empirically—that we currently see life and ourselves as "but a poor reflection as in a mirror."[70] The paradoxes Jesus introduces in the story of humanity's redemption peak a Dreamer's curiosity and tendency to wonder "what if." Thus, they accept and believe that "God chose the foolish things of the world to shame the wise; God chose the weak things of the world to shame the strong."[71] Dreamers embody and thus quietly permeate those around them with a deep sense of peace and acceptance. "So we fix our eyes not on what is seen, but on what is unseen. For what is seen is temporary, but what is unseen is eternal."[72]

## *Beyond the Immediate—Mary, Mother of Jesus and Daniel*

Certainly it is difficult or impossible to draw an entire personality structure from the brief descriptive accounts in Scripture of Mary, the mother of Jesus. But Mary exhibits particular qualities of a Dreamer in her quiet submission to God's will during an encounter with the angel Gabriel. When she receives perhaps the most shocking news in human history—that she will carry the Savior of the World—Mary responds: "I am the Lord's servant. May it be to me as you have said."[73] It is a response of obedience and surrender. But it is also a response laced with the language of a Dreamer— "may it be to me…" Dreamers often have a sense of life "happening" to them—out of their control and therefore beyond the reach of much more than contemplation and submission. In one supernatural moment, Mary receives an unexpected shift in the direction of her life with humility and a passive, quiet acceptance.

Mary's Dreamer qualities are evident again later on in Luke's account of the birth of Jesus. "But Mary treasured up

---

[70] 1 Corinthians 13:12, New International Version.
[71] 1 Corinthians 1:27, New International Version.
[72] 2 Corinthians 4:18, New International Version.
[73] Luke 1:38, New International Version.

all these things and pondered them in her heart."[74] The introspective tone of this description of Mary's response to the flurry of events surrounding Jesus' birth—a supernatural conception, angelic proclamations, shepherds arriving to worship, a birth in a stable—suggest a reflective nature that takes time to consider the larger picture even amidst chaos.

In the Old Testament world of visions and dreams, diviners and wise men, enchanters and magicians, Daniel was set apart by an eerily perceptive ability to interpret dreams that had not even been told to him.[75] Even more unusual, Daniel attributed this divine ability as a gift of the "God in heaven who reveals mysteries."[76] The King of Babylon, King Nebuchadnezzar, said of Daniel's reputation:

> "Are you Daniel, one of the exiles my father the king brought from Judah? I have heard that the spirit of the gods is in you and that you have insight, intelligence, and outstanding wisdom. The wise men and enchanters were brought before me to read this writing and tell me what it means, but they could not explain it. Now I have heard that you are able to give interpretations and solve difficult problems."[77]

Daniel simply saw the world through different eyes. He had uncommon wisdom, a perspective abounding with an awareness of the supernatural. In abstract metaphors, strange images, and disturbing dreams and visions, Daniel imagined the depth and divine meaning underneath the superficial layers. Seeing beyond the immediate and temporal, he trusted God to carry out the larger picture even if it meant his life was at stake.

## CATALYZERS: THE CHARISMATIC INITIATOR

Because of their persuasiveness and ability to connect with a wide variety of individuals, Catalyzers generally excel in any kind of career involving salesmanship. They use their sharp eyes and minds to intuit what kinds of tactics might work with different customers, changing their approach like a

---

[74] Luke 2:19, New International Version.
[75] Daniel 2:13, 27-28, New International Version.
[76] Daniel 2:28, New International Version.
[77] Daniel 5:13-16, New International Version.

chameleon depending upon what is needed or will bring about the desired result. Because of their God-given ability to see and act upon opportunities, Catalyzers are often found at the forefront of a new project, initiative, or business venture. These are the individuals who encourage others to "strike while the iron is hot!" and to take risks that will pay off big in the long run. Since they are more concerned with feeling alive than feeling stable, Catalyzers might also be found in high-risk jobs, whether the danger is financial or physical. They get a thrill out of a wide variety of adrenaline filled situations, from leading a group of scuba divers through shark infested waters to investing and following the stock market. Because of their charisma and natural confidence, they also fit well into positions of leadership where they are able to motivate others to move in a new and exciting direction.

Within the church, Catalyzers might be drawn to ventures like planting churches that require initiative and more than a little risk and boldness. In commissioning His disciples to spread the Gospel throughout the known world, Jesus was full of the confidence, direction, and vision characteristic of a Catalyzer. Those with a good deal of Catalyzer energy are not "thin-skinned" to the possibility of failure or rejection; thus they are not afraid to forge ahead even in the midst of uncertainty to "close the deal." Whatever they choose to do as a career, ministry, or hobby, it will be strongly flavored with action, intensity, and a pinch of charm to get them out of any sticky situation. "For the Kingdom of God is not a matter of talk but of power," [78] Paul told the church at Corinth. Catalyzers live out this sense of power and possibility for change in tangible ways, constantly aware of opportunities to advance the Kingdom. "Be very careful, then, how you live—not as unwise but as wise, making the most of every opportunity, because the days are evil."[79]

### Risky Business—Caleb and Jacob

Caleb, son of Jephunneh, used his God-given ability to boldly take chances and risks in wholehearted obedience to the Lord. Of the twelve spies sent to survey Canaan and bring a report of the Promised Land to the rest of Israel, only Caleb

---

[78] 1 Corinthians 4:20, New International Version.
[79] Ephesians 5:15, New International Version.

and Joshua son of Nun had the faith and the boldness to motivate the people to action. With daring confidence in what God had said could be done, "Caleb silenced the people before Moses and said, 'We should go up and take possession of the land, for we can certainly do it.'"[80] Caleb's words ring with a willingness to risk complete obedience and call others to direct action with charismatic confidence, even in a situation of apparently insurmountable obstacles.

Caleb's fellow spies, however, did not have the same eagerness to do the seemingly impossible. Paralyzed by fear and practicality, the other spies declared, "All the people we saw there are of great size. We saw the Nephilim there…we seemed like grasshoppers in our own eyes, and we looked the same to them."[81] Yet Caleb saw the situation differently, exhibiting his willingness to put it all on the line, take bold, decisive action, and motivate others to do the same.

Caleb's vitality and enthusiasm for a challenge did not decrease with age. Even at the age of 85, Caleb showed the same motivating confidence, charisma, and boldness of his youth: "I am still as strong today as the day Moses sent me out; I'm just as vigorous to go out to battle now as I was then. Now give me this hill country that the Lord promised me that day. You yourself heard then that the Anakites were there and their cities were large and fortified, but, the Lord helping me, I will drive them out just as he said."[82]

Jacob, one of the patriarchs of the nation of Israel, also showed considerable energy in his Catalyzer floor. Yet as evidenced by Jacob's life, these natural, God-given strengths can be twisted or misused for our own self-advancement or selfish gain, resulting in the negative behaviors of Distress that we'll consider more in Chapter 9.

## ENERGIZERS: THE CREATIVELY YOUNG AT HEART

In order to stay constantly animated and engaged, Energizers require a degree of stimulation and expression in their work just as in every area of their lives. Because they receive energy from playful contact and have a childlike nature, Energizers generally enjoy working with children and

---

[80] Numbers 13:30, New International Version.
[81] Numbers 13:32-33, New International Version.
[82] Joshua 14:11-12, New International Version.

animals. You can often find Energizers in jobs that utilize their creative minds and free spirits, such as graphic design, visual art, or advertising. Many Energizers are natural performers or entertainers; stand-up comedians, dancers, actors, and other performing artists are likely to have considerable energy on their Energizer floor.

On the job, they need someone or something against which to push in a healthy way; thus Energizers do well working in teams and get energy from the interpersonal interaction. Energizers are invaluable in a "brainstorming" session, unafraid to think way outside the box. Because they get bored easily, Energizers also like an occupation that offers some degree of variety and allows for spontaneity and change.

The Energizer's bold acceptance of his or her uniqueness models a freedom found only in the Spirit. As they delight in and seek to experience life fully, Energizers invite others into that delight with a joyful, childlike zest. Energizers also have the capacity to experience the spectrum of emotions in life and enter into each moment with wholehearted abandon. Thus they have the capacity to "rejoice with those who rejoice; [and] mourn with those who mourn."[83]

Those with a high amount of Energizer energy are not subject to the same sorts of "boxes" or limitations as others who are more traditional or logical. Their desire to bounce or react against the assumed or accepted sometimes sends Energizers off in new directions. The unpredictable Energizer can be indispensable in creatively bringing the Kingdom of God to earth in the here and now.

When doubters or skeptics tried to corner Jesus with a question which begged one of two answers, Jesus would innovatively present a *third* option—one no one else had even considered as a possibility. This "third option" often went against the religious conventions or expectations of the day, creating quite a "stir." In a world where foreseeable options often look equally undesirable, Energizers use their humor, optimism, and off-the-wall creativity to bring about the unexpected.

---

[83] Romans 12:15, New International Version.

## Reaction and Restoration—Simon Peter

Of the many labels that might be attributed to Peter, one that *never* comes to mind is neutral. Whether he was royally messing up or boldly proclaiming the Good News of Jesus before thousands, Peter responded wholeheartedly in every situation without holding any of himself back. Peter, like all of us, cannot be defined as one pure type or caricature. But his strong reactions, energy for the Kingdom, and tendency to question or rebel against what was said reveal a prominent Energizer floor in his personality throughout the Gospel accounts and the building of the early church.

When Peter sees Jesus walking across the water of the lake, he responds by calling out, "Master, if it's really you, call me to come to you on the water!" Then Peter jumps right into the water, overcome by his response to Jesus' miraculous presence.[84] When Jesus later tells Peter He is going to wash Peter's feet, Peter reacts immediately and strongly: "No, you shall never wash my feet." Upon Jesus' reply—"Unless I wash you, you have no part with me"—Peter immediately retorts with equal fervor on the opposite end of the spectrum, proclaiming with gusto: "Then, Lord, not just my feet but my hands and my head as well!"[85] Several moments pass in an emotion-filled meal with Jesus and his closest friends. When Jesus tells Peter that no one can go where He is going but must follow later, Peter pushes against the statement: "Lord, why can't I follow you now?"[86] Just like a strong Energizer, Peter reacts to the opposing forces present, hearing "later" and immediately wondering "but why not *now*?"

These intense responses get Peter in trouble as the night wears on in the Garden of Gethsemane. Peter sees Jesus being threatened, pulls out his sword, and impulsively cuts off the ear of the high priest's servant in front of a detachment of Roman soldiers and important officials! At the end of the same night, a fearful Peter sneaks into the courtyard outside of Jesus' late night trial before Jewish religious leaders. When asked three separate times whether he is a disciple of this Jesus of Nazareth, Peter responds with increasingly strong and impassioned denials of what he is *not*! After the third

---

[84] Matthew 14: 28-30, The Message.
[85] John 13:6-9, New International Version.
[86] John 13:36-37, New International Version.

inquiry, "Peter got really nervous and swore: 'I never laid eyes on this man you are talking about!'"[87] When the rooster immediately announces Peter's betrayal just as Jesus predicted, Peter weeps bitterly, expressing the full force of his grief and shame.

Can you begin to see the passionate personality and reactionary nature of Peter clearly revealed in a snapshot of one significant night? Peter goes from saying he will lay his life down for Jesus to denying any association with him. His quick reactions lead to substantial mistakes and consequential deep shades of remorse and regret, but Jesus does not leave Peter there in his shame. In a beautiful scene of forgiveness and restoration, the resurrected Jesus gives Peter the chance to respond three times with declarations of love, "wiping out" his three denials and confirming Jesus' acceptance of Peter. Interestingly, Peter is given the task of proclaiming Jesus to the Jewish people as the promised Messiah of the Old Testament. This unconventional Energizer, uniquely designed to challenge the status quo and suggest new and creative approaches to doing life, becomes the rock of the early church in Jerusalem.

## "Providentially Equipped"

In general, God has uniquely designed us with specific gifts or Character Strengths that are a part of our make-up as individuals. These Character Strengths that are simply "true of us" must be recognized as having their source in God's unique design for us. When we submit these gifts to His will, God can and will use our strengths for the Kingdom in the ways in which they were intended. God used Mary's eternal mindset and willing submission to bring the Savior into the world. He transformed Paul's zealous, passionate dedication to persecuting Christians into a commitment to spreading the Gospel. Peter's energy and eagerness were given direction and focus in establishing a church under the new covenant in Jerusalem.

None of these individuals were perfect, sinless, or superhuman. Rather, God is exceptional at using exactly who we are to accomplish the purposes He has. And this includes

---

[87] Mark 14:71-72, The Message.

using every aspect of our lives—our greatest strengths as well as our weaknesses, our painful pasts and our hidden failures, our cultural, religious, political, socioeconomic backgrounds—to creatively work for redemption. As author Brennan Manning puts so beautifully:

> "Despite our physical cracks, intellectual limitations, emotional impairments, and spiritual fissures, we are providentially equipped to fulfill the unique purpose of our existence."[88]

A beautiful design unfolds as we trust God to use who we honestly are, in the entirety of our stories—we come alive as we find purpose in serving Him, and we also experience God's steadfast commitment to our maturity and healing. Author Donald Miller says, "If I have a hope, it's that God sat over the dark nothing and wrote you and me, specifically, into a story, and put us in with the sunset and the rainstorm as though to say, *Enjoy your place in my story. The beauty of it means you matter, and you can create within it even as I have created you.*"[89]

---

[88] Manning, Brennan (2009). *Ruthless Trust* (pp. 145-146). New York, NY: HarperCollins.
[89] Miller, Donald. (2009). *A Million Miles in a Thousand Years* (pp. 59). Nashville, TN: Thomas Nelson, Inc.

# 05 | *Personality Structure*

As unique and precious Image-Bearers of our Creator, we all reflect the character and glory of God in different ways depending upon how God has ordered and ordained our personalities. Thus far we have considered ways in which individuals with the Character Strengths of six different personality floors might contribute to the healthy functioning of a ministry, business, church, or family. But now, let's consider how all six of these floors interact with one another to make up the complete personality of *each individual*. We are not simply one personality floor or another; rather, our personalities are made up of far more complex combinations. How do the six personality floors function as the components that comprise the **Personality Structure**[90] of an individual?

In the chapter, we will introduce the *Process Communication*® and *Process Spiritual*™ *Models* as a means to understand how your personality has been designed. Dr. Kahler referred to one's **Personality Structure** as the specific and uniquely designed stacking and ordering of these six personality floors and the amount of "energy" you have available in each personality floor.[91]

To better understand this complex design, let's stop by a successful kite production company located downtown in the

---

[90] From Kahler, T. (1982, 1996). *Process Communication Management Seminar*. Little Rock, AR: Kahler Communications, Inc.; adapted by permission.
[91] From Kahler, T. (1979). *Process Communications Model*™ *(In Brief)*. Little Rock, AR: Taibi Kahler Associates, Inc.; adapted by permission.

business district: "B. Franklin Kites, Inc." We will use this six-story business as a metaphor for understanding how each of the six personality floors can be stacked in your Personality Structure and how the particular *order* of your floors shapes your personality.

## WELCOME TO B. FRANKLIN KITES, INC.

At the corner of E. Broadway and Central Street sits a six-story, red-brick office building. Flanked on either side by a quaint little coffee shop and an investing firm, this plain-faced building houses a manufacturing company that creates, develops, constructs, and sells kites. B. Franklin Kites, Inc. was named after Benjamin Franklin's famous experiment, which utilized a kite to attract lightning during a storm. As Christmas approaches and you scratch your head wondering what to buy for your picky, seven-year-old niece, you decide to step inside and take a look.

On the **first floor** of B. Franklin Kites, Inc., you find the Human Resources/Customer Service department. Upon entering the building, you feel immediately welcomed and comfortable. The employees of the first floor department care personally about your satisfaction and are excellent at relating to others. Their skills as peacemakers come in handy when dealing with the rare disgruntled customer or interpersonal employee conflicts.

The Accounting and Purchasing Department occupies the **second floor** of B. Franklin Kites, Inc. These individuals are skilled at handling details, crunching data and numbers, and keeping track of quantitative trends, statistics, and other information in a logical and analytical manner. Wandering amongst the cubicles, you notice Excel spreadsheets open on countless computers and desks that are obviously operating on their own system of organization and neatness.

The **third floor** of B. Franklin Kites, Inc. is dedicated to the Quality Control department. There is a seriousness about the atmosphere of this department that suggests an environment of dedication and commitment to a job well done. This department contains individuals who are good at following rules, maintaining high standards, and making sure every single kite, no matter how big or small, is of exceptional quality. A few qualified individuals on this floor are also responsible for risk management and compliance, making sure that B. Franklin Kites, Inc. flawlessly meets all the fire, safety, and health codes applicable to this business.

You step onto the **fourth floor** of B. Franklin Kites, Inc. only to be bumped in the head with a kite shaped like a flying taco. Rubbing your head in a slight daze, you dimly hear someone exclaim with enthusiasm: "Welcome to Product Testing and Development!" This department interacts with and experiences the product itself, engages in spontaneous play, and brainstorms about creative ways to make kites more fun.

The **fifth floor** is almost empty, as many of the Sales and Marketing representatives of this department are out on the job, selling kites to anyone who will listen. Adept at making a convincing sales pitch, these charismatic and convincing individuals work on commission and prefer to set their own rules and schedules in the building.

The top floor of B. Franklin Kites, Inc. deals with Production, Shipping, and Innovation. The **sixth floor** seems an appropriate place for members of this department, who prefer to receive clear instructions and then be left alone to complete the tasks of sewing, cutting, and packing the kites. This department is also the seat of great ideas, however; an employee on this floor came up with the innovative idea of how to use recycled materials to make a new line of "green" kites.

In order to run with maximum efficiency, a business like B. Franklin Kites, Inc. cannot be concerned with only one aspect of its business. What if B. Franklin Kites, Inc. were a single story stucco building with only a Quality Control department inside? What about customers who need to talk about potential employment opportunities with the company? How will anyone know about these kites unless someone gets out of the corporate office and sells them? Who will make sure these kites are actually fun and thus marketable?

To see every department in your tour through B. Franklin Kites, Inc., you had to visit six different floors. That's a whole lot of stairs. Thankfully, the smart designers of B. Franklin Kites, Inc. equipped this building with an elevator,[92] allowing for more efficient access to the different departments as needed. Thus if I want to make sure every kite has been appropriately designed, I can hop onto the elevator and ride up three floors to the Quality Control Department. If I need to talk to someone about possibly increasing prices for the kites, I take the elevator to the Accounting and Purchasing department. To talk with a Human Resources representative, I need only walk through the front door.

Of course, not every building with six floors is designed in the same way. For a business concerned primarily with retail and walk up sales, it would make more sense to make the Sales and Marketing department more readily accessible for employees and customers. The investing firm next door to B. Franklin Kites, Inc. has Accounting and Purchasing on the bottom floor, as they deal primarily with numeric trends and statistics. Because this particular kite manufacturing company tends to encourage a great deal of personal interaction, Customer Service and Human Resources is the most easily accessible department.

Each of the six floors of B. Franklin Kites, Inc. has a specific, identifiable role within the overall functioning of the business of making and selling kites. And the design of the building itself—the accessibility of the various departments—is specifically suited to the type of business being conducted. So what does B. Franklin Kites, Inc. have to do with your personality, with unique designs, with becoming and serving as you were created to do? The different departments of this kite manufacturing company, B. Franklin Kites, Inc., contain characteristics representative of the Character Strengths of the six personality floors we discussed in Chapters 3 and 4. Depending upon how God uniquely designed you, the six personality floors in your Personality Structure will be ordered in a certain way to accomplish "the good works, which God

---

[92] From Kahler, T. (1996, 2012). *Process Communication Model® Seminar—Seminar One: Core Topics.* (pp.16). Little Rock, AR: Kahler Communications, Inc.; adapted by permission.

has prepared in advance for you to do."[93]

The warm, compassionate, sensitive **Harmonizer** makes a caring Human Resources/Customer Service representative. The logical, responsible, and organized **Achiever** has all the tools necessary to be efficiently employed in the Accounting and Purchasing Department. The observant, dedicated, conscientious **Persister** serves as an excellent Quality Control manager on the third floor. The spontaneous, creative, and playful nature of the **Energizer** makes him or her the perfect tester of the "fun potential" of the product. The Sales and Marketing Department is likely to flourish and grow under the adaptable, persuasive, and charming **Catalyzer**. And the calm, reflective, and imaginative **Dreamer** is satisfied with the clear and tactile tasks of the remote sixth floor dealing with Production, Shipping, and Innovation.

## Personality Structure

As a caring Master, God has indeed planned "good works" for us to do as uniquely designed individuals. And as a brilliant Architect, God has intentionally constructed our individual Personality Structures for *our* good and for the accomplishment of *His* good purpose. Though there are six personality floors, these floors are arranged in each individual differently according to our unique callings and the particular talents required. With six personality floors available, there are a stunning **720** possible combinations just in the order of one's Personality Structure![94]

**Example: Personality Structures**

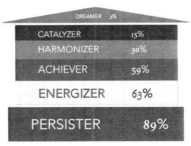

All Personality Structures/Condominiums adapted and used with permission from Kahler, T. (1988, 1992, 2000, 2004). *The Mastery of Management*. Little Rock, AR: Kahler Communications, Inc.

---

[93] Ephesians 2:10, New International Version.
[94] From Kahler, T. (1996, 2012). *Process Communication Model® Seminar—Seminar One: Core Topics.* (pp.16). Little Rock, AR: Kahler Communications, Inc.; adapted by permission.

## Your Base Floor

In the *Process Communication Model®*, Dr. Kahler identified the bottom floor of the Personality Structure as the **Base**.[95] You can think about your Base floor as "home base" in your personality. God laid your Base floor at the bottom of your Personality Structure as the *Foundation*[96] upon which everything else is built. Your Base is the initial and defining floor of your personality that will be readily seen or identified by others; it's the sign out in front of your store advertising the core of who you are and what you do. The Base floor of your Personality Structure is present and evident early in childhood development and remains your Base floor throughout your life.[97] The remainder of your Personality Structure "order" is generally set by age seven.[98]

BASE — stable core of who you are

According to your unique design, your Base floor will be the most readily accessible for you. Think back to Chapter 3 discussing the specific Character Strengths of each of the six personality floors. Remember Riley, who had a joyful, childlike spirit and a contagious zest for life that affected even a sullen teenager? Riley is an excellent example of an Energizer Base. Your Base floor is so central to who you are that we sometimes identify a person by that aspect of his or her personality alone, such as "Elise is a Harmonizer," or "Geoffrey was a Persister." What we really mean when we use this phrase is: "Elise has a Harmonizer Base. The qualities of the Harmonizer floor are central to who she is. However, Elise is not only a Harmonizer; it is simply her strongest and most easily identifiable personality floor."

---

[95] From Kahler, T. (1988, 1992, 2000, 2004). *The Mastery of Management*. Little Rock, AR: Kahler Communications, Inc.; adapted by permission.
[96] In his earlier works, Dr. Maris referred to Kahler's "Base" term as one's "Foundation." We will be using the PCM® term Base in this book. From Maris, R. (1996). *Your Great Design*. Little Rock, AR: Transpersonal Technologies, L.L.C.
[97] From Kahler, T. (1996, 2012). *Process Communication Model® Seminar—Seminar One: Core Topics*. (pp.16). Little Rock, AR: Kahler Communications, Inc.; adapted by permission.
[98] From Stansbury, P. (1990). Report of Adherence to Theory discovered when the Personality Patterns Inventory was administered to Subjects Twice. Little Rock, AR: Taibi Kahler Associates, Inc.; adapted by permission.

## Example: Personality Structure with Energy (%)

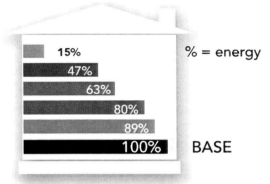

You will feel comfortable, natural, and energized when operating out of the Character Strengths and attitudes of your Base personality floor. Dr. Kahler referred to the ease or difficulty with which one can "access" a particular floor of the Personality Structure (and its correlating characteristics) as the amount of **energy** available for that personality floor.[99] The amount of energy is represented in the graph of your Personality Structure by the length of the horizontal bar on that floor, indicated by a percentage. You will have the greatest amount of energy—and thus the longest horizontal bar—in your Base floor.

## Energy and Elevators

To allow for greater efficiency, B. Franklin Kites, Inc. is equipped with an elevator. This elevator allows employees access to various floors other than their "Base" department. Your Personality Structure is also equipped with an **elevator** that allows you to access the Character Strengths and other qualities of the six different floors in your Structure.[100]

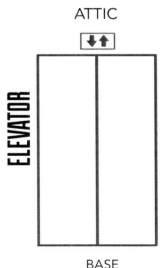

---

[99] From Kahler, T. (2008). *The Process Therapy Model: The Six Personality Types with Adaptations.* Little Rock, AR: Taibi Kahler Associates, Inc.
[100] From Kahler, T. (1996, 2012). *Process Communication Model® Seminar—Seminar One: Core Topics.* (pp.16). Little Rock, AR: Kahler Communications, Inc.; adapted by permission.

In order for this elevator to function properly, you need to consistently meet the Psychological Needs of your Phase floor, Base floor, and Stage Floors, which will be discussed in greater depth later in this book.[101] For now, just know that in order to communicate with others who are differently wired than you or to access less familiar Strengths in your Structure, it is important for you to get your Needs met in healthy ways.

Any personality floors for which you have anywhere from 76-100% energy are places you like to hang out.[102] This could apply solely to your Base personality floor. However, according to your unique design, this could include all six floors! These floors with higher amounts of energy—as indicated by the percentages and horizontal bars in your Personality Structure—are easily accessible and leave you feeling energized. It is natural to experience and relate to the world through these floors in your personality. When called upon, you can and will readily operate out of the Character Strengths associated with these floors, hopping on and off the elevator without much effort.

At times in life, circumstances or relationships may require you to leave your Base in order to access the Character Strengths of a different floor of your personality. In order to visit these other floors in your personality, you will need to expend a little (or a lot of) energy by taking the elevator. If your particular Psychological Needs are being met, taking the elevator up one floor is not a big deal and may not require much more energy than hanging out in your Base. For some individuals, however, even moving up one floor takes considerable effort. These people tend to be "specialists" with their gifting concentrated primarily on one personality floor—that of their Base floor.

Floors of your Personality Structure in which you have 50-75% energy are not quite as strongly utilized but still readily accessible.[103] You can operate out of the Character Strengths of these floors without too much strain or excessive loss of energy, though it will not be quite as "natural" as accessing floors for which you have more energy. Riding the elevator to

---

[101] From Kahler, T. (1996, 2012). *Process Communication Model® Seminar—Seminar One: Core Topics.* (pp.57). Little Rock, AR: Kahler Communications, Inc.; adapted by permission.
[102] From Kahler, T. (2008). *The Process Therapy Model: The Six Personality Types with Adaptations.* Little Rock, AR: Taibi Kahler Associates, Inc.
[103] From Kahler, T. (2008). *The Process Therapy Model: The Six Personality Types with Adaptations.* Little Rock, AR: Taibi Kahler Associates, Inc.

these floors too frequently may begin to feel a little tiring, particularly if your Psychological Needs are depleted.

For all—specialists or not—the farther up you are asked to go in your Personality Structure in order to relate, work, etc., the more energy you are likely to expend and the more likely you will be to move into negative thoughts and behaviors. Floors in your personality for which you have 26-50% energy become more difficult to access.[104] That elevator ride begins to feel more and more tedious. If you stay on these floors very long, you will likely need to go back to your stronger personality floors to regain your energy.

## Attic Floors

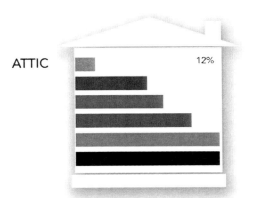

The least accessible floors of your personality have been arranged intentionally closest to the top of your Structure and are thus harder to visit. If you have less than 25% energy on a particular floor of your personality, you will find it very difficult to access the Character Strengths or Perceptions (particular points of view) characteristic of this personality floor.[105] Dr. Kahler identified these areas of your Personality Structure with less than 25% energy as **Attics**.[106] Similar to an attic in your home, these Attics in your Personality Structure might be hard to access and tiring to remain in for a length of time, yet they also hold things (such as Strengths) that you may need occasionally.

Let's make this a little less theoretical and a little more tangible. What does this arrangement of your Personality Structure and its various energies look like?

Suppose you were reading the discussion of each of the six personality floors earlier and identified strongly with the characteristics of the Catalyzer floor. You love adventure,

---

[104] From Kahler, T. (2008). *The Process Therapy Model: The Six Personality Types with Adaptations*. Little Rock, AR: Taibi Kahler Associates, Inc.
[105] From Kahler, T. (2008). *The Process Therapy Model: The Six Personality Types with Adaptations*. Little Rock, AR: Taibi Kahler Associates, Inc.
[106] From Kahler, T. (1982). *Process Communication Management Seminar*. Little Rock, AR: Kahler Communications, Inc.; adapted by permission.

adapting well to new situations. You are uniquely gifted to persuade others to see things your way and have thus headed up some valuable initiatives. Knowing these things about yourself, you apply to B. Franklin Kites, Inc. for a position in Sales and Marketing. You're going to sell these kites like they are the hottest new product on the market. You're going to convince your customers that they've simply "got to have it!"

But the only available position is as a "Kite Technician" on the sixth floor, which is concerned primarily with Production, Shipping, and Innovation. This particular job depends upon the strengths of the Dreamer personality floor, which is an Attic in your Personality Structure. Because you desperately need a job, you take the position. So you stick it out for the first four days of sitting in one seat by yourself and operating a sewing machine for eight solid hours. After seemingly endless hours of no adventure, no contact, and no change, you are completely fried. Exhausted. Miserable. And lashing out at your fellow employees, who seem strangely peaceful and content about their sixth floor confinement.

In this case, you are being asked to spend uncomfortable amounts of time in an area of your Personality Structure that is an Attic, and the result is constant distress for you and for everyone around you. You beg the administration at B. Franklin Kites, Inc. for a transfer. You are moved to the Accounting and Purchasing Department on the second floor, which requires the logical, analytical, detail-oriented tendencies of the Achiever personality floor. You are still not being asked to use your Character Strengths as a Catalyzer Base. But happily, you have 81% energy in the Achiever floor of your personality, which the Accounting and Purchasing Department relies upon heavily. Though your job is not directly related to using the qualities of your Catalyzer Base, you have enough energy in this Achiever floor to access its Character Strengths with considerable ease. You find a tremendous amount of satisfaction in balancing checkbooks and are competent in your ability to contribute to the company's financial decisions. And with a little hang-gliding on the weekends, you fulfill your desire for adrenaline soaked adventure and excitement outside of the workplace.

It is true that a business cannot be comprised of purely one department. (You cannot "sell" kites unless someone is actually making kites, for instance). But it is also true that businesses specialize. A business that tries to "do it all" rarely does anything well—how many kite making, financial planning, catering, family counseling restaurants do you know of? Your individual personality cannot be boxed into one pure personality "type," but God has arranged your Personality Structure with its varying energies with a particular specialty and calling in mind.

Your Base personality floor is available to you all the time. You can be comfortable there, spending all the time you want without tiring or needing to visit another floor. Ministry and service flowing from your personality Base feel naturally fulfilling and organic, echoing with a deep sense of "This is what I was made to do!" Conversely, the Attics of your Personality Structure are areas of your personality that may well have very little available energy and consequently leave you drained, stressed, or distressed.

Your Base floor houses the Character Strengths that flow naturally from the way God has designed your personality. God also intentionally crafted you with a corresponding way of viewing and experiencing the world around you, which uniquely equips you to fulfill your purpose. We will explore these **Perceptions**[107] in the next chapter.

---

[107] From Kahler, T. (1979). *Process Communications Model™ (In Brief)*. Little Rock, AR: Taibi Kahler Associates, Inc.; adapted by permission.

# 06 | Perceptions

DO YOU SEE TWO FACES, OR A VASE?

What do you see when you look at this image? Does this image contain a vase? Or two faces in profile looking at one another?

The answer is yes.

Depending upon which details you attend to, what you consider to be foreground or background, what visual cues you prioritize as important, you might clearly see one image before you are capable of perceiving the other. But both interpretations of the image are equally correct and represent legitimate perceptions; there is no right (or wrong).[108]

IT IS SIMPLY A MATTER OF PERCEPTION.

## WITHIN GOD'S DESIGN

As part of God's special preparation and gifting of His creatures, He has given each of us a particular way of perceiving the world. We find evidence of different types of perception—that is, varied ways of sorting and understanding information—throughout the animal kingdom. Owls can see

---

[108] Image taken from "Optical Illusions and Pictures." [Website]. Retrieved from http://www.123opticalillusions.com/pages/Facevase.php

very well in the dark but cannot perceive colors. Eagles attend to tiny movements from incredible heights but cannot see in the dark. Deer do not see color but are exquisitely sensitive to the slightest movement. In each instance, the mode of perception given to each creature is uniquely linked to that animal's purpose, crafted by an intelligent and loving Creator. The same specificity and gifting of perception is true of human beings as Image-Bearers and reflectors of divine character. Just as we are created with a particular set of Character Strengths and gifts to offer the Kingdom, we are also designed with a corresponding Perception.

In his original research, Dr. Kahler identified six distinct **Perceptions,** each of which correspond to the six Personality Types or floors in the Personality Structure: *emotions, thoughts, opinions, inactions, actions and reactions.*[109]

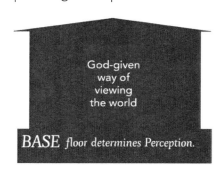

Our **Perception** serves as the grid through which we take in the world and filter our experiences. This lens is fundamental to how we see life and remains constant, as it connects to our unchanging Base personality floor. In addition to describing how we naturally take in information, our Perceptions also influence how we respond to the world around us, affecting how we engage in relationships as well as our preferences in communication. As you become more familiar with this model, you will be able to discern another's Base by the telltale cues that express an underlying Perception.[110]

## Perceptions at B. Franklin Kites, Inc.

We've established that each of the six floors of B. Franklin Kites, Inc. specializes in handling a different but necessary

---

[109] From Maris, R. (1996). *Your Great Design*. Little Rock, AR: Transpersonal Technologies, L.L.C.. Kahler, T. (1979). *Process Communications Model™ (In Brief)*. Little Rock, AR: Taibi Kahler Associates, Inc.; adapted by permission.
[110] From Kahler, T. (1996, 2012). *The Process Communication Model® Seminar—Seminar One: Core Topics.* (pp. 9). Little Rock, AR: Kahler Communications, Inc.

part of the business. In order to accomplish the diverse tasks involved in designing, making, and selling kites, every floor in B. Franklin Kites, Inc. requires a different type of attention—specific "glasses" so to speak for filtering through what is essential for the job at hand and what can remain unnoticed or overlooked. These different "glasses" are views of others and the world, identified by Dr. Kahler as the six Perceptions for each Personality floor or Type.[111]

As people skilled in dealing with and taking care of people, the hospitable Human Resources and Customer Service representatives on the first floor are specifically gifted in attending to personal needs. They intuit the emotional state of each customer individually and can then respond to that customer's needs accordingly with sensitivity and compassion.

This kind of emotional perceptivity characteristic of the first floor employees would not be as helpful for the representatives in Accounting and Purchasing. These data-crunching employees need to view their jobs through a meticulous attention to details involving facts, logic, and calculations. The Accounting and Purchasing Department employees are skilled at their jobs because they naturally take in information through an analytical, fact-oriented perception. When a customer is trying to get his order straightened out, anger, disappointment, or even praise might all be interpreted as "noise" distracting from the pertinent data and task at hand. By tuning out what is unnecessary, these employees can efficiently solve the problem.

Third floor employees in the Quality Control department are well served by their attention to standards and values. Skills in perceiving data or relating to people might be helpful for a Quality Control employee, but ultimately their job requires statements of opinion about which products are of high quality and which ones are not up to par. Thus their tendency to immediately perceive what is "not right" is essential for the success of their department.

Perceptions are quite different on the fourth floor Product Testing and Development Department, where fun and humor reign! One well-intentioned employee from Quality Control often meets unexpected "attitude" when he points out that

---

[111] From Kahler, T. (1979). *Process Communications Model*™ *(In Brief)*. Little Rock, AR: Taibi Kahler Associates, Inc.; adapted by permission.

Zoe, a fourth floor "Fun Tester," has missed her parking space by half a foot again. It may be off by a full foot or two tomorrow…on purpose. In order to do their job well, these fourth floor employees don't need to be caught up in calculations or in standards of quality. They need to pay attention to what is creative, engaging, and unique about their product!

The employees working in Sales and Marketing on the fifth floor constantly perceive opportunities to market their product, paying attention to chances to take action and make a sell! Attending to customer comfort would not be bad for these employees, but it is less important for their job than having their eyes on the lookout for opportunities to take quick and decisive action.

And those folks in Production, Shipping, and Innovation? They pay attention to their thoughts and reflections, following rabbit trails that interest them. Human Resources employees might be lonely up on the sixth floor and long for more active human interaction; Product Testers would likely be bored. But the ability of these innovators to "zone out" and be present to their own thoughts allows them to take great pleasure in simple tactile tasks like sewing and cutting.

## PERCEPTION: A GOD-GIVEN LENS

Each of the six Perceptions is deeply rooted in an underlying belief about the world and how I am meant to operate within it. Yet because these beliefs are central to who we are, they can be difficult to distinguish as our given means of *perception* rather than objective reality. "It is extremely difficult for most people to recognize which ideas are governing their life and *how* those ideas are governing their life. This is partly because one commonly *identifies* his or her own governing ideas with reality, pure and simple," said Dallas Willard.[112]

Simply put, we often believe that how **we** see the world is exclusively how it is. Each of the six personality floors sees and experiences the world through a different lens colored by a particular belief:[113]

---

[112] Willard, Dallas. (2002). *Renovation of the Heart* (pp. 97). Colorado Springs, CO: NavPress.
[113] Beliefs adapted by permission from Kahler, T. (1988, 1992, 2000, 2004). *The Mastery of Management*. Little Rock, AR: Kahler Communications, Inc.; adapted by permission.

// The Harmonizer **feels**: "If we can learn to love and care for each other well, the world will be a warm and wonderful place."

// An Achiever **thinks**: "If people would get their facts straight and think logically before acting, all of us would be more productive, therefore making the world a better functioning place."

// A Persister **believes**: "If everyone would learn the rules of life and obey them, then the world would be a safe and wonderful place for us all."

// The Dreamer **reflects**: "As long as I am given time and space to reflect and explore interesting thoughts, the world is a peaceful and enjoyable place."

// The Catalyzer **acts**: "If everyone were willing to just do it and take a few risks, then the world would be a more exciting place."

// An Energizer **reacts**: "If everyone would just lighten up and not take themselves so seriously all the time, the world would be a more joyful place."

*Which glasses are you wearing?*

## EMOTIONS

Those who have a Harmonizer Base view the world through the lens of their **emotions**.[114] They respond first with the heart, considering how others might feel or be affected. Empathetic to the core, they are able to put themselves in someone else's shoes and literally feel what that individual might feel. Harmonizers are highly intuitive and sensitive to the subtle hints and changes in mood and emotion around them. Because of this emotional perceptivity and their genuine empathy and concern for others, Harmonizers will often adapt themselves without even trying in order that others will feel special, cared about, and noticed. This innate response to adapt and please can be also be a struggle when twisted in the service of oneself, as you will see in Chapter 9 on Distress.

---

[114] From Kahler, T. (1988, 1992, 2000, 2004). *The Mastery of Management.* Little Rock, AR: Kahler Communications, Inc.; adapted by permission.

## Logical thoughts

Achievers view the world through the lens of their logical **thoughts**.[115] Responding initially and primarily with a logical intellect, Achievers are analytical, objective, and sequential thinkers. Those with Achiever Bases naturally gather data in situations unemotionally through their senses. They then use their objectivity, common sense, and keen minds to come to rational, well-thought out conclusions. Achievers efficiently manage details and sort information into reasonable categories. They employ logic to reach the best solution to any problem, relying upon predictable patterns such as "cause and effect" or "if…then" thinking.

## Opinions

Persisters view the world through the lens of their **opinions**.[116] With a deep and steady system of internal values, Persisters consistently evaluate their external world against that internal grid of principles and convictions. Unlike the Harmonizer who has an intuition or impression and literally checks in his or her heart for confirmation, or the Achiever who takes a digital picture in his "mind's eye" and jots down descriptive and relevant details, the Persister scrutinizes closely how things are and compares them to an internal "template" of how things *should* be. Those with a Persister Base are thus particularly attuned to what does not fit or needs to be changed. Through an observant (although not necessarily objective) filter of strong convictions and definite opinions, Persisters often classify ideas, people, and situations, as good or bad, right or wrong, black or white.

---

[115] From Kahler, T. (1988, 1992, 2000, 2004). *The Mastery of Management*. Little Rock, AR: Kahler Communications, Inc.; adapted by permission.
[116] From Kahler, T. (1988, 1992, 2000, 2004). *The Mastery of Management*. Little Rock, AR: Kahler Communications, Inc.; adapted by permission.

## INACTIONS (REFLECTIONS)

Dreamers view the world through the lens of their **inactions** by reflecting.[117] For those with a Dreamer Base personality floor, thoughts need not be externally stimulated or couched in logical or sequential terms. Dreamers prefer to turn their eyes inward into an imaginative world of possibilities, abstractions, metaphors, or ideas. Without feeling drawn into action or pressured to "do," Dreamers can ask "What if?" in innovative ways. They typically await clear direction or encouragement before moving from reflection and passivity to decisive or external action. In order to outwardly engage with others, Dreamers must take their elevator to access a different personality floor.

## ACTIONS

Those with the Catalyzer personality floor as their Base view the world through the lens of their **actions**.[118] With highly attuned senses and perceptive observation, Catalyzers move through life constantly scanning situations for the right moment to take action. When action does occur, it is characterized by immediacy and decisiveness. They are watching for a chance to act out as a catalyst—to put opportunities and resources together to make things happen. Because Catalyzers feel alive in moments of quick adrenaline or intense stimulation, they typically seek out opportunities where it is necessary to think or react quickly, seize the moment, or put everything on the line. And when such opportunities are not present in the current situation, they move on to a fresh setting.

---

[117] From Kahler, T. (1988, 1992, 2000, 2004). *The Mastery of Management*. Little Rock, AR: Kahler Communications, Inc.; adapted by permission.
[118] From Kahler, T. (1988, 1992, 2000, 2004). *The Mastery of Management*. Little Rock, AR: Kahler Communications, Inc.; adapted by permission.

## REACTIONS (LIKES AND DISLIKES)

Energizers view the world through the lens of their **reactions**—particularly their likes and dislikes.[119] Rather than the empathy of the Harmonizer, the digital picture of the Achiever, the template of the Persister, the inner pond of the Dreamer, or the sharp, opportunity-seeking eyes of the Catalyzer: the Energizer Base's ever-present perspective is more like a video game—"Watch what happens when I push this button...!" For an Energizer, the external world serves as a surface against which to push and get a reaction. Energizers perceive life as full of opposing forces, responding with strong and almost immediate feedback such as "I love it" or "I hate it." With a deep sense of independence and individuality, Energizers often define themselves by what they are **not** and boldly challenge conventions or the status quo.

## ADVERTISING WHO WE ARE

The false belief that we all see the world in the same way leads to inevitable frustration. If I expect everyone to be like me—to talk just like me, to think just like me, to value exactly what I value—miscommunication and disappointment will reign in my life. It's a little like expecting my eyes to perceive the same sensory cues as my nose: it is illogical to reprimand my nose for not seeing a circle or get angry with my eyes for failing to smell something burning. The human body simply isn't made to function this way, and expecting it to do so is a false expectation that sets us up for constant disappointment. As we communicate and live in collaboration and community with other people, we notice that people do indeed see, experience, and respond to the world in unique and often polar opposite ways. And this, my friends, is a *good* thing!

We typically advertise our core beliefs about the world—rooted in our foundational Perceptions—in the ways or "currencies" through which we communicate. Dr. Kahler

---

[119] From Kahler, T. (1988, 1992, 2000, 2004). *The Mastery of Management.* Little Rock, AR: Kahler Communications, Inc.; adapted by permission.

identified the "currency" used by each of the six Personality Types or floors as: *compassion, logic, values, imagination, charm, and humor*.[120] In the *Process Spiritual Model*™, we refer to these currencies of communication as "Advertisements."[121] These currencies or Advertisements are evident in our habits of communication, whether verbal or non-verbal. Becoming aware of these cues is not a "fool-proof" method, a relational shortcut, or a means of stereotyping unique individuals into oversimplified categories. Rather, we are using what is observable in our communication styles to understand not only the *content* of what we say but also the *process* of what we say. Dr. Kahler contends that:

"HOW WE SAY SOMETHING IS SO MUCH MORE IMPORTANT THAN WHAT WE SAY."[122]

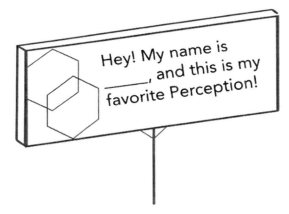

All "currencies"/advertisements adapted by permission from Kahler, T. (1996, 2012). *The Process Communication Model® Seminar—Seminar One: Core Topics.* (pp. 5). Little Rock, AR: Kahler Communications, Inc.

When speaking from the Harmonizer floor of our personalities, words are used like a soft blanket—a means to provide comfort, warmth, and emotional nurturance. Through kindness, consideration, and encouragement, Harmonizers gently suggest that we spend our energy learning how to get along and help one another feel good about ourselves. This is evident not only in the words chosen by Harmonizers but also

---

[120] From Kahler, T. (1988, 1992, 2000, 2004). *The Mastery of Management.* Little Rock, AR: Kahler Communications, Inc.; adapted by permission.
[121] From Maris, R. (1996). *Your Great Design.* Little Rock, AR: Transpersonal Technologies, L.L.C.
[122] From Kahler, T. (1996, 2012). *The Process Communication Model® Seminar—Seminar One: Core Topics.* (pp. 22). Little Rock, AR: Kahler Communications, Inc.

in their unconscious tones, postures, gestures, and facial expressions. Thus every aspect of communication—verbal and non-verbal—clearly communicates that Harmonizers care about feelings, valuing their own emotions and the emotions of others. Their eyes speak of relational interest and warmth; their foreheads and eyebrows are often lifted in a half moon shape, silently but actively communicating understanding and acceptance.[123] The Harmonizer's currency in communication is **compassion.**[124]

Operating under the guidelines of equality and logic, Achievers fill their words with the invocation to think first. An individual with an Achiever Base wants to deal in facts and figure, timetables and schedules, predictability and control. In communication, they ask questions in order to know the details and then use logic to solve problems. Over time, an individual with a strong amount of Achiever may develop parallel lines across the middle of the forehead, non-verbal residue from the Achiever's unconscious expression of thought and analysis.[125] Their currency in communication is **logic.**[126]

Individuals with a Persister Base at the foundation of their Personality Structure are likely to not only advertise their perspective through their words but also to work to convert others to their worldview. Promoting a cause of justice, ethics, and fortitude of character, Persisters deeply believe that the safety and well-being of our world is dependent on people believing the right thing and faithfully adhering to those beliefs. Their words explicitly preach as much; they are never hesitant to express their beliefs or clearly communicate their strict standards. When weighing an external event or belief against an internal standard, individuals with Persister Bases will furrow their eyebrows, creating two vertical parallel lines that advertise a forming judgment or opinion.[127] Their currency in communication is **values.**[128]

---

[123] From Kahler, T. (1996, 2012). *The Process Communication Model® Seminar—Seminar One: Core Topics.* (pp. 12). Little Rock, AR: Kahler Communications, Inc.
[124] From Kahler, T. (1996, 2012). *The Process Communication Model® Seminar—Seminar One: Core Topics.* (pp. 5). Little Rock, AR: Kahler Communications, Inc.
[125] From Kahler, T. (1996, 2012). *The Process Communication Model® Seminar—Seminar One: Core Topics.* (pp. 10). Little Rock, AR: Kahler Communications, Inc.
[126] From Kahler, T. (1996, 2012). *The Process Communication Model® Seminar—Seminar One: Core Topics.* (pp. 5). Little Rock, AR: Kahler Communications, Inc.
[127] From Kahler, T. (1996, 2012). *The Process Communication Model® Seminar—Seminar One: Core Topics.* (pp. 11). Little Rock, AR: Kahler Communications, Inc.
[128] From Kahler, T. (1996, 2012). *The Process Communication Model® Seminar—Seminar One: Core Topics.* (pp. 5). Little Rock, AR: Kahler Communications, Inc.

A Dreamer is unlikely to actively "advertise" anything. Through their thoughtful, introspective, reflective Perception, Dreamers imply that they enjoy imagining possibilities, looking at things in different ways, and spending time with their own ideas and imaginings. Sometimes the Dreamer's most telling form of communication is a thoughtful silence implying an internal world of musings. What is *not said* is often more communicative than what is stated out loud. Their silence is not so much a "Keep Out" sign as it is a simple request to "Please Don't Walk on the Grass." An individual with a Dreamer Base, content to muse and wonder internally, can often appear to the outside world like a blank slate or the still surface of a pond with very few facial wrinkles or ripples.[129] Their currency in communication is **imagination**.[130]

Strong Catalyzers exude a sense of action and urgency through their words, facial expressions, and body language. Created to act quickly, boldly, and persuasively, the Catalyzer declares: "We've talked enough; let's do something!" Their verbal cues are clear and decisive statements aimed at making things move—and now. Nonverbally, individuals with Catalyzer Bases often have a ruddy complexion and communicate persuasion with a raised eyebrow, charming smile, confident posture, or overall aura of charisma.[131] Their currency in communication is **charm**.[132]

Energizers radiate intensity, vibrancy, and playfulness. Viewing life as a brilliant spectrum of experiences, emotions, and new sensations, an Energizer's language unapologetically and playfully shouts: "I have strong likes and dislikes! I either love something or I hate it. NO middle ground for me." Energizer Base individuals have free and full facial expressions, blatantly advertising the exact state of their current reactions—whether utter frustration or complete joy. These reactions are particularly evident in the Energizer's eyes and mouth through defined smile lines and laugh lines.[133] Of course, the expression may change within only a few seconds!

---

[129] From Kahler, T. (1996, 2012). *The Process Communication Model® Seminar—Seminar One: Core Topics.* (pp. 13). Little Rock, AR: Kahler Communications, Inc.
[130] From Kahler, T. (1996, 2012). *The Process Communication Model® Seminar—Seminar One: Core Topics.* (pp. 5). Little Rock, AR: Kahler Communications, Inc.
[131] From Kahler, T. (1996, 2012). *The Process Communication Model® Seminar—Seminar One: Core Topics.* (pp. 15). Little Rock, AR: Kahler Communications, Inc.
[132] From Kahler, T. (1996, 2012). *The Process Communication Model® Seminar—Seminar One: Core Topics.* (pp. 5). Little Rock, AR: Kahler Communications, Inc.
[133] From Kahler, T. (1996, 2012). *The Process Communication Model® Seminar—Seminar One: Core Topics.* (pp. 14). Little Rock, AR: Kahler Communications, Inc.

Their currency in communication is **humor**.[134]

**Table 2:** Identifying Perceptions (Base) Through Language

| Base | Perception | Phrases | % of population |
|---|---|---|---|
| Harmonizer | Emotions | I feel; In my heart I know; I understand how you feel; Are you comfortable?; I'm sad about… | 30% (75% F; 25% M) |
| Achiever | Thoughts | I think; Who/what/when/where/how?; What options…?; If this, then this; Does that mean…? | 25% (75% M; 25% F) |
| Persister | Opinions | I believe; In my opinion; You ought to; I admire and respect; I value; You should… | 10% (75% M; 25% F) |
| Dreamer | Inactions | I need time to reflect; What if…?; I need space; I need to wait for more direction; Wait and see… | 10% (60% F; 40% M) |
| Catalyzer | Actions | Do it; What can we do right now?; Make it happen; Give it your best shot; Get to the bottom line | 5% (60% M; 40% F) |
| Energizer | Reactions | I love it/I hate it; No matter what, I'm going to be me; Because it's fun!; Wow, that's awesome!; That really stinks! | 20% (60% F; 40% M) |

From Kahler, T. (1988, 1994, 2000, 2004). *The Mastery of Management.* Little Rock, AR: Kahler Communications, Inc.; Kahler, T. (1996, 2012). *The Process Communication Mode® Seminar—Seminar One: Core Topics.* (pp. 6). Little Rock, AR: Kahler Communications, Inc.; adapted by permission.

## APPLICATION: LEARNING NEW LANGUAGES

As we become increasingly aware of why we communicate as we do, we mature into a deepening understanding that these varied Perceptions are good and necessary gifts that enrich and expand our experience of life! In God's grace, we can grow to appreciate and value the diverse ways we have been gifted to view and respond, approaching others with increased patience and a willingness to grow in our attempts at communication. But admittedly, this kind of awareness takes time, patience, and grace. It is a process much like learning to speak a new language. As Dallas Willard explains:

---

[134] From Kahler, T. (1996, 2012). *The Process Communication Model® Seminar—Seminar One: Core Topics.* (pp. 5). Little Rock, AR: Kahler Communications, Inc.

"To learn a language, as for the many even more important concerns of life, we must resolutely *intend* the vision, if it is to be realized. That is, we must initiate, decide, bring into being, those factors that would turn the vision into reality."[135]

Anyone who has tried to become fluent in a second language inevitably experiences certain hurdles, obstacles, and moments of frustration. One does not begin to think and respond naturally in German after studying the language for two weeks or two months. Time, repeated exposure, and an intentional choice to continue learning are necessary in developing an ease in communication. It could take months or even years before this student of language responds in German as though responding in his or her native language.

The same kind of effort, care, and process applies to learning to speak and hear other Perceptions. Though we might have a "native language" of Perception (the Perception from our Base personality floor), we are not doomed to be unilingual. We can learn to recognize and even to speak from another's Perception. Initially this might feel like trying to converse in a completely foreign tongue. The language of the heart does not automatically communicate effectively with the language of actions or the language of opinions. Those who experience life through rational thought might be frustrated at the inaction and rambling reflections of their less logical or more abstract brothers and sisters. How many of your conversations are peppered with exclamations like, "You're not even listening to me!" or "You just don't understand!"? Hearing a spouse talk about his frustrations is one thing. But actually *listening* can require a shift in the way you intentionally filter and perceive not only the **content** of what is being said but also **how** it is being conveyed.

IN OTHER WORDS, WE PAY ATTENTION NOT ONLY TO THE **WORDS**, BUT ALSO TO THE **MUSIC** BENEATH IT.

Remaining ignorant of another's Perception or stubbornly refusing to look from another's perspective can keep you in a relational deadlock, while expanding your languages can lead to meaningful, freeing communication in your relationships.

---

[135] Willard, Dallas. (2005). Living a Transformed Life Adequate to Our Calling. Previously unpublished for *The Augustine Group*. Retrieved from http://www.dwillard.org/articles/artview.asp?artID=119

## A Conversation in Two Languages

As the youngest of four brothers, I returned home from my sophomore year of college relatively unscathed. I hadn't gotten in any exceptional trouble to speak of and had high enough marks in my classes. From my Harmonizer Base Perception of emotions, I pictured my first reunion with my father in six months through relational terms of the heart. I had painted a grand scene in my mind: My father would be happy to see me. Maybe he would say he was glad I had come home after so long or ask about my college friends. Perhaps my father would even pull me in for a hug or one of those manly slaps on the back that fathers are so fond of bestowing on their sons.

I stepped through the front door and held my duffle bag in my right hand, meeting my father's eyes in the foyer.

"Do you need a haircut?" my father questioned immediately, his eyes scanning over my appearance with an increasingly furrowed brow. "And don't you need to tuck in your shirt?"

My heart started to sink.

"And you haven't shined your shoes since you left home," my father finished with a disapproving shake of his head.

What had been a potentially glorious reunion now felt to me like a parade of failures, a checklist of ways that I had already disappointed my father within three seconds of my arrival. I remembered again why my visits home grew increasingly farther and farther apart. What I did not realize until years later was that my father had been showing me love in the way that he knew how.

As a parent with a Persister Base, my father felt responsible for modeling and instilling in his boys a sense of honor, dedication, and respectability. My father compared the picture standing in front of him to the internal template of a successful young man he had constructed through years of experience. Taking one look at my disheveled mop of hair and scuffed shoes, he thought, "I haven't done my duty. This boy doesn't look prepared to go out into the world. No one's going to hire him, and he won't be able to be successful unless I shape him up a bit."

Reflecting back on my father's love with this expanded perspective, I can now say, "The positive side of that [way of communicating love] was that he wouldn't let me get in a car with bad tires because he wouldn't want me to get hurt. He made sure he put money back and he sacrificed and did whatever he could to make sure all four of his sons went to college, which he didn't get to do." I learned to appreciate the sacrificial way my father provided for and loved me, even though it was not my "native language."

In this case, the language of the heart and the language of opinions spoke *past* one another. What communicated love to my father felt like criticism and disappointment to me. Both my father and I were attempting to communicate with each other through Perceptions that were completely foreign to our natural ways of seeing the world.

## BLINDSPOTS

We will refer to these unfamiliar Perceptions as **Blindspots**—less prevalent or underdeveloped Perceptions associated with any of the floors of our personality that qualify as Attics (less than 25% energy).[136]

Communicating out of a Blindspot can lead to ineffective communication or even miscommunication. My father had a Harmonizer Blindspot; the language of the heart and emotions felt unnatural to him, and if called upon frequently, utilizing this Harmonizer energy would leave him feeling drained. His Persister Base also influenced his Perception and style of communication, making him unquestioningly sure that his particular way of viewing the situation was right. Our unique ways of viewing the world are at the core of how we communicate with others—not only the ways in which we see the world but also the ways in which we do *not*.

Yet none of us are doomed to miscommunication or merely trapped within our own eyes and forever limited by our Blindspots. Communicating with people who have similar Perceptions will likely feel more natural or less effortful. Yet as we inevitably engage with completely opposite Perceptions or ways of experiencing and relating to the world, we have the divine opportunity to put aside our needs and comfort for

---

[136] Maris, R. (1996). *Your Great Design*. Little Rock, AR: Transpersonal Technologies, L.L.C.; From Kahler, T. (1982). *Process Communication Management Seminar*. Little Rock, AR: Kahler Communications, Inc.; adapted by permission.

the sake of another. In short, we have the chance to choose sacrificial love.

Consider this possible interaction between an Achiever father and his teenage daughter who has just been dumped by her boyfriend. As an individual with an Achiever Base and a Harmonizer Attic, the father views the world through a filter of logical thought and has a Harmonizer Blindspot, meaning he has very little access to Harmonizer energy and its corresponding Perception of emotions. In orienting himself to the world, this father considers cause and effect and relies on rational understanding and simple computation of the facts to make decisions and solve problems.

His daughter, operating in deep distress out of her Harmonizer Base personality floor, views the world through the lens of her heart and emotions. She has an Achiever Blindspot and will not naturally communicate in the language of facts, data, and logic. Instead this Harmonizer daughter is longing for her daddy to hold her and tell her that she is lovely and worthwhile simply because of who she is, no matter what this boy says. If the father interacts simply out of his innate Perception, his best attempts to love his daughter will likely result in severe miscommunication and leave her feeling misunderstood or confused.

Through tears, the daughter manages to sob, "He broke up with me."

Her father responds. "How long have you been dating?"

"Four months," she sniffles, obviously trying to pull herself together.

"I see. That's less than half a year. And how many boys are in your grade, as compared to girls?"

She stares at him more than a little bewildered. "I don't know. More boys than girls, I guess."

The father nods again. "Well, then the statistics are with you. And the odds are, at least 30% of these guys are interested in you. That's in your grade alone, to say nothing of the other three grades and those possibilities. So the probability is that you won't have trouble getting another date. You might date many different people during your next years of high school."

The daughter swallows hard and feels her shoulders rounding forward in defeat and dejection.

"It doesn't make sense to spend much time being sad on

this guy," her father concludes with a pleasant but factual tone.

For anyone who has ever counseled a heartbroken teenage girl, this kind of response looks either insensitive or unbelievably unaware. From within his own eyes of logical thoughts, this father was simply gathering information to build to the analytical conclusion that his daughter would date again and thus lessen her sense of sadness. But he responded to her in the way *he* would have preferred, oblivious to her completely different set of needs and heart-guided, rather than head-guided, perceptions. It's an understandable and common error of miscommunication, because naturally our own Perception is the only one with which we are initially familiar. Any other lens feels foreign and perhaps even significantly uncomfortable.

Under stress, we tend to become less flexible in our Perceptions and modes of communication, seeing fewer options or possible paths of response. Under the stress of seeing his daughter's emotions and not knowing how to help (aka "make them go away"), this Achiever father is more likely to resort to his strongest avenue of communication—his logic. Yet in her current state of stress, the Harmonizer daughter will also find it more difficult to receive communication in a language of Perception other than her own. The "process" of his interactions—that is, the **how** of what he said more than the "what"[137]—fixated on the facts and ignored his daughter's emotions, implicitly implying to her: "Don't feel; think like I do." [138] Though the message is not literally stated, its implications ring clear. Harmonizers don't miss communicative subtleties and thus feel more "stupid" and less loveable at the end of such exchanges.[139]

But in this instance, what if the father had been more aware of his daughter's sensitive heart and emotional experience of life and been presented with the choice to intentionally (and rather sacrificially) shift his perspective to see through her Perception? What would that look like?

---

[137] From Kahler, T. (2008). *The Process Therapy Model: The Six Personality Types with Adaptations*. Little Rock, AR: Taibi Kahler Associates, Inc.

[138] From Kahler, T. (1997). The Transactional Analysis Script Profile. Little Rock, AR: Taibi Kahler Associates, Inc..

[139] In this instance, the "Channels of Communication" between father and daughter are mismatched, and thus miscommunication occurs. The Achiever father is communicating in his Requestive channel, asking his daughter for information; whereas she is communicating in her Nurturative channel, expressing emotion. From Kahler, T. (1996, 2012). The Process Communication Model® Seminar—Seminar One: Core Topics. (pp. 33-39). Little Rock, AR: Kahler Communications, Inc.

Perhaps rather than asking questions aimed at gathering data, he might have embraced her and listened while she gave voice to those emotions. He would have the opportunity to show her love in the way she is most likely to receive it, through affirming touch and words of encouragement about her inherent value as a person as well as her importance to him. Such a purposeful shift in his Perception and language of communication would have been a stretch, particularly if he is new to the idea or has very little Harmonizer energy himself. The reality of emotions as such a powerful force might not make any sense to him, and trying to identify with those feelings and speak the language of the heart will likely feel unfamiliar or even uncomfortable. But ultimately, this kind of sacrifice would result in his daughter feeling and receiving the love and support he wants to show her.

### *No Greater Love Than This—Multilingual Love*

If you have ever spent time in a country that is not your home, you know that you can be overwhelmed with the amount of new stimuli—unfamiliar sights, smells, sounds, customs. All of this is often compounded when you are unable to speak the language of that region. Instead you wander about using over-exaggerated non-verbal cues, utter broken sentences from your pocket phrase book, and hope for the best. Suddenly in the midst of a crowd, your ears pick up a familiar cadence. In a manner of seconds, you realize that someone is speaking, and for the first time in minutes, hours, or months, you actually understand! There is a sense of immediate comfort in hearing your language spoken. You feel connected to whoever is speaking, whether you know him or her or not. You feel renewed confidence in your ability to communicate. And you feel something else that is incredibly powerful and soul regenerating in nature: you no longer feel alone.

And so it is with the language of Perceptions. In a practical, everyday kind of way, intentionally reaching out in communication to another with an unfamiliar Perception is exactly the kind of sacrificial love that Jesus mentions in the Gospel of John: "Greater love has no one than this, that he lay down his life for his friends."[140] Such sacrifice might

---

[140] John 15:3, New International Version.

happen on a large scale in the actual physical substitution of one's life in place of another's life. Jesus modeled this kind of extreme, costly love—an action infused with enough power to conquer sin and death, transform individual lives, and change the course of history. "This is how we know what love is," Jesus' dear friend John affirms, "Jesus Christ laid down his life for us. And we ought to lay down our lives for our brothers."[141]

But this laying down of our lives is not necessarily a one-time event, a literal martyrdom of our physical selves. These little deaths of self are called for countless times a day in seemingly small decisions about how we interact with others. Choosing to step into an uncomfortable place for the sake of another is an act of intentional love, even in a conversation that feels as ordinary as a father comforting a broken-hearted daughter. In the moment that she enters the room with tear-stained cheeks and red eyes, her father has the chance to set aside his own lens and step into her world for a moment.

In this moment, he has a chance to honor her unique design and respond to who she is as Jesus would. As Thomas Merton suggests, "If we love one another truly, our love will be graced with a clear-sighted prudence which sees and respects the designs of God upon each separate soul."[142] What a quiet but significant sacrifice for a daughter who is unlikely to care about the statistical probability of a date in the future but is sure to remember the way her daddy simply held her and let her cry.

Becoming "multilingual" in different Perceptions than your own embodies the selfless love that Jesus commands for his followers—a selfless love that He modeled. As God, Jesus saw life through a lens unlike anyone else. He discerned the hidden depths, wounds, and hopes within the hearts of men and women to a degree that they were not even aware of within themselves. And also as someone fully human, Jesus sometimes seems to intentionally change his tone, his focus, the language of his "Perception" depending upon a particular individual's most effective mode of communication.

---

[141] 1 John 3:16, New International Version.
[142] Merton, Thomas. (2002). *No Man Is an Island* (pp. 9). New York, NY: Mariner Books.

## Through the Lens of Grief—John 11

"Now a man named Lazarus was sick. He was from Bethany, the village of Mary and her sister Martha...the sisters sent word to Jesus, 'Lord, the one you love is sick.'"[143]

The situation looks unquestionably dire. Lazarus is on the edge of death, and his sisters Mary and Martha are worried enough about Lazarus and confident enough in Jesus' response to send a personal message about "the one Jesus loves." According to an account within the Gospel of Luke, we know that Jesus had a personal relationship with this family. When Jesus passed through the village of Bethany, Martha had opened up her home to Jesus and his disciples. From the little information recorded about her, Martha seems to exhibit characteristics associated with the Achiever floor of her personality—responsible, organized, concerned with work and accomplishment. At the same household gathering, Martha's sister Mary forgoes responsibilities as a hostess to simply be with Jesus and give him her undivided attention. Mary's natural mode of responding suggests she values the relationship, intimacy, and personal connection associated with the Harmonizer floor of her personality.

Four excruciating days pass as the sisters wait for Jesus to respond to their message. Lazarus dies and is buried. Finally Jesus arrives outside of Bethany. Martha hears of Jesus' arrival and rushes out to meet him. As an Achiever Base, she wants to gather more information. In the face of death and grief, Martha needs to *understand*.

"Lord, if you had been here, my brother would not have died. But I know that even now God will give you whatever you ask."[144] Embedded within Martha's first comment upon seeing Jesus is the "if/then" logic typical of an Achiever Perception. Martha has seen evidence of Jesus' miracles and knows him to be capable of healing. **If** Jesus had come in time, Martha reasons, **then** He could have healed Lazarus and prevented him from dying. It doesn't make sense.

Jesus could have responded to Martha in a number of ways. Conscious of and attuned to Martha's Perception, however, Jesus answers Martha in her language of facts and data. "Your brother will rise again," he states candidly.

---

[143] John 11:1,3, New International Version.
[144] John 11:21-22, New International Version.

Martha, still viewing the situation through the lens of her intellect, sees Jesus' comment not as a promise or as a deeper reality but as a simple statement of fact. Drawing upon what she knows, Martha responds, "I know he will rise again in the resurrection at the last day."

With intention and care, Jesus then invites Martha to see *beyond* her natural Perception. He moves from the logical to the personal, from the factual to the relational, from exchanging information to revealing who He is. "I am the resurrection and the life." He effectively directs Martha to move her focus from the questions of what, why, and how to the ultimate question of *whom*. **If** Jesus Himself is the resurrection and life, **then** He has power over death itself. Jesus is operating out of a different system of logic and rules than those that confine this world. Throughout their interaction, He both meets Martha where she is and invites her to expand her eyes to see more than the easily observable or calculated facts.

While Martha sought out Jesus for information, Mary remains at the house. John, the author of the account, mentions that Mary is surrounded by a group of mourners who are comforting her and follow her to the place where Jesus waits. In the midst of her grief, she leans into the support of others and chooses community over isolation.

Jesus' interaction with Mary is completely different from his previous conversation with Martha. Whereas Martha approached with a deep need for understanding couched in logical terms, Mary collapses at Jesus' feet weeping. Her experience of Jesus' delay throbs not with questions to understand on an intellectual level but with intense, tear-drenched sensations of the heart.

> "LORD, IF YOU HAD BEEN HERE,
> MY BROTHER WOULD NOT HAVE DIED."

And Jesus' response? To weep. To engage fully in Mary's grief (and His own, as one who was fully human and had lost a dear friend) and feel the depth of the pain and loss. He does not comfort Mary with the realities and facts that made sense to Martha, bringing her a sense of calm in the midst of chaotic loss. He simply joins Mary in her grief. There could be no more sensitive response to the empathetic and tender heart of a hurting Harmonizer than to be fully present to and part of the emotion of the moment.

## MIRRORS OF GOD—REFLECTING GOD'S CHARACTER THROUGH OUR PERCEPTIONS

Our Perceptions work hand in hand with the rest of our design to make us perfectly suited for the work God prepared, beforehand, for us to do. As with our Character Strengths, these Perceptions also serve to reflect—although dimly and imperfectly—the multi-faceted attributes of God's character to each other. He calls Himself good and just, slow to anger, jealous, steadfast, rich in mercy, eternal, patient, peace-giving, righteous, orderly, powerful.[145] He never, ever changes, and yet the depths of His character are complex, unfathomable, and many-layered. He shepherds, disciplines, comforts, and counsels us. He is Love and Life itself. He is Jehovah Jireh, the One who Provides, and Jehovah Rapha, the Healer.

And just as He is the Creator, He is also the Redeemer of that which has been lost, twisted, or stolen. As His Image-Bearers, we are in the midst of a glorious redemption of the broken creation of which we are a part. Scripture promises a complete restoration that has yet to be fully realized for the groaning earth.[146] And Jesus lived, died, and raised himself from the dead in order to reconcile the separation between man and God—a reconciliation that has both already happened and is ongoing.

God woos us individually, personally, passionately, and persistently. Like a lover slowly getting to know the character of the Beloved, we may be initially drawn to parts of God's character that speak to the ways in which we personally experience and respond to life. We are by no means getting a complete picture of who God is, but we are intrigued. We are drawn in and captivated.

The Harmonizer responds and draws close to the God who fully knows and unconditionally loves us. The sensitive, compassionate Harmonizer heart hears the tender call for intimate relationship and leans into a God who cares infinitely about His people and feels affectionate toward His children,

---

[145] See Psalm 103, Psalm 116:5-6, Psalm 136.
[146] See Romans 8.

the same God who holds us in His hands and wants us to call Him "Abba, Father"—Daddy.[147]

As Achievers search for a logical design in the midst of chaos, they find a God who promises "[I am] not a God of disorder/confusion but of peace."[148] Though His ways not always fully comprehensible, Achievers take comfort in a God who is in ultimate and competent control of an intricate, detailed plan. This capable, sovereign God invites us to turn the work over to Him.

Persisters are drawn to God as a protector and upholder of justice, the ultimate standard with which we are to align our lives and ourselves.[149] He defines that which is full of purpose and worthy of our investment, remaining faithful, true, and trustworthy regardless of our infidelity or inadequacy. And He willingly paid the ultimate sacrifice of His very life for that which He valued—His name, His glory, His people.

Dreamers gather under the protective shelter of God's wings with a sense of safety and provision. As they already feel they are not quite a part of this world, they resonate with an awareness of a God who is weaving an infinitely larger picture than we might see on the surface level or even be able to imagine.[150]

When Catalyzers glimpse even a part of the picture that is the daring rescue of creation, they find infinite opportunities for decisive action and risk. God invites them into a story that is larger, bolder, and more exciting than any drama of self-destruction or self-promotion.[151]

Energizers are intrigued by how Jesus always challenges what the religious guys say, questioning the way things have been done and pushing against traditions or assumptions by introducing a new and creative response. They relate to a God who has an incredible sense of humor and creativity and delight in what He has made, inviting them and others into a vibrant, full life.[152]

As Image-Bearers, we have the beautiful privilege to reflect—imperfectly and incompletely—different aspects of who God is. In selflessly standing behind truth and conviction

---

[147] Romans 8:15.
[148] 1 Corinthians 14:33, New International Version; New American Standard Bible.
[149] Psalm 33:5; 106:3.
[150] Ephesians 3:20-21.
[151] 1 Corinthians 4:20.
[152] John 10:10.

regardless of personal consequence, a Persister might reveal God's commitment and faithfulness to a Harmonizer who has hitherto only seen justice as cruel or mean. The vibrant joy and zest for life that naturally exudes from an Energizer bubbles over and frees an Achiever to see God as interested in more than just "getting the job done" but in relishing each moment.

In simply being who God created us to be, we are participating in that glorious redemption—the fleshing out of the fullness of God's character to ourselves and to each other. We act as vessels to introduce one another to a God who is bigger and broader than our own Blindspots. Loving one another invites us to grow, mature, and expand. As the adage says, "The eyes are the windows to the soul." If our Perceptions are the eyes through which we see the world, they are also reflections of what is occurring at the deepest core of our being. And in broadening the windows of our Perceptions—in seeing and reflecting God for one another in intentional and sacrificial acts of love—our souls themselves are expanded.

# 07 | *Psychological Needs*

The way of the Kingdom requires trust. Trust that we are called to more than mere survival. Trust that there is more to life than just "getting by." Jesus declares, "I have come that they may have life, and have it abundantly...I have come to give them a rich and satisfying life."[153] The "*them*" to whom Jesus refers is US! Trust enables us to free our attention from ourselves, focused on *living into* being the kind of people who are investing in *serving* the Kingdom with abandon.

Trust deepens with increasing knowledge of and intimate experience with the One whom we serve. Among His many names, God calls Himself Jehovah Jireh, the One who promises to provide for our needs and who has indeed provided for His children throughout the ages. Ultimately, as Dallas Willard said, "it is love of God, admiration and confidence in his greatness and goodness, and the regular experience of his care that frees us from the burden of 'looking out for ourselves.'"[154] In Chapter 9 on Distress, we will explore what happens when we fail to trust God and choose instead to distort our gifts and purpose in an effort to take care of ourselves.

If we consider that our loving Creator God purposefully designed us to live into our particular Character Strengths and to experience life through a specific Perception, it follows that we are often called to *serve out of* those Strengths enabled by that Perception. And that service is deeply satisfying. It is

---

[153] John 10:10, New American Standard; New Living Translation.
[154] Willard, Dallas. (2002). *Renovation of the Heart* (pp. 70). Colorado Springs, CO: NavPress.

even more—it is *full-filling*. Let's say I'm employed in caring for the home of a wealthy and kind Master. By nature, I am a gardener. I'm gifted with a green thumb, and I receive deep pleasure from interlacing my fingers in the rich, dark soil. Something in my spirit comes alive as I nurture seeds and watch these plants grow. I have never felt so satisfied. My Master knows my propensity for gardening, and thus He graciously encourages me to spend a great deal of my time in the garden plot beside the house. He recognizes that I will be most productive when my work is most fulfilling.

And, as a Master who knows me and loves me deeply, He also cares that I experience pleasure and joy as I do what I was created to do. And in the *doing*, I am *being* who He made me to be. Just as He delights in who I am, He loves to watch me delight in the work He has given me to do.[155] Does this mean I'll never have to pluck the feathers from an unruly chicken or balance the household checkbook if those tasks are unappealing to me? Certainly not. But if I love my Master and recognize His goodness, I do those tasks with the same spirit of obedience and gratitude that I have as I tend the plants that I love like my own children.

## Psychological Needs: God's Gifts and Provisions

In His graciousness and provision, God, as our good and loving Master, allows us to experience energy and fulfillment as we do His work. He also allows us to **desire** certain sources of energy or satisfaction in a way that encourages our dependence on Him to meet our needs. Desiring these sources of energy is more than a preference; rather, our **Psychological Needs** are integral to the way that God designed us. We were made to desire and gain energy from meeting our Psychological Needs as we experience God's pleasure in doing what we were created to do! Dr. Kahler's research originally drew the connection between the **Psychological Needs** of the six Personality Types and the negative or "Distress" behaviors associated with not getting those needs met in healthy ways.[156] I conceptualized this

---

[155] Ephesians 2:10.
[156] From Kahler, T. (1988, 1992, 2000, 2004). *The Mastery of Management.* Little Rock, AR: Kahler Communications, Inc.; adapted by permission.

relationship somewhat differently in the *Process Spiritual Model™*, viewing Kahler's "Needs–Distress" relationship from a Christian worldview.[157]

**Table 3: Psychological Needs**

| Personality Floor | Psychological Needs | Existential Question |
|---|---|---|
| **Harmonizer** | Recognition of Person Sensory | Am I lovable? |
| **Achiever** | Recognition of Work Time Structure | Am I in control? |
| **Persister** | Recognition of Work Conviction | Am I valued? |
| **Dreamer** | Solitude | Am I safe? |
| **Catalyzer** | Incidence | Am I on my own? |
| **Energizer** | Contact | Am I acceptable? |

From Kahler, T. (1988, 1992, 2000, 2004). *The Mastery of Management.* Little Rock, AR: Kahler Communication, Inc.; adapted by permission.

Your individual Psychological Needs—the activities or interactions that you find particularly satisfying as well as necessary for energy and health—are predictable based on your Personality Structure. In thinking about your individual Personality Structure as discussed in Chapter 5, recall that you have easier access to the characteristics of the bottom floors of your Structure. Thus in the course of our lives, we will first experience the Psychological Needs of our Base personality floor. You will likely have enjoyed or sought out these Psychological Needs for as long as you can remember.

## PHASE FLOOR

Dr. Kahler labeled the site of your primary Psychological Needs as your **Phase** floor, the first floor in your Personality Structure that exhibits less than 100% energy.[158] If the bottom

---

[157] From Maris, R. (1996). *Your Great Design.* Little Rock, AR: Transpersonal Technologies, L.L.C..
[158] From Kahler, T. (1988, 1992, 2000, 2004). *The Mastery of Management.* Little Rock, AR: Kahler Communications, Inc.; adapted by permission. From Kahler, T. (1982). *Process Communication Management Seminar.* Little Rock, AR: Kahler Communications, Inc.; adapted by permission.

floor of your Personality Structure has less than 100% energy, then this floor is currently functioning as your Base floor as well as your Phase. When Base and Phase are the same, you will experience the Psychological Needs of your Base as primary.[159]

Base & Phase Needs Different   Base & Phase Needs Same

## A Heart Check

Though we may not be consciously aware of the *why* behind our actions, we will unconsciously move into activities, jobs, relationships, etc. which seem to provide the certain Psychological Needs we desire. When receiving these Needs becomes our focus, rather than doing and enjoying the work we were created to do, our heart's orientation shifts, and we become self-serving. The fruit of our lives comes up barren and sun-scorched. These Psychological Needs are meant to point us toward God, not to make us satisfied apart from God.

When we pursue the "good works" planned for us, however, using the gifts God built into our design, our lives will resonate with a sense of "fullness." We feel energized. Satisfied. Motivated. And our ability to receive this kind of pleasure or deep satisfaction from living into and serving out of who we are uniquely designed to be is a gift of *grace*. Grace allows us to gratefully receive Psychological Needs that energize and motivate us, all the while recognizing that they are *gifts* from the One who provides for all of our needs. God graciously allows these Needs to add the richness of trusting Him to our lives, and perhaps, to let us know we are headed in the right direction. It's not simply a matter of feeling good.

---

[159] From Kahler, T. (1996, 2012). *The Process Communication Model® Seminar—Seminar One: Core Topics.* (pp. 57). Little Rock, AR: Kahler Communications, Inc.

## Feeling God's Pleasure

As a young man in Scotland, Eric Liddell discerned a call from God to go to China as a missionary. Yet in 1924, Eric Liddell ran in the summer Olympics in Paris. Liddell's sister questioned his chosen Olympic path, uncertain how training and competing as a world class runner fit into God's calling on Eric's life. Liddell responded with the heart of a man confident in who he was created to be:

> "I WAS MADE FOR CHINA, BUT GOD ALSO MADE ME FAST, AND WHEN I RUN, I FEEL GOD'S PLEASURE."[160]

Liddell's gifting as a runner was not separate from God's calling for him; rather, God used Liddell's fame as a runner to pave the way for otherwise impossible access for his mission in China. God wove these seemingly disparate callings into a life oriented toward His will and pleasure. And Liddell felt God's pleasure as he lived into his particular gifting!

Let's take a deeper look into what Psychological Needs Dr. Kahler has identified each phase floor desires or finds uniquely motivating, energizing, and satisfying. Remember: because you are a unique combination of all six personality floors, you might identify with several of these Psychological Needs. You might also notice that your Needs have shifted at different seasons of your life.

## PSYCHOLOGICAL NEEDS: IN DEPTH

### Harmonizers—Recognition of Person and Sensory

The Harmonizer floor of your personality thrives on relationships, engaging through intimate sharing and sensitive, transparent, emotional vulnerability with others. For someone with a Harmonizer Phase or Base, to be recognized as a worthwhile and lovable individual simply for being *who he or she is* feels energizing and necessary. This "recognition of person" is different than being acknowledged for hard work

---

[160] Hudson, Hugh (Director). (1981). *Chariots of Fire* [Motion picture]. United Kingdom: Allied Stars Ltd., Enigma Productions.

or accomplishments or strong beliefs and values. Individuals in a Harmonizer Phase long to be valued for their identities as precious and special individuals. They deeply desire to give and receive unconditional love.

Additionally, the Harmonizer floor of your Personality Structure is motivated by pleasant **sensory** experiences and comfort. For an individual with a good deal of Harmonizer energy, a soft fleece blanket, a vanilla scented candle, or a particularly juicy peach opens up new mediums in which to experience and enjoy God. Atmosphere and environment can boost Harmonizer satisfaction through shaping overall mood; warmth, comfort, music, and beauty speak to and motivate this floor of your personality in special ways.

When we begin to look at these Psychological Needs as demands that we must fill on our own rather than trusting God to provide us with lasting satisfaction, our emotional equilibrium is thrown out of balance. For instance, it is healthy for someone with a Harmonizer Phase to receive energy from feeling appreciated for who she is. But when this desire for positive affirmation becomes the focus in and of itself, the Harmonizer floor feels particularly vulnerable to negative or even neutral feedback.

From this mindset, if you don't say that I am worthwhile, then I cannot accept myself as lovable.[161] I begin to measure my own lovability by how well I feel I am loving others, a perception dependent upon how much others are continually confirming that I am loving them well. The recognition of person that feels so affirming to the Harmonizer floor is meant to be a gracious source of energy rather than the dominating center of one's life.

Understanding the nature of these Psychological Needs can steady the Harmonizer's sensitive heart and make him less circumstantially dependent on external affirmation (or lack thereof) from others. Thus true maturity for the Harmonizer floor looks like being the exact person who one was created to be regardless of feedback, relying on God for steadfast, unconditional love.

---

[161] Dr. Kahler identified two different behavioral life positions that are present in Second Degree Distress. The behavioral life position exhibited by the Harmonizer in this instance is "You're OK, I'm not OK." These behavioral life positions incorrectly assume that we cannot all be "OK" simultaneously. Kahler, Taibi. (1982, 1996). *Process Communication Management Seminar*. Little Rock, AR: Taibi Kahler Associates, Inc.

### Achievers—Recognition of Work and Time Structure

Whereas the individual with a Harmonizer Phase or Base desires to be loved simply for who he or she is, individuals in an Achiever Phase are motivated by **recognition of their work**. Because the Achiever floor is meticulous in execution and quality, these individuals have their own stringent standards for what kind of work is acceptable and what quality of work is not up to par. External acknowledgement of their high-quality work, exceptional attention to details, competence in following things through to the end, and clear thinking can energize those in an Achiever Phase to give of themselves to accomplish whatever is required.

Because the individual with an Achiever Phase or Base is constantly calculating and managing details, he or she is particularly sensitive to issues of **Time Structure**. Having a handle on their schedule and a sense of control over planning when, how, and where they spend their time is extremely important to the sense of well-being for those with strong Achiever floors in their personalities. For Achievers Bases or Phases, hearing "Well done, good and faithful servant" from the lips of the Living God is the most meaningful confirmation imaginable of a life well lived in diligence.

### Persisters—Recognition of Work and Conviction

Those with a Persister Phase floor (or Base if Base/Phase are the same) also experience a deep desire for external, explicit **recognition of their excellent work**. Unlike the Achiever personality floor, however, someone in a Persister Phase seeks respect and acknowledgement that *commitment and deep convictions* are the underlying factors motivating one's service. They are concerned with the "why" behind what they are doing. It is the Persister floor of our personalities that motivates individuals to dedicate themselves to what they believe is worthwhile.

For Persister Phases and Bases, a respectful recognition that their strong and steadfast **convictions** and beliefs are central to their character and consistent with their actions is highly satisfying. When someone they trust or respect recognizes the consistency, dedication, and sacrifice with which they live their lives, individuals with a Persister Base or Phase experience being validated, worthwhile, and motivated to continue sacrificially giving. They are energized when believing that they are living with integrity according to their convictions.

### Dreamers—Solitude

The Dreamer floor of your personality finds itself energized by significant periods of **solitude** for quiet reflection and stillness. Those in a Dreamer Phase need to retreat from the world in order to recharge, allowing themselves the imaginative space to play with "what ifs" and endless possibilities. Solitude could include a calm activity with one's hands, like carpentry work, knitting, or putting together a model airplane. Solitude could look more like meditation and a practice of clearing one's mind. Solitude could involve spending quiet time in a peaceful, natural environment and thus reaffirming the "smallness" of who we are in light of the magnitude of the universe. Or a Dreamer might pursue solitude as a means to ponder ideas and come up with innovative solutions to problems.

### Catalyzers—Incidence

Individuals with a significant amount of Catalyzer energy experience a particular need for high bursts of adrenaline and action in a relatively short period of time. Kahler's *Process Communication Model®* labels this quality "incidence."[162] The strong Catalyzer floor also

---

[162] From Kahler, T. (1988, 1992, 2000, 2004). *The Mastery of Management*. Little Rock, AR: Kahler Communication, Inc.

thrives in the thrill of the moment and appreciates the freedom to operate outside of a routine, quickly seizing the chance to self-direct their opportunities, expectations, time schedules, etc. Those with Catalyzer Phases or Bases are also satisfied by the chance to network and connect others in pursuing a new opportunity, often providing motivating energy, vision, and direction at the outset. Whatever they are doing, individuals with Catalyzer Phases/Bases are motivated by a fast pace that gets their adrenaline pumping.

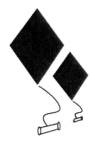

### Energizers—Contact

The Energizer personality floor experiences full, vibrant life when receiving and giving healthy amounts of playful, physical and verbal **contact**. Contact could include everything from good-natured teasing to a playful punch on the arm. External stimulation is needed for this personality floor to feel alive and eager to spill that energy and joy onto others around them. They feel most motivated and energized when surrounded by noise, color, people, toys, and activity. Energizers are wholly and energetically present to the moment at hand, fully experiencing and delighting in each sensation, interaction, and reaction.

Someone in an Energizer Phase may also make contact with the world through unique self-expression. Thus they often gravitate toward the visual or performing arts. Those with strong amounts of Energizer energy function most freely in environments and situations where individuality is both encouraged and recognized. Energizer Phases and Bases need to be seen as distinct individuals, unique beings who are unlike anyone else who has come before or who will come after them. An Energizer fully submitted to God's loving provision for the Psychological Need of contact is incredibly fluent in reflecting God's pleasure in His creation to others.

## A VISIT TO B. FRANKLIN KITES, INC.

To more fully understand Psychological Needs, let's revisit B. Franklin Kites, Inc.! Angelo has been faithfully working on the third floor Quality Control department for the past 17 years. Due to his Persister Base, Angelo sees the world and his job through the Perception of his strongly held opinions. This Perception enables him to function out of his strengths in making keen observations and upholding high standards of quality. Angelo catches any and every mistake made in the design and production of the various types of kites. He sometimes makes suggestions for how to improve parts of the company's procedures and infrastructure that he believes are not up to par. In his 17 years of work, Angelo has exhibited incredible integrity and dedication. Though Angelo is not the official head hauncho on his floor, the Quality Control department has nevertheless flourished under the leadership of his character.

Angelo's boss notices that the more he verbally and publicly recognizes the quality of Angelo's work, the more satisfied and productive Angelo tends to be on the job. Two years ago at the company Christmas party, Angelo was presented with a plaque for "15 years of Outstanding and Dedicated Service." By 7:30 am the next morning, the plaque was hanging in a prominent position in Angelo's office. Because Angelo is also in a Persister Phase, recognition of his work and his convictions invites Angelo to experience being particularly valued and respected, allowing him to gain personal satisfaction in doing his job with excellence and integrity. Angelo's work situation is an excellent example of how receiving Psychological Needs associated with either our Phase or Base personality floors allows us to function at maximum capacity, truly living out our gifting and using our strengths to serve those around us.

Gretchen used to feel fulfilled at work in B. Franklin Kites, Inc. Her workspace in the corner of the sixth floor Production, Shipping, and Innovation department allowed her to tend to her tasks of sewing and cutting kites in relative quiet and solitude. Her boss understood that Gretchen was most comfortable and productive when she told Gretchen directly what she wanted and then left her alone. Gretchen always did exactly what was asked of her, and she secretly relished the isolated condition of her work and its repetitive physical nature, which allowed her time and socially vacant space in which to daydream. Her hands deftly wove the thread in and out of the fabric, creating seams and giving shape to the kites, adding colorful patterns and fluttering tails. But in her mind…in her mind she could wander down untold paths, explore imaginary worlds, muse over "what ifs" like mental play-dough, explore unending possibilities, and keep herself peacefully entertained for hours on end.

That was before the merger. Before the restructuring of the company, the shuffling of positions, the waiting with baited breath to see who would stay and who would be unemployed. Before the loss of Gretchen's safe haven on the sixth floor and her subsequent move to a cubicle on the third floor Quality Control department, surrounded by noise and people and traffic.

Gretchen's new boss personally needed others to verbally affirm that her work was excellent and of the highest quality and thus gave the same motivating feedback publically to her employees. Even though Gretchen's well-meaning supervisor attempted to give "positive rewards," telling Gretchen she was doing a good job and patting her on the back, Gretchen's productivity slipped. Almost imperceptibly at first, Gretchen failed to finish any one project. And while she unsuccessfully juggled a hundred loose ends, it didn't occur to Gretchen to ask for help. Increasingly she lost all motivation to come to work. It was much more appealing to call in sick and then to not even call in at all, to stay at home and imagine a different world. Anything was better than the reality.

Gretchen's situation is a good example of how Psychological Needs serve both as an energizing result of living into one's design or as a potential drain when unfulfilled or when trying to be someone else. Due to her Dreamer Base and Phase, Gretchen thrives in an environment where she is allowed solitude to work and to think. Receiving her Dreamer Psychological Need allows her to operate out of her Character Strengths and stay in a healthy, energized spot without much effort. When her Psychological Need was no longer available, as when Gretchen was transferred to a different work environment, Gretchen began to show distressed behavior characteristic of her Dreamer personality floor. Without the recharging times of solitude, Gretchen met her deep need for quiet and reflection in an unhealthy way by pulling further and further away from reality and disconnecting altogether. Without clear direction, Gretchen spread her attention in such a way that she could not complete or finish even a simple task.

## Square Peg, Round Hole—Wrong Needs

Not aligning ourselves to receive the Psychological Needs associated with our Phase and Base floors within our Personality Structure can potentially drain us or leave us more vulnerable to exhibiting predictable patterns of distress. Life experience tells us that what motivates or provides energy to one individual does not necessarily have the same effect on another. While Gretchen's boss was attempting to motivate her employees by providing the Persister Psychological Needs that she personally needed, employees like Gretchen actually received no motivation from positive verbal feedback.

While physical touch for one individual may affirm a sense of value or connection, to another it seems too intimate, familiar, or intrusive. There are some whose minds light up at the chance to make color-coded lists, who thrill at crossing off plans accomplished, who experience satisfaction in shutting a perfectly balanced checkbook. Yet if everyone felt motivated by managing such details, we would hardly need professional accountants or financial advisors. Everyone would be counting down the days until tax season rather than frantically hiring someone to "handle" finances. In reality, we are simply not all longing for, motivated, or energized by the same things.

So what happens when we receive Psychological Needs that are not particularly energizing or effective? What if I as someone with an Achiever Phase deeply desire recognition of my consistent, high-quality work but am instead constantly given playful punches on the arm and good-natured, teasing remarks? Though this playful contact would likely fill someone with an Energizer Phase floor with satisfaction and energy, it will not serve the same purpose in meeting my Achiever Psychological Needs. The Achiever floor of my Personality Structure will not view this playful contact as a Psychological Need of any sort and will not experience the same kind of fulfillment. In fact, depending upon how much Energizer energy I have available in my Personality Structure, numerous encounters of playful contact might drain my resources rather than replenish or nourish them.

**What one person needs might actually be counterproductive for another.**

Angelo's love of Quality Control and pleasure in public recognition was a completely different experience for Gretchen. On an even more basic level, consider a general personality trait like introversion versus extroversion. An introverted individual might be thrilled by a simple, quiet night at home. He dreads B. Franklin Kites Inc.'s upcoming Christmas party. His extroverted friend, however, has been counting down the days until the party. She feels energized at the thought of a night of being around others while dancing, laughing, and sharing stories. Conversely, the last three nights spent at home alone have left her sinking into a slight depression! One Psychological Need is not more or less valid than another; they are simply different.

*Plaques and Hugs*

As a second grade elementary school teacher, Mrs. Stacey loves her job. She is in a Harmonizer Phase and thus responds to the Psychological Needs associated with that floor of her personality, including recognition of person and sensory. She loves sweet cards out of the blue from friends, taking long baths at the end of long days, and spending time making a warm, delicious apple pie to share with her neighbors. The Persister personality floor is in the Attic of Mrs. Stacey's Personality Structure, meaning she has little or no access to the Character Strengths or Perceptions of this floor. Looking at Mrs. Stacey's Personality Structure, we can predict that receiving Psychological Needs associated with the Persister floor—recognition of work and conviction—will not be motivating for her.

"For excellence in work, for 21 years of exemplary service, for her part in the implementation of our Free Lunch program nine years ago, we would like to formally recognize and applaud Mrs. Stacey," Principal Martin spoke into the crackly microphone.

Applause erupted throughout the auditorium, and Mrs. Stacey blushed furiously and made her way to Principal Martin. Principal Martin gave her a courteous nod, and then his voice boomed into the microphone again.

"In honor of Mrs. Stacey's work, we will be displaying this plaque," he removed the gold plaque from its wrapping and held it high, "in the front hallway. Thank you, Mrs. Stacey."

Principal Martin turned to Mrs. Stacey again and clapped with respectful appreciation.

Mrs. Stacey waited for a warm feeling to spread through her as she stared at the plaque, but all she experienced was the continued, furious blushing of her cheeks. She wanted to get back to her classroom, hug her second graders, and finish teaching syllables.

The assembly ended, and Mrs. Stacey made a beeline back to the second grade hall. Her sensitive heart tugged at the sight of Cooper, a particularly small second grader who was in Mrs. Tatum's class next door. Cooper sat, hugging his knees to his chest, in the small space under the water fountain.

"Hey, Cooper," Mrs. Stacey bent down to meet his eyes.

"Hi, Mrs. Stacey," he mumbled, his chin tucked down at an angle as his eyes studied the speckled tile floor.

"Do you feel okay, Cooper?" Mrs. Stacey put her hand on Cooper's thin shoulder.

Cooper proceeded to spout off a list of miserable grievances from tummy aches to math troubles to playground disputes. Mrs. Stacey listened attentively and finally invited Cooper out from his hiding spot.

"What was all the clapping for, Mrs. Stacey?" Cooper asked as he took her hand to crawl from under the water fountain.

"Oh," Mrs. Stacey shrugged. "They gave me a gold plaque."

"Why?" Cooper looked confused.

"You know, I'm not sure," Mrs. Stacey replied. Why indeed? What did a gold plaque even mean? Her reward was this—the children holding her hand, the bellies that were not hungry at lunchtime, the impulsive instances of 'I love you, Mrs. Stacey'. "I guess it's kind of like when we give you stickers for doing something good."

Cooper chewed on his lip thoughtfully. "Oh. You do deserve a sticker, Mrs. Stacey. Lots of them!" He broke into a grin and threw his arms around her knees with a squeeze.

"May I tell you a secret, Cooper?" Mrs. Stacey patted his head tenderly. "I'd rather have *that* hug than a hundred gold plaques!"

## LOVE LOOKS LIKE...MOTIVATING OTHERS

If we can make some predictions about what each individual will desire, need, and be motivated by based upon an awareness of his or her Personality Structure, then we have the opportunity to apply this knowledge to our relationships. Just as we have chances to lovingly switch to another's Perception in order to communicate effectively, we can also become specific and intentional in the Psychological Needs we offer to others. Rather than only offering the Psychological Needs that we might find most satisfying, we can lovingly make informed choices based on the unique design of each individual.

> // An observant friend notices that his pastor particularly receives recognitions of his commitment to his ministry. This friend, out of love and a desire to add to his pastor's sense of satisfaction in his calling, makes an intentional effort to publicly affirm his pastor's steadfast work.
> // After several months of marital therapy, a husband and wife make the decision to consciously become more aware of each other's needs. As an extension of this conversation, the wife sets up a sky diving experience for her husband who has been craving excitement. The husband makes an intentional effort to tell his wife that he loves her at least ten times a day, honoring her Harmonizer Need for unconditional recognition and love.

Much like the challenge of learning an unfamiliar Perception to better understand another's perspective, intentionally offering unfamiliar Psychological Needs is like learning a new dialect of love. This choice on our part to expand and grow can invite others out of a place of unhealthy or destructive attempts at self-motivation to an experience of deep satisfaction and healthy behavior.

### *Loving Outside of the Box—Hayden's Story*

Hayden was driving everyone crazy—and it seemed to be on purpose. This was the fourth parent-teacher conference that his mother had attended this school year, and the litany of offenses Hayden had committed was like a scratchy record on a broken gramophone. "Hayden will not remain in his seat.

Hayden bothers the other children, pinching them, shooting spit wads, and more. Hayden makes jokes or talks at inappropriate times." On and on the list went. Things weren't much better at home, and Hayden's mother was at the end of her rope.

Hayden's mother knew Hayden had a prominent Energizer floor. As she watched Hayden's behavior more closely, she began to notice little signs and tentatively put the pieces together. For instance, if Hayden played tackle football with his brothers before dinner, he was much less resistant to sitting at the table and even to taking his dish to the sink when asked. Or if she tickled him when he said no to cleaning his room, he was much more likely to actually do it than if she gave him stern, logical reprimands. When she let him paint one wall of his room like a mural rather than insisting he curb his creativity by coloring within the lines on paper, Hayden seemed to flourish and bloom. The same energy that had been overflowing in negative ways transformed into a brightness and zest for life that lit up the dinner table and kept the family in constant stitches.

At the next scheduled parent-teacher conference time, Hayden's mother grinned at his fourth grade teacher and offered a suggestion: "Elbow him every now and then. He likes the playful contact, and if he just gets enough of that, he will be much more manageable in class. And show this painting to his art teacher, the one who always scolds him for mixing colors or painting outside of the lines." Hayden's mother held up an impressive painting—a messy, chaotic, expressive, obvious display of talent. "He just wants to be able to express himself without having to fit in a box. I think if he can do that, he'll stop painting on the other kids when she's not looking…"

With his disruptive behavior in the classroom and at home, Hayden was trying to receive the Psychological Needs of his Energizer Phase on his own. In other words, he was not receiving what he needed to function out of maximum health and satisfaction. According to the Psychological Needs linked to his Energizer Phase/Base floor, Hayden needs contact. Without a positive outlet for receiving that Psychological Need at the core of his Energizer floor, Hayden did whatever possible to receive negative contact (scolding, spanking, disciplinary attention) and express himself even if only in defiance and opposition. Hayden's mother recognized that when Hayden received his Psychological Need in positive ways, he had no need for the negative patterns of distress he exhibited in their absence.

## PSYCHOLOGICAL NEEDS AS *NEEDS*?

The word *needs* can have a loaded connotation. Yet part of living into our unique, God-ordained designs means admitting that we have legitimate and specific needs. Recognizing that individuals are motivated differently can be a significant step in self-acceptance as well as greater relational understanding.

Our Psychological Needs indicate what fulfillment looks like for us as uniquely designed individuals; conversely, they also provide clues as to what will leave us feeling dissatisfied. Just as consistently meeting our Psychological Needs leads to healthy, energizing consequences, *not* receiving our Needs over time will have a negative behavioral result. Dr. Kahler has discovered the personality concept that when a Psychological Need is not met positively, a person will attempt to get this same Need met in a predictable, distressful way.[163]

In the *Process Spiritual Model*™, I expand upon Dr. Kahler's idea by suggesting that our attempts to meet our own needs will often result in a distortion of our greatest Character Strengths.[164] As Hayden's story demonstrates, failure to receive our primary or Phase Psychological Needs may lead us to act and meet these needs in unhealthy ways by distorting our Character Strengths. We'll talk more about what these predictable patterns of behavior[165]—and the Deceptions underlying these behaviors—look like when we consider Distress in Chapter 9.

### *Looking for Love in the Wrong Places*

Marybeth was raised in a family where there was no room for verbal affirmations of love or appropriate physical touch or affection. Her parents rarely if ever reached out to hug her.

---

[163] From Kahler, T. (1996, 2012). *The Process Communication Model® Seminar—Seminar One: Core Topics.* (pp. 57). Little Rock, AR: Kahler Communications, Inc.
[164] From Maris, R. (1996). *Your Great Design.* Little Rock, AR: Transpersonal Technologies, L.L.C..
[165] From Kahler, T. (1996, 2012). *The Process Communication Model® Seminar—Seminar One: Core Topics.* (pp. 57). Little Rock, AR: Kahler Communications, Inc.

Though they provided for Marybeth's physical needs, sent her to a top-notch school, and paid for her music lessons, Marybeth never heard her parents verbally affirm that they loved and cared for her simply because of who she was. Marybeth's Harmonizer Psychological Need for recognition of person remained constantly depleted. In fact, this desire or need was even looked down upon by her family as a sign of weakness or oversensitivity.

Unable to get her Needs met in a healthy way at home, Marybeth began getting into heavily physical romantic relationships and lying to her parents about her activities so that they would remain externally pleased with her. Marybeth craved the temporary satisfaction she received from feeling loved and sought it out. Ultimately, Marybeth ended up feeling as though she *needed* this kind of affirmation to function and grew increasingly desperate to find it—even if that meant in unhealthy ways or non-safe places.

How do we reconcile the truth that God is truly all we need with the reality that, as humans, we do still experience desires or needs? We experience these needs at such a depth that if we are not able to receive these Needs in healthy ways, we will act in ways that could even harm us in order to get these Needs met! People who are truly trusting in God to be sufficient *still* might function better when receiving a good dose of appropriate physical affection. Others crave and thrive on time alone and feel more energized when they receive this kind of solitude, even when they are deeply connected to and dependent on God. Do these tendencies indicate a lack of faith in God's sufficiency? In other words, is truly **needing** these Psychological Needs wrong?

In their brilliant and insightful work, *TrueFaced*, authors Thrall, McNicol, and Lynch suggest that we have a distorted understanding of *needs as sin*. We easily fall into the trap of believing it is wrong or weak to *need* something. Not so, these authors insist—going so far as to equate meeting our spiritual and emotional needs with meeting our basic needs for water, air, and sustenance.[166] We have needs, and we have needs for a reason.

---

[166] Thrall, B., McNicol, B., & Lynch, J.S. (2004). *TrueFaced* (pp. 85). Colorado Springs, CO: NavPress.

## The Ultimate Need

In order to not miss the forest for the trees, I think it's important to add this caveat: The ultimate Need is connection to God. Ultimate fulfillment comes as a result of connection with God.

Though particular floors of our personalities might experience different Psychological Needs, we are all linked by this common and desperate need for God. Our very lives depend upon an extravagant redemption that cannot be earned. We are all powerless on our own to heal the sin-distorted rift between who we are and who we were created to be. The humble, the broken, and the honest all readily admit that though we might try, though we might see intermittent success, though we might be able to keep up appearances for a little while—we cannot be sufficient for ourselves. We cannot "get by" on our own. We need help!

Consider Jesus' story about the Pharisee who exalted his own righteousness rather than admitting his need for God. In the Jewish culture of Jesus' day, the Pharisees were the cream of the crop: the smartest and most fastidious men in following the strict requirements of the Old Testament Law. By external appearances, these Pharisees *needed* very little from anyone—even God. Compare this religious, socially elite man to a nearby tax collector, a profession notorious for greed and traitorous disloyalty to the Jewish people for one's own personal (and often dishonest) financial gain. Looking at a tax collector in undeniable need of visible repentance, forgiveness, and life transformation, "the Pharisee posed and prayed like this: 'Oh, God, I thank you that I am not like other people—robbers, crooks, adulterers, or, heaven forbid, like this tax man. I fast twice a week and tithe on all my income.'"

In other words, "I thank you that I am completely self-sufficient, that I have no struggles, that I am fiercely independent and thus have no need for a community or a God of grace."

Jesus continues, "Meanwhile the tax man, slumped in the shadows, his face in his hands, not daring to look up, said, 'God, give mercy. Forgive me, a sinner.'"

In other words, "God...I need you. Desperately."

Jesus gives the story an unexpected twist—its hero is the

tax collector, not the Pharisee. Jesus insists that this Pharisee was in grave need to be rescued from his illusion of godliness and his blindness to his own desperate condition. The tax collector, Jesus says, was made right with God. Jesus wraps up the story with this truth: "If you walk around with your nose in the air, you're going to end up flat on your face, but if you're content to be simply yourself, you will become more than yourself."[167] Until we admit that we do have needs—and that we are incapable of doing life all alone—we cannot fully *live into* who we were uniquely designed to be.

## *Putting it in Perspective*

Remaining in a healthy, grace-filled, satisfied place thus means doing our part to keep our unique Psychological Needs in their proper perspective. Like all of life, it is ultimately a matter of the heart. As the Pharisee's story illustrates, ignoring these needs because we are "above them" or "too spiritual" or fully sufficient in ourselves leads to a place of isolation, pride, and deep dissatisfaction.[168] In reality, we are not meant to be fully independent from one another but rather to be *inter*dependent as a community of believers in Christ, as the family of God, as the Body of Christ.[169] We are not meant to live as the sole suppliers of our own needs. In a bold move of trust, God has chosen to use His Body of believers as one of the primary agents through which He meets our individual and communal needs. We, as Christ's Church, as the living temples of His Spirit, are the imperfect conduits through which God shows us grace, comforts us, forgives us, and invites us to love and be loved.

Helping to cultivate environments where needs can be shared, understood, validated, and met in fruitful ways fosters an atmosphere of love and acceptance. Non-love—born either of ignorance or judgment—assumes that others have the same needs as we do, demanding that others must receive love and energy in the same ways that we do. It takes time to discover what encourages a uniquely designed individual to come alive and to appreciate the multitude of Psychological Needs God has built into his diverse people.

No particular Psychological Need is better than another or

---

[167] Luke 18:9-14, The Message.
[168] Thrall, B., McNicol, B., & Lynch, J.S. (2004). *TrueFaced* (pp. 86). Colorado Springs, CO: NavPress.
[169] We will talk more about the Body of Christ in Chapter 11.

any more or less holy. To devalue what motivates another individual—whether it is solitude or high excitement activities or sensory comforts—is to overlook a chance to appreciate and serve another child of God. On the other hand, to sacrificially offer what you know will be motivating to another individual is building up the beautifully diverse community of Christ in a powerful way.

God does not ask us to pretend—to Him, to ourselves, or to others—that we are not needy. Living as though we have no needs—and thus also denying the presence of the sin that occurs when we attempt to meet these "non-existent" needs negatively—ultimately keeps us from giving and receiving love. Again, *TrueFaced* authors Thrall, McNicol, and Lynch describe this link between need and love beautifully: "Without needs," they suggest, "we cannot experience love—we cannot know when we are being loved."[170] For if we are never in conscious need, how can we recognize when another is sacrificing on our behalf? If we are never in need, our ability to be washed and soaked in gratitude for God's gracious provision will be forever stunted and limited. And there is always the risk that if we are never in need, we will be deceived into believing (like the Pharisee) that we do not need even God Himself.

Let's consider the other end of the spectrum in regards to Psychological Needs. Denying our needs is not honest or healthy. Yet if we make these Psychological Needs idols—i.e., "I cannot live without this," "It is my entitled right for everyone to provide for these needs," "I can be happy apart from God as long as these needs are met"—we end up in a place of equal dissatisfaction. As with most things in life, there is a balance here that requires "keeping in step with the Spirit."[171] Appreciating and attending to Psychological Needs requires a heart surrendered and turned toward God.

God has the ability to be invested in and attending to the smaller picture and the bigger picture perfectly and simultaneously. In the smaller picture, He is infinitely interested in the redemption and fullness of your individual life as He shapes you to look more like His Son Jesus. He is also weaving all our individual stories into His epic, grand restoration of all creation.

---

[170] Thrall, B., McNicol, B., & Lynch, J.S. (2004). *TrueFaced* (pp. 86). Colorado Springs, CO: NavPress.
[171] Galatians 5:25, New International Version.

OUR STORY IS ALWAYS INTENSELY **PERSONAL**
AND **ABOUT SO MUCH MORE** THAN JUST OURSELVES.

With this in mind, it is true to say God has uniquely designed us to experience a deep motivation from and satisfaction in the work He has given us as individuals. It is also true to say that receiving these Psychological Needs is not a closed circuit or the end in and of itself. As our needs are graciously met and we feel satisfied, we are empowered and enabled to share ourselves and our gifts in service. So it *is* about our satisfaction, and it is also about infinitely *more*. It is about this satisfaction transforming us into individuals reaching out in love, boldness, and grace to those around us.

As Image-Bearers, we are given the privilege and responsibility to encourage and support one another, to pass on the good word: "You are loved," "You are admirable," "I love your creativity," "It is good to have peace and solitude," "You inspire me," and even, for now, "Well done, good and faithful servant."

# 08 | Phasing: Rewiring

*"There has never been the slightest doubt in my mind that God who started this great work in you would keep at it and bring it to a flourishing finish on the very day Christ Jesus appears."*[172]
*"And yet, O LORD, you are our Father. We are the clay, and you are the potter. We all are formed by your hand."*[173]

Have you ever experienced an "awakening?" Perhaps you felt an undeniable longing for a grand and even dangerous adventure. It confronted you like a splash of cold water upon your face, demanding that you pay attention or otherwise drown in monotony. Or perhaps your awakening felt more like the subtle autumn stirring of rustling leaves, so still that you hardly noticed the movement at first. But its whisper lodged in your soul, and you cannot ignore the quiet doubt, the discontent, the desire for "more."

Regardless of how you personally experience change—whether it is welcome or uncomfortable, expected or unpredicted—we as human beings are constantly confronted with the reality that change is an ever-present part of our lives. In our environment, in our relationships, and even in our own selves, life is ever shifting, ever moving forward, dynamically changing seasons. In the midst of the apparent chaos of change is the guiding hand of the good and loving

---

[172] Philippians 1:6, The Message.
[173] Isaiah 64:8, New Living Translation.

Master Potter, who takes all things and works them together for the refining of our character, for our transformation into His likeness, and for our ultimate good.

As you allow God to work in you and with you in becoming more fully His, there are times in life when you might begin to feel open to a variety of new experiences or types of satisfaction. You may notice new trends or emerging patterns in what feels motivating to you on personal and professional levels.

Perhaps your view of God broadens to make space for your developing perspective. You experience longings for things that hitherto did not feel central to you or your experience of life. You might also become restless or dissatisfied with how life has always been and experience discomfort at this shift. And you might employ new ways of dealing with distress if you attempt to fulfill these needs in unhealthy or misguided ways.

> // A previously content stay at home mom begins to feel increasingly restless and longs to return to work, where she has control over her schedule and is recognized for her productivity. She is experiencing a desire for the Psychological Needs of recognition of work and time structure in the Achiever floor of her personality.
>
> // A corporate executive who has lived his life in the pursuit of career success and accolades from colleagues begins to feel empty and for the first time strongly desires warmth and intimate companionship, to be loved for himself and not for his external activity. Although he and others might identify this abrupt change as a "midlife crisis," it may signal a genuine movement from the Psychological Needs of his Achiever or Persister floors into previously uncharted Harmonizer territory.
>
> // A formerly playful child loses a close family member and constantly seeks out solitude, months and even years after the initial grief has passed. Trauma and an emotionally charged experience result in this Energizer Base child moving into his Dreamer personality floor and deeply desiring the Psychological Need for solitude.

# Phasing & Phase Changes

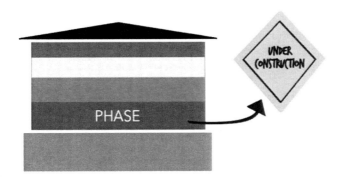

In the previous chapter, we identified your Phase floor as the site of your primary Psychological Needs. Initially, the Needs of your Base and Phase are the same. But for some individuals, God instigates an internal shift in motivation. In his *Process Communication Model®*, Dr. Kahler refers to these shifts in personality—or instances of experiencing new Psychological Needs—as **Phase changes**. [174] When you undergo a Phase change, you will still enjoy and need the Psychological Needs of your Base floor, but those Base Needs will likely feel secondary to meeting your newly arising Phase Psychological Needs. Thus your Phase floor is the aspect of your personality that God is currently awakening. It is as though God is "rewiring" your desires, making adjustments in your internal power sources to woo you into experiencing the next floor in your Personality Structure.

Have you ever lived in a home while it was under any sort of renovation, like a rewiring of your electricity? Or worked in a business in the midst of a major reworking of a particular department? These renovations are often uncomfortable, surfacing all sorts of new needs, questions, and even coping patterns to deal with the inherent stresses of change. Yet whether in business, ministry, relationships, or personal growth, change—when submitted to God's loving care—is inevitable and healthy. Authors Thrall, McNicol, and Lynch powerfully highlight the essentiality of being open to change

---

[174] Kahler, T. (1996, 2012). *The Process Communication Model® Seminar—Seminar One: Core Topics.* (pp. 57). Little Rock, AR: Kahler Communications, Inc.

in the life of a Christian:

> "...your destiny requires that you be a maturing person. The Father wants us to mature into 'the likeness of His Son,' because he can't release us into his dreams for us unless we are maturing."[175]

Though few would disagree that maturity resulting from change is a good thing, it is tempting to cling to what "has always worked" and thus get ourselves stuck in familiar patterns. Yet at times in life, we encounter circumstances or events that we have no idea how to handle. All our old tactics and tricks come up short as we try to cope with and handle new longings and motivations that are unfamiliar. It is in these moments that God lovingly walks with us as we experience the Psychological Needs of the Phase floor in our personality, wooing us into further exploring the qualities of this floor.

Experiencing a desire for new Psychological Needs might feel like a surprise or a definite shift. You will begin to find a new pleasure or feel an unexpected longing for activities, interactions, or experiences that had not previously felt so satisfying. It is as though the Holy Spirit "awakens" a longing or sense of incompleteness *in order to* move us toward developing a greater understanding of and appreciation for other floors in our Personality Structure.

According to Kahler's PCM®, a Phase change most often occurs in the wake of emotional distress or tragedy which triggers an underlying issue that the individual must resolve.[176] When confronted by this unresolved issue, an individual can either 1) deal with that issue authentically, in which case the individual will not Phase, or 2) further avoid the issue and thus enter a period of intense distress. Dr. Kahler refers to this process of experiencing distress in the midst of a Phase change as **Phasing**.[177]

About two-thirds of individuals will experience a Phase change at some point in their lives, moving from experiencing the Psychological Needs of their Base as primary to the Needs of a new Phase floor.[178] For the remaining third, the

---

[175] Thrall, B., McNicol, B., & Lynch, J.S. (2004). *TrueFaced* (pp. 15). Colorado Springs, CO: NavPress.
[176] Kahler, T. (1997). *The Advanced PCM Seminar*. Little Rock, AR: Kahler Communications, Inc.
[177] Kahler, T. (1996, 2012). *The Process Communication Model® Seminar—Seminar One: Core Topics*. (pp. 58). Little Rock, AR: Kahler Communications, Inc.
[178] Kahler, T. (2008). *The Process Therapy Model: The Six Personality Types with Adaptations*. (pp. 109). Little Rock, AR: Kahler Communications, Inc.

Phase personality floor will remain the same as the Base personality floor throughout one's life. Whether or not you phase through all six floors of your personality or maintain the same Base/Phase floor throughout life does not determine whether you are more or less healthy than other individuals. It might indicate, however, that you have particularly honed skills in your Base Perception and its associated Character Strengths but will have more difficulty expending energy in relationships or tasks that call upon other personality floors. What ultimately matters is trusting God to faithfully lead you in *living into* who He created **you** to be.

As we have already considered, each of the six floors in your Personality Structure understands God and the world differently—through a particular Perception with specific Character Strengths that are integral to who you are. These Character Strengths and Perceptions are connected to your Base personality floor, the bottom floor of your Personality Structure which contains the most available energy. Your Base personality floor is the first floor of your personality to develop as a child, and the corresponding Character Strengths and Perception of the Base personality floor will also remain constant throughout one's life.[179]

Remember: though one's personality can continue to grow or change throughout life, the overall **order** of your Personality Structure and the particular stacking of your personality floors remain stable, regardless of how many times you may experience a Phase change.[180] Your Personality Structure has been divinely constructed; to move these floors would require a total rebuilding or rearrangement of the entire structure.

For those who do experience a Phase change, this change always occurs in the ascending order of one's Personality Structure.[181] That is, one's first Phase change will be into the personality floor that has the next highest energy after the Base floor.[182] Experiencing a Phase change is a shift in what you find motivating. God stirs up new longings and needs to

---

[179] From Kahler, T. (1996, 2012). *The Process Communication Model® Seminar—Seminar One: Core Topics.* (pp. 9). Little Rock, AR: Kahler Communications, Inc.
[180] Stansbury, Pat. (1990). Report of Adherence to Theory discovered when the Personality Pattern Inventory was administered to Subjects Twice. Little Rock, AR: Kahler Communications, Inc..
[181] From Stansbury, P. (1990), "Report of Adherence to Theory discovered when the Personality Patterns Inventory was administered to Subjects Twice", Little Rock, AR: Taibi Kahler Associates, Inc.: adapted by permission.
[182] From Kahler, T. (1996, 2012). *The Process Communication Model® Seminar—Seminar One: Core Topics.* (pp. 58). Little Rock, AR: Kahler Communications, Inc.

which you were previously not "plugged in." Thus as you Phase, you will begin to experience an increasing desire for the Psychological Needs associated with the new Phase floor of your personality most strongly. In fact, feeling unfamiliar longings or developing new interests is often a good "hint" that you are beginning to phase. You might also encounter new responses to stress as you seek to understand why you are experiencing these changes.

The degree to which you experience the Psychological Needs of your Phase floor correlates with the amount of energy you already have available in that personality floor. For instance, if you have 85% energy in your Dreamer Phase floor, you might highly identify with the Psychological Needs of your Dreamer. But if you have only 50% or less energy in this Phase floor, these Psychological Needs and Character Strengths will not feel as familiar and might be newly developing.

As you get in touch with the Psychological Needs of your Phase, you are also open to *enjoy* in ways you have not hitherto experienced. There are newly opened avenues through which you can feel satisfied or fulfilled in your work, in your relationships, in your recreation and play, and in your perception of God and how He meets your needs. Let's return to the middle-aged corporate businessman who phases into the Harmonizer floor of his personality and begins to experience a longing for the associated Psychological Needs—in this case, recognition of person and sensory. This successful business executive who was previously satisfied to live with integrity and provide for his family now begins to wonder if they love him.

As this man phases into his Harmonizer floor, he does not simply feel a newly developing need for sensory comfort; he also receives new *enjoyment* from it—acknowledging and delighting in the warmth of the fire, the smell of the cinnamon candles, the softness of the fireside blanket. And perhaps the "I love you's" from his children now create a deeper sense of satisfaction in him than those words previously did. From his Harmonizer Phase floor, this businessman and father both longs for and recognizes the unconditional acceptance inherent in these simple words and can perhaps respond by pouring into the relationship differently than he did before. Experiencing the Needs of his Harmonizer Phase enables him to relate, experience, and express love in a new way.

A college student phasing into the Persister floor of her Personality Structure now experiences a growing sense of purpose and gets involved in a human rights organization on campus. She is energized by pouring her time into raising awareness and feels newly satisfied as her awakening Psychological Needs are met. Whereas before she did not understand the long, tedious hours her roommate poured into organizing campaigns for awareness and advocacy, she now experiences a profound respect and admiration for her friend. Their friendship and mutual respect, strengthened by commitment to a meaningful cause, deepen as a result of understanding. Experiencing the Psychological Needs of her Persister Phase floor might also open up new subjects of interest to this student, who decides to pick up a minor in global health issues.

## STAGE FLOORS

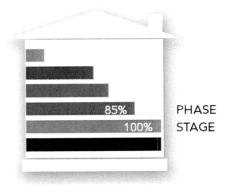

In addition to experiencing new kinds of Psychological Needs and new methods of displaying and coping with distress (which we will discuss in the next chapter), an individual who is phasing into a new personality floor has the potential to develop greater access to the Character Strengths associated with that floor of one's personality.

According to Dr. Kahler, if one successfully *phases through* a Phase personality floor—resolving key issues in a healthy way after periods of long distress—then that personality floor will become what is known as a **Stage**.[183] Any personality floor above your Base for which you have 100% energy is a Stage floor and indicates that you have, at some point in your life, gone through the process of Phasing. In that season of your life, you might have experienced new longings

---

[183] From Kahler, T. (1988, 1992, 2000, 2004). *The Mastery of Management*. Little Rock, AR: Kahler Communications, Inc.; adapted by permission.

or needs than you had previously.

Once you phased through this floor, it was no longer the primary site of your Psychological Needs or Distress, but the Character Strengths and Perception of this personality floor are readily available and accessible to you. This Stage has been "lived in," so to speak, and you can easily ride your elevator to access this Stage floor's particular qualities without expenditure of great effort. The personality floor with the next highest energy under 100% following the Base and the Stage will now be considered your Phase.[184]

Norah has always had a warm and sensitive heart guiding her life. But as she entered her teenage years, Norah began to experience a need to assert her independence and express herself. Though Norah's compassion or desire to love and be loved never disappeared, the sweet compliance of her childhood transformed into acts of rebellion and pushing the edge. In this case, Norah's **Base** personality floor (Harmonizer) remained the same, but she entered a **Phase** in adolescence (Energizer). As Norah left home and began living outside of the realm of her parents' care, she began to authentically face the Energizer Phase issue of responsibility, eventually phasing through her Energizer floor.[185]

The next floor in Norah's Personality Structure with less than 100% energy was her Persister floor. Imagine Norah's surprise when her most immediate instinct as a mother twenty years later is not to be playful with her children but rather to protect them and invest in them a deep sense of values and commitment. Becoming a parent (and subsequently having to confront the issues of fear and trust) has moved Norah into a new **Phase** (Persister).

At this point, Norah has a Base personality floor (Harmonizer), a Stage personality floor (Energizer), and a new Phase personality floor (Persister). She can access the Perception and Character Strengths of her Harmonizer and Energizer floors, but her most immediate Psychological Needs, her Phase issue, and her pattern of distressed behaviors are now related to her Persister floor.

---

[184] From Kahler, T. (1996, 2012). *The Process Communication Model® Seminar—Seminar One: Core Topics.* (pp. 58). Little Rock, AR: Kahler Communications, Inc.
[185] Dr. Kahler identified "Phase issues" for each of the six Personality Types. From Kahler, T. (1997). *The Advanced PCM Seminar.* Little Rock, AR: Kahler Communications, Inc.

## Rewiring: New Energy Sources

We have talked about Phasing as a rewiring of your internal energy sources. Have you ever attempted electrical rewiring in your house? Not only do you risk getting shocked, but you also experience the same kind of discomfort that accompanies any kind of home repair—an interruption to daily life which requires a number of adjustments, sacrifices, and rearrangements. This "rewiring," particularly in the human soul, always requires some disruption of what "has been" and thus can be painful. As you move into a new Phase, you may experience a desire or even unconscious pull to turn your life upside down, as what was once satisfying now seems layered with emerging and insistent new desires. How should you handle these shifting needs and sources of motivation in your personality? Sometimes, God may be calling you to make radical and bold life changes. At other times, however, you might not have to turn your world upside down to handle a Phase change. You may instead have to turn the way you view *your place in the world* upside down.

### Rediscovering Purpose

Gene was approaching thirty-five years of employment as a punch press operator for boat dashboards. As someone with a Dreamer Base, Gene received a deep sense of pleasure and peace from the quiet, hands-on, steady environment required for his job. As a kid out of high school, Gene worked his way over the span of three decades from low man on the totem pole to a laborer with seniority, significant health benefits, job security, and a growing retirement fund. His steady job and health insurance had seen his wife through two different surgeries, and with his current income, Gene was sending his second daughter to college next year.

One February, a subtle shift began to ripple through Gene's psyche, creating wrinkles where there had been only smooth acceptance, stirring up longings where contentment had reigned. As Gene phased from his Dreamer Base into his Persister personality floor, he could not understand why the work that had previously been ideal and fulfilling now felt dissatisfying. Even more distressing than the daily grind was

Gene's growing sense of despair as he looked back over his life and made evaluations and judgments. Through the lens of his current Persister Phase Psychological Needs, Gene evaluated the first fifty-three years of his life and saw nothing of significant value. He saw no lifelong cause for which he had sacrificed, no external recognition of his work from those he respected, nothing that validated him as a man of value and conviction.

"I feel like my whole life has been worthless," Gene shared with his wife. "What good have I done as a punch press operator? I have wasted my life and my purpose."

Yet Gene felt stuck. Pragmatically, he could not leave his job. The benefits were too good, his family was depending upon his consistent financial provision, he was too close to retirement—the reasons piled up like an insurmountable tower. Looking ahead, Gene saw only purposeless work and a shiftless, valueless existence. At his wife's encouragement, Gene went to see a therapist.

"My life has been meaningless. Without purpose. Wasted," Gene looked disgusted with himself and life in general. "But I simply can't turn everything upside down. I'm stuck."

The therapist leaned forward, searching Gene's eyes. "Gene," he began slowly. "There are countless things of value that you have done in your life. As you experience new Psychological Needs, it is important to recognize what has *already been true* of who you are all along."

Gene looked skeptical.

"You have financially supported your wife through several surgeries. You have been a faithful and dedicated employee. Your conscientious saving over the years allowed your two children to go to school debt free," the therapist continued. "But all of that is what has come before. And now...*now*...you still have valuable work ahead. Do you realize how those young men at the factory look up to you? They are hungry for a mentor, a man of character and integrity like you, whether they know it or not. Many of them don't come from families where their fathers stayed and provided. Many of them haven't held jobs for thirty-five days, much less thirty-five years. They need to see what dedication looks like in action. They need to watch the integrity of a man who has been and continues to be faithful to his wife."

Gene fought back unexpected tears. "I see."

"Whether you are the head of a non-profit promoting a global cause or a punch press operator in a small town, who you are and what you do as a result is *still* valuable. It has meaning. I believe that if you go to work tomorrow with that mindset, if you see the lives you can influence for good because of your character, you will no longer be convinced that your life has been or will continue to be void of meaning."

The rearrangement associated with Phasing might result in a complete life readjustment—a change in careers, location, etc. Or, as in Gene's case, it might call for a significant shift in perspective, a fresh framework through which to view your life in light of new Psychological Needs.

Ever heard a similar story? Or perhaps you have felt it yourself. Significant changes or shifts in what you want, what you long for, what leaves you feeling excited or empty. Perhaps you have watched a spouse undergo this change and evolve into what feels like a completely different person than the one you married. When there is no deeper understanding or point of reference for what is happening at the core, this internal shifting that Dr. Kahler identified as a Phase change can lead to a helpless feeling. But take comfort in this truth: Phasing, though painful, is never out of God's control or beyond the scope of His plan and care. Experiencing a new Phase floor is not essential in order to be a growing or maturing individual; for some, God has already designed and highlighted that which is needed for the good works He has planned for us. For these, a Phase change might never occur.

But for others, a Phase change is part of God's plan for uncovering another layer of our unique design. We do not have to fear these changes, unfamiliar as they may be. It is a little like a woman suddenly desiring to learn to swim for the first time at the age of sixty, only to find that she has had the capacity to be an incredible swimmer all along. This skill (and the desire to acquire that skill) simply had not yet been "awakened", not nurtured until now. And it took a little work, some concentrated learning and humility, in order to fully access this "newfound" ability. These internal shifts in motivation are instances of God wooing us to further expand an aspect of who He has *already* created us to be in order to accomplish what He intends in and through us. "Being confident of this, that he who began a work in you will carry it on to completion until the day of Christ Jesus."[186]

So what is truly at the root of any Phase change?

Shifting into a new Phase floor does not only entail developing new sources of motivation in one's personality; it often involves healing core beliefs or wounds that we have carried for years. Though Phases are often recognizable by the presence of newly developing Psychological Needs, these Needs themselves do not start the change. They are not the catalyst for the Phase; they are merely evidence that a Phase is occurring. At the core of each Phase change lies an attempt to resolve an underlying **Phase issue**, which varies depending upon the personality floor undergoing the Phase change.[187] Dr. Kahler has identified the "Phase issues" of each of the six personality floors as follows:[188]

**Table 4:** Potential Phase Issues

| Phase Floor | Phase Issue |
|---|---|
| Harmonizer | Anger |
| Achiever | Loss |
| Persister | Fear |
| Dreamer | Autonomy |
| Catalyzer | Abandonment |
| Energizer | Responsibility |

From Kahler, T. (1997). *The Advanced PCM Seminar*. Little Rock, AR: Kahler Communications, Inc.; used with permission.

If you are never confronted with a situation or circumstance that demands you deal with the issue of your particular Phase personality floor, you will not undergo the period of distress known as **Phasing** or shift into a new Phase floor. For example, the Achiever floor's Phase issue is loss. If, as someone with an Achiever Phase, you do not experience a significant loss, you will not be asked to deal with this issue

---
[186] Philippians 1:6, New International Version.
[187] Kahler, T. (1997). *The Advanced PCM Seminar*. Little Rock, AR: Kahler Communications, Inc.
[188] Kahler, T. (1997). *The Advanced PCM Seminar*. Little Rock, AR: Kahler Communications, Inc.

and thus will remain in an Achiever Phase for the entirety of your life. By that same token, if you are in an Energizer Phase and experience loss, it will not cause a Phase change as this is not the crucial issue for Energizers to resolve.

Long-term distress lasting anywhere from six months to two years generally precedes a Phase change, which requires resolving one's Phase issue.[189] This Phase change occurs after a period of intense distress known as Phasing, which can last anywhere from two years to a lifetime depending on how long it takes one to authentically confront and deal with his or her Phase issue.[190]

Phasing can be a means through which God heals parts of yourself that you have "lost" along the way or rejected. At some point in your life, you may have shut down the elevator entrance to a certain floor and all of its associated characteristics because you felt you had to protect, limit, or deny aspects of yourself in order to survive. Perhaps you were told that boys don't cry and subsequently shut down or denied all access to your emotions and heart; yet all the while you built up a repressed anger about being unappreciated for who you are. Or your attempts at self-expression and creativity were ridiculed in a family where reason ruled supreme, so you disowned your childlike nature and grew up fast; yet you internally continue to rebel and refuse to commit at the level of your heart. In essence, we can try to "re-create" ourselves and our worlds in order to fit what we perceive to be the right kind of image or environment.

## PHASE ISSUES: TWO CHOICES

According to Dr. Kahler, when you *are* confronted with the issue associated with your Phase personality floor, you have two choices.[191] You can feel the authentic emotion associated with that issue, depending upon God's grace for healing and seeking out safe relational spaces through which to process your pain, hurt, disillusionment, and more. Perhaps as a Persister Base, you were deeply wounded or betrayed by a family member or friend and have had trouble trusting ever

---

[189] Kahler, T. (1997). *The Advanced PCM Seminar*. Little Rock, AR: Kahler Communications, Inc.
[190] Kahler, T. (2008). *The Process Therapy Model: The Six Personality Types with Adaptations*. (pp.162). Little Rock, AR: Kahler Communications, Inc.
[191] From Kahler, T. (2008). *The Process Therapy Model: The Six Personality Types with Adaptations*. Little Rock, AR: Taibi Kahler Associates, Inc.

since. Now as a college student, you expect your roommates to be perfect because when they are not, you face the reality that they too might be untrustworthy. You must confront the Persister Phase issue of *fear* before moving to a new Phase. Moving toward freedom and away from fear might mean uncovering, naming, and facing this difficulty in trusting others. Facing this Persister Phase issue of fear authentically would allow you to "phase through" your Persister floor, gaining access to its Character Strengths, receiving enjoyment from receiving its Psychological Needs, and gaining new perspective through its Perception.

Or perhaps confronting your Phase issue asks you to access experiences and emotions that you have shut off since childhood, remembering the disconnected self. At the suggestion of his therapist, one successful physician took the *Servants by Design*™ profile [192] (based upon the *Process Spiritual Model*™) to find he showed a great deal of energy in the Dreamer floor of his personality. In a therapy session, the physician expressed disbelief or confusion at the results. As his therapist began to further explain the imaginative Dreamer who enjoys solitude and thinking of things in different or unusual ways, the physician began to weep. The doors to a locked floor he had not visited since his adolescence swung open and flooded him with familiar images and ideas and possibilities long denied.

Through tears, he said: "I remember when I was fourteen, I looked around at other people and thought 'people like me are going nowhere. I can't be like I am'." Rather than claiming his imaginative, reflective nature, he learned early in life to protectively mis-use his Dreamer ability to remain unaffected by simply "numbing out" and denying or repressing this aspect of his God-given personality.

When we deny aspects of our unique designs, we miss out on becoming and serving from the fullness in which we were created to live. We feel the gap between who we *think* we are supposed to be and who we were *created* to be. And we feel the exhaustion or hopelessness associated with constant pretending. Recognizing and reclaiming these disowned or lost floors of our personality plays a vital role in walking toward wholeness and healing.

---

[192] Maris, R. and Richardson, J. (2002). *Servants by Design Profile*. Little Rock, AR: Transpersonal Technologies, L.L.C.; this profile has been updated as the *Freed to Be Me: A Servant by Design*™.

Experiencing your authentic emotions can be extremely painful and make you feel small and vulnerable, but resolving this core issue paves the way to healing and wholeness. In this wholeness, the Holy Spirit works you toward the completion of His specific design for you. When this kind of grace-soaked process occurs, you will successfully *phase*. This Phase personality floor now becomes a Stage, and the next highest floor in the Personality Structure becomes the new Phase personality floor.[193] You could remain in this new Phase floor for a short amount of time or for the rest of your life, depending on whether you are asked to face the new Phase issue or not.

What is your second choice when confronted with the specific issue of your Phase? You can avoid the issue through a carefully constructed façade of "cover-up emotions" and maladaptive behaviors, avoiding the call to dig too deep into the soul-garden for fear of the dirt or worms you might find. It is a rigorous and sometimes relentless process, asking you to unlock parts of your heart and memories for God to heal. Ultimately, it requires that you surrender false beliefs and cognitive distortions about the world and allow God to redefine you and your reality. It is no small call! Until you allow yourself to feel the *authentic* emotion associated with your Phase rather than hiding behind the cover-up feelings, you will fall prey to the Deceptions and Distress behaviors associated with the Phase floor of your personality.[194]

When God woos us to develop the next floor of our Personality Structure, these issues relentlessly echo deep within our consciousness, in the hidden places of our hearts and minds. We may be afraid to openly seek the answers to our questions, but we constantly attempt to find them unconsciously through our interactions, in our work, and in our relationships. Through our actions or inactions, in our deepest thoughts and the resonant chambers of our hearts, we look to God with these questions on our lips. And if we are ever to move toward healing and wholeness, we must look to God to answer these issues with His truth, in His timing, in His way.

---

[193] From Kahler, T. (1996, 2012). *The Process Communication Model® Seminar—Seminar One: Core Topics.* (pp.58). Little Rock, AR: Kahler Communications, Inc.
[194] From Kahler, T. (1982, 1996). *Process Communication Management Seminar.* Little Rock, AR: Taibi Kahler Associates, Inc.

The following table shows the Phase issues of all six personality floors and the associated cover up emotions that Dr. Kahler has discovered.

**Table 5:** Unresolved Phase Issues & Cover Up Emotions

| Phase Floor | Phase Issue | Cover-Up Emotion | Avoids: |
|---|---|---|---|
| Harmonizer | Anger | Sadness | Conflict |
| Achiever | Loss | Frustrated Anger | Dependency |
| Persister | Fear | Righteous Anger | Vulnerability |
| Dreamer | Autonomy | Impotence | Involvement |
| Catalyzer | Abandonment | Vindictive | Commitment |
| Energizer | Responsibility | Vengeful | Accountability |

From Kahler, T. (1997). *The Advanced PCM Seminar.* Little Rock, AR: Kahler Communications, Inc.; adapted by permission.

## *Ben's Story: Risky Business*

In working through the process of Phasing and its associated issues, the individual and all those intimately connected to him are likely to experience the discomfort, the growing pains, and potentially even the deep wounds that accompany the process.[195]

Ben and his wife Naomi, who have been married for seven years, experienced this struggle. Ben has a Harmonizer Base but phased into his Catalyzer floor right after college. He met and married Naomi two years later. When Naomi entered into life with Ben, she knew to expect an element of risk. As Ben continued to develop his Catalyzer Phase over the years, Ben experienced an increasing desire for the Psychological Need for incidence associated with his Catalyzer floor. He loved to engage in physical activities such as ice climbing and snowboarding. Ben's draw toward Psychological Needs for

---

[195] From Kahler, T. (1996, 2012). *The Process Communication Model® Seminar—Seminar One: Core Topics.* (pp.58). Little Rock, AR: Kahler Communications, Inc.

challenging, risk-taking behaviors, combined with Naomi's Persister Base and Phase, had always caused some tension in their marriage, as Naomi believed Ben was being needlessly unsafe. She personally had no desire for such risk, and Naomi's growing edge in the relationship was learning to accept Ben's need for excitement and challenge.

But something significant had shifted after Ben's father died seven months ago. The death had been brutally sudden; Ben's fifty-six year old father had died in seconds from a heart attack that no one had seen coming. Naomi knew the father-son relationship had been anything but close; following his parents' divorce, Ben had painfully few memories of his father from his early childhood onward.

In the car on the way home from his father's funeral, Ben remarked to Naomi:

"Shouldn't have surprised anyone that he just up and left. It's what he does. He leaves."

Naomi took a deep breath, disturbed by the callousness in Ben's voice. "He didn't leave you on purpose," she finally replied.

Ben's face showed no response as his grip tightened on the wheel.

Since that day, Ben's "risk-taking" behavior escalated exponentially. What had been one or two nights of snowboarding a week exploded into a multitude of high-risk, high-stakes behaviors. Naomi watched their bank account dwindle and learned from one of Ben's friends that Ben had taken to visiting the nearby casino every few weeks. When Naomi confronted him, Ben lashed back in anger and told her to "Get over it. It's just money. You spend it too." Speeding tickets piled up. Recently Ben had informed her that he wanted to try base-jumping. And he was spending more and more late nights at the office, something he refused to discuss with Naomi.

The loss of his father triggered Ben's core Catalyzer Phase issue—that of abandonment.[196] At some level, Ben believes his father's death was a final stab at an unhealed wound from years of feeling abandoned. Rather than acknowledging his fear of abandonment, Ben responds by covering up with vindictive emotions, feeling bitter, spiteful, and unforgiving.

---

[196] Kahler, T. (1997). *The Advanced PCM Seminar*. Little Rock, AR: Kahler Communications, Inc..

And rather than meeting his Catalyzer Psychological Needs in healthy and productive ways, Ben enters into a predictable spiral of distress, abusing his strengths in an attempt to avoid his wound.

For reasons he himself might not even understand, Ben is seeking out high amounts of adrenaline in short periods of time, such as speeding, taking financial risk, or flirting with an affair at the office. Ben's attempts to take care of himself and his hurt rather than leaning into the All Sufficient One are wreaking havoc on his life and in his heart. Before Ben can move through this process of Phasing and experience a Phase change, he must face his Catalyzer Phase issue and feel the honest emotions associated with that issue, depending on God—the One who promises, "I will never leave you nor forsake you."[197]

"I know, Elise. But I don't know how to reach him right now. It's like he's a different…" Naomi stopped mid-sentence at the sound of the garage door. "He's home from work. I'll let you know how it goes."

"I'll be praying," Elise replied.

Naomi hung up the phone and noted that her posture felt stiff and rigid. She hoped she was doing the right thing. She just wanted to be doing the right thing—for Ben, their marriage, their family. Maybe even for her.

"Ben, will you come in here?" Naomi tried to make her tone easy and hide the edges of expectation in her vocal cords.

Ben was unknotting his tie as he flopped down beside her on the other side of the couch. "Yep?"

Naomi took a deep breath. She was never one to beat around the bush. "It's after ten o'clock, Ben. It's the fourth night in a row you've come home late from work. Anything going on I should know about?"

Ben looked back at her with a fairly blank expression, his cool stare inviting Naomi to feel intimidated. "What are you trying to say?"

Naomi shook her head. "I'm trying to get you to communicate about what is going on inside you. You used to talk about things. Now it's like a brick wall. And I'm tired of waiting up at home for you, wondering where you are, if

---

[197] Joshua 1:5, New International Version.

you're safe, if you're alive."

"Then don't."

"You're different, Ben. Ever since your father died, some kind of struggle has been happening under the surface. What's going on? Are you unhappy? Why won't you talk to me?"

Ben set his tie on the couch and flashed Naomi a defensive look. "What do you mean, different?"

"You put over half our savings in risky investments without telling me. You've gotten two speeding tickets in the past three months. One for going ninety-seven miles per hour, Ben. Ninety-seven! You'd rather spend your time schmoozing the big money clients and spinning tales about buying a winter home near Breckenridge so we can ski in the winter and 'live the high life.'" Naomi took a breath. "That's not the man I married."

Ben's face was hard. "I don't see anything wrong with any of those things. I'm just trying to have some excitement in my life. You want excitement, don't you? Don't expect me to just work a nine-to-five job, come home and watch sitcoms, take my vitamins, go to bed, and do it all over again every day, year in and year out. You just can't expect that of someone."

Naomi felt herself wanting to snap. She folded and unfolded hands incessantly.

"You're dying in this life. Admit it!" Ben leaned forward.

"Ben," Naomi's tone was measured and felt wooden, though she believed every word she said. "I made a commitment to you, no matter what. I believe we can work through this. I will stick it out."

## Phase Issue Resolution

Phasing highlights our dependence on God for wholeness and healing. When we attempt to handle unfamiliar needs on our own, we end up in a rut of self-defeating behaviors that hurt ourselves as well as those around us. But when you lean into the grace available to you as you walk the road of healing and integration, you emerge with a broadened perspective on who God is and how He abundantly meets your needs. He truly does desire for you to *live into* your unique design as you *serve Him* with abandon. This free service flows from an identity marked by healing.

Let's return to Ben's story to see how a Phase issue might be resolved.

The death of his father brought Ben face to face with the Catalyzer Phase issue of whether or not he can risk himself in real intimacy with another or whether he will be abandoned first. Ben's Psychological Need for incidence (frequent adrenaline) accompanied by his risk- taking behaviors make little sense, until one realizes that he is unconsciously testing the waters for whether or not he will be abandoned by those closest to him. His unconscious mind wonders, "My father left me. Will you leave me too?" In the midst of distress, the individual going through a Catalyzer Phase believes the Deception: "I'm only okay if you're being strong."[198] In other words, we must all fend for ourselves, because no one else will take care of us. This is a false but painful lesson that Ben learned early on in life when his father left. In an attempt to avoid getting hurt, an individual in a Catalyzer Phase might push others away or use manipulation to prove this Deception true.

As his distress and confusion deepen, Ben takes his harmful and distressing behavior—his disregard for rules and his risk-taking actions—even farther to the point where his flirtations at work progress to a short-term affair.[199] He still loves Naomi but feeds on the twisted thrill of keeping secrets and having an intense interaction that requires no emotional risking or intimacy on his part. Without utter dependence on God's wisdom to further understand and heal the issues raised within the process of Phasing, extreme, prolonged distress will cause significant and possibly permanent damage to Ben's relationships, career, health, finances, etc.

Ben's process of Phasing could have a variety of different endings. Perhaps Naomi finds out about the affair, and the marriage falls apart. Utterly devastated and suffering from shattered trust, Naomi leaves. At the bottom of every Phase issue is a destructive payoff.[200] For Ben, that payoff is that he acts in such a way that the very thing he fears most actually happens—his wife rejects or "abandons" him. Thus Ben

---

[198] Kahler, T. (1982, 1996). *Process Communication Management Seminar*. Little Rock, AR: Taibi Kahler Associates, Inc. From Maris, R. (1996). *Your Great Design*. Little Rock, AR: Transpersonal Technologies, Inc..
[199] These behaviors are indicative that Ben has moved into second and even third degree distress in Kahler's Distress Sequence. Kahler, T. (1982, 1996). *Process Communication Management Seminar*. Little Rock, AR: Taibi Kahler Associates, Inc.
[200] Kahler, T. (1982, 1996). *Process Communication Management Seminar*. Little Rock, AR: Taibi Kahler Associates, Inc.

abandons his wife (whether literally or metaphorically) before she can "abandon" him. With the loss of that chance for intimacy, Ben might be likely to continue in his risk-taking and reckless behaviors, leaving a relational wake of pain. He will remain stunted in this kind of distress until, through God's grace, he boldly faces his Phase issue.

But what if Naomi, his wife, finds out about the affair and gives herself some separation from Ben without abandoning him? What if she somehow reaffirms her commitment to stay with him regardless? What if Ben does not receive his destructive payoff but instead receives undeserved grace? There is the chance that Ben will confront this deep fear of intimacy and admit his wrong to Naomi. A chance that they will work to reconcile and trust God to heal the deep wounds they both have. A chance that their bond of intimacy will be strengthened rather than broken.

As Ben re-learns that he will not always be abandoned by those he loves, he is simultaneously freed to forgive his imperfect father for his past abandonment and to commit or bind himself to others. In the coming years, Ben is able to speak into the lives of other young men and women who have been abandoned. Though the growth process was painful, Ben can now live, free and healed, more fully into the design God gave him. This is the power of our ever-redeeming God to give us as His people "a crown of beauty for ashes, a joyous blessing instead of mourning, festive praise instead of despair. In [our] righteousness, [we] will be like great oaks the Lord has planted for his own glory."[201]

In this difficult but redemptive scenario, Ben will be able to successfully complete the process of Phasing through the Catalyzer floor of his personality. He will still have greater access to and understanding of the Character Strengths of his Catalyzer floor and can see the world through that Perception if necessary in order to communicate (though never as naturally as the Perception of his Harmonizer Base), but Ben will no longer experience his most immediate Psychological Needs there or habitually exhibit Distress out of that floor of his personality.[202] It is possible that Ben will never go through the process of Phasing again. Or perhaps God will again woo

---

[201] Isaiah 61:3, New Living Translation.
[202] From Kahler, T. (1996, 2012). *The Process Communication Model® Seminar—Seminar One: Core Topics.* (pp.58). Little Rock, AR: Kahler Communications, Inc.

him to a different floor of his Personality Structure, and a new type of healing will take place.

In the previous story, Ben's distress was linked most specifically to working through the issue associated with his Catalyzer Phase. Individuals who do not undergo a Phase change at some point in life do not experience the same kind of disruption and distress associated with confronting a Phase issue.[203] Yet it is evident that every individual still experiences **distress** to some degree on both a daily basis and over a lifetime. Whether a momentary twinge of anxiety, an irritating encounter, or a prolonged pattern of destructive behavior, we move in and out of varying degrees of negative thoughts, feelings, and behaviors throughout our lives. In the next chapter, we'll look at the possible Deceptions that can move us from a place of *living into and serving out of* our unique designs to one of desperately trying to meet our own needs at all costs.

It all goes back to belief.

---

[203] From Kahler, T. (1996, 2012). *The Process Communication Model® Seminar—Seminar One: Core Topics.* (pp.58). Little Rock, AR: Kahler Communications, Inc.

# 09 | Distress: The Great Distortion

What happens if you pull the leaves off of a weed in your flowerbed but leave the root intact? You would be a little naïve to be surprised when the weed still flourishes, drawing nutrients under the ground to feed its root system while you destroy its petals on the surface. What happens if you have a respiratory infection but treat only the symptoms of fever, the sore throat, or the fatigue associated with the bigger problem? Your fever might break, or you may have a little relief from your scratchy throat for a few hours; meanwhile, the root cause behind all of your symptoms has gone untreated. Without pinpointing the infection itself, your sore throat will return in a matter of hours and perhaps even get worse!

Though imperfect, this is a good framework through which to begin thinking about Distress. If we want to experience real and lasting change in our lives, we cannot simply "clean up" behaviors without asking **why** we are acting as we are. Polishing up your actions without heart transformation is much like pulling a few petals off a growing weed; instead, God must unearth sin by the roots to form a new ecosystem of nourishment for your soul. He must carefully, methodically weed out false or destructive counterfeits of "truth" and plant new seeds of His Truth in their place.

## THE QUESTION

Every behavior is rooted in a belief—no matter how old or unconscious this belief is. Ultimately, changing behavior requires a journey into the heart. And as Dallas Willard said, "What is in our heart matters more than anything else for who we become and what becomes of us."[204]

> THE QUESTION RESONATING IN THE DEPTHS OF EVERY HUMAN HEART—WHETHER A HUSHED WHISPER OR A SHOUT OF CHALLENGE—IS "CAN I TRUST YOU, GOD?"

This question subtly infiltrated the hearts and minds of the Image-Bearers of God all the way back in the Garden of Eden. Dallas Willard points out the root of Eve's deception when she ate of the fruit from the Tree of the Knowledge of Good and Evil:

> "When [Satan] undertook to draw Eve away from God, he did not hit her with a stick, but with an idea. It was with the idea that God could not be trusted and that she must act on her own to secure her own well-being."[205]

The deception, then, to which we as human beings are vulnerable, is that God cannot be trusted. When we believe this lie, when we remove ourselves from trusting God's word about who He is, when we feel cut off from the protection and sovereignty of a God who wants to "prosper us and not to harm us"[206]—we are vulnerable to a host of other deceptions. We begin to believe God is either not strong or not loving. Perhaps He is simply not mighty enough to take care of His children, or He does not really exist at all. Perhaps He exists but is removed and distant, like an uncaring or apathetic cosmic force. Or perhaps He is a God who is out for Himself, quick to become angry and eager to punish us for His amusement.

Looking at life through any one of these worldviews, it is painfully obvious that we as human beings must then meet our own needs apart from God. It becomes necessary for us to believe that we can be, should be, and actually want to be self-sufficient. Life's all about us, and it's all up to us. Anyone

---

[204] Willard, Dallas. (2002). *Renovation of the Heart* (pp. 16). Colorado Springs, CO: NavPress.
[205] Willard, Dallas. (2002). *Renovation of the Heart* (pp. 100). Colorado Springs, CO: NavPress.
[206] See Jeremiah 29:11.

who has lived in this lie of self-sufficiency for any length of time recognizes, whether consciously or unconsciously, how exhausting this deception is to maintain. For we are certainly not God, and we daily encounter situations, relationships, and a demanding self that are impossible to control. It's like paddling upstream against a deadly strong current. You are far more likely to get tired and surrender to the stream, or to pull another underwater to save yourself, than you are to make it to the bank safely.

## DRIVEN OR LED?

Our belief regarding this question—Can God be trusted to meet my needs and take care of me?—determines which one of two paths we will walk in our lives.

WILL I BE **DRIVEN** TO DEFINE AND MEET
MY OWN NEEDS AT ANY COST?
    OR WILL I BE **LED** INTO A LIFE OF PURPOSE AND SERVICE
        WHERE MY NEEDS ARE UNDER GOD'S CARE? [207]

Let's take a walk down these two paths to explore where each might lead.

What if God *is* utterly trustworthy? If I believe that trusting and seeking God abundantly meets my deepest needs, then I will be *led* into a life of purpose. Being led feels like a loving invitation, a hand extended in relationship, a beckoning to walk with God together on a journey. As Jesus said to his closest friends, "Steep your life in God-reality, God-initiative, God-provisions. Don't worry about missing out. You'll find all your everyday human concerns will be met."[208] If I stake my life on the belief that God is trustworthy and capable of taking care of me, I will be released to use my gifts to joyfully fulfill my calling—living into and serving from the unique design of my Character Strengths, my Psychological Needs, and my Perception.

My understanding of who God is removes the anxiety of constantly questioning "who I am," for I know that I am His first and foremost. My identity rests secure in what He says about me. Thus in my relationships with others, I will move increasingly toward intimacy and authentic sharing. I can

---

[207] From Maris, R. (1996). *Your Great Design*. Little Rock, AR: Transpersonal Technologies, L.L.C.
[208] Matthew 6:33, The Message.

afford to be vulnerable, because my worth and value rest in God's loving care. While I will not look to others to give me ultimate fulfillment, I can gratefully receive God's provision for my needs through the love and generosity of others. Empowered by the Spirit, I can do the same for them—noticing and meeting the needs of others sacrificially as I am able.

In communication, I am free to be honest and open about my struggles and needs as well as verbal in my praises of God's faithfulness. Because I am living in humble trust upon God, there is no shame in admitting that I am dependent upon His grace and goodness for all I am and have—no need to prove, to perform, to compete. Gratitude is the theme of my song as I am gently *led* into a life of fulfillment and service to God and others. For those who are led by a loving God, "the tenor of their lives becomes one of humble and joyful thanksgiving."[209]

If, however, I believe that it is up to me to define and meet my needs apart from God, I will be *driven* to do so in any way I can. Rather than living into and serving from my design, I will be focused on utilizing the resources of my Character Strengths and Perception in order to meet my Psychological Needs for my own personal gain. When I am *driven* rather than led, I believe I must compete for limited resources in order to momentarily satiate my needs. I am interested in surviving with the least amount of pain rather than growing, flourishing, and giving. I will particularly twist and distort my *strengths* to serve myself rather than God. Because my Character Strengths are consistent with my Personality Structure, the misuse of these Character Strengths will occur in predictable ways. This distortion of my design will lead to unhealthy relationships where I focus on what I can get or take from others in order to meet my needs. My worth and the worth of others are constantly in question.

Kahler's *Process Communication Model*® postulates that miscommunication occurs as we wear masks in order to get what we want, to hide the depth of our need, to cover up pain with the illusions of self-sufficiency or cynicism.[210] Ultimately, we will act out in predictable patterns of distress

---

[209] Manning, Brennan (2009). *Ruthless Trust* (pp. 34). New York, NY: HarperCollins.
[210] Kahler, T. (1982, 1996). *Process Communication Management Seminar*. Little Rock, AR: Taibi Kahler Associates, Inc.

over which we feel we have no control. If we continue on this path, we are pushing onward toward self-destruction like a runaway train without any brakes barreling toward the edge of a cliff.

We walk these paths over the course of our lives, but we also walk them moment-by-moment in the choices we make hundreds of times throughout a day. For each action, there lies an intersection of choice: will I be driven or led? Will I trust God or myself? On the surface, small, daily decisions to use our unique designs to serve ourselves and momentarily, temporarily satisfy our own needs appear quite miniscule or insignificant. It is because these choices are connected to a deeper deception that they are actually symptoms of a rot, an unreality, a worship of self at the level of the soul. And when we are all our own gods, stumbling blindly in the darkness of deception, our wills to "get our own way" inevitably clash. Miscommunication breeds in the swamps of these deceptions like mosquitoes in a stagnant, sweltering puddle, resulting in unpleasant consequences.

## Distorted Character Strengths

In our discontented attempts to find fulfillment and worth apart from God, we will use the greatest advantage at our disposal—our Character Strengths—to serve ourselves. Thus each personality floor's manifestation of the deception of self-sufficiency often looks like a misuse or twisting of those aspects of our design that were meant for God's delight, our satisfaction, and the bringing of God's kingdom. We take our greatest strengths—parts of our unique design meant to give God pleasure and to find meaningful purpose in service to His kingdom—and make them desperate weapons of self-service and manipulation.

A man with a warm and compassionate heart uses his sensitivity to make sure others like him rather than to genuinely empathize and care for others. Another with intellect and competence uses these God-given abilities to over-detail everything and everyone. A woman of deep commitment wears her convictions like an unfriendly badge of invulnerability to hide from fear of letting others down. The imaginative mind turns further and further inward on itself to worship fantasy and illusion rather than offering its ideas to transform reality. A couple with great capacity for risk and motivation use their charisma and intimidation to manipulate others for their own self-serving purposes. The joyful creativity of the childlike spirit uses reactivity as a wall against responsibility.

## *Jacob's Wrestling Match*

Remember Jacob, considered one of the fathers of the nation of Israel? His path from second-born son to patriarch was littered with self-promotion and the distortion of his natural gifts for his own gain. Yet God skillfully redeemed even Jacob's selfishness for His perfect plan.

Jacob has lived a life defined by a matter of seconds. Because his twin Esau came out of the womb first, he has the privilege of receiving the birthright from their father Isaac and all the benefits of being the firstborn son. On one not-so-special afternoon, Jacob's brother Esau returns from a long, hot day of hunting with an insistent rumbling in his belly. Esau is hungry and impatient, and as a result, careless. In this moment of Esau's weakness, Jacob sees a chance to change his situation and seizes the opportunity. Jacob withholds some steaming, aromatic stew and gives Esau a calculating glance: "First sell me your birthright." Jacob asks Esau to swear an oath selling his birthright in exchange for some bread and lentil stew. And suddenly, in an instance of shrewd and decisive action, Jacob has transformed his status—from second-born son to the inheritor of the birthright.[211] He pulls a similarly conniving stunt near the end of his father Isaac's life, taking advantage of Isaac's blindness and tricking his father into giving Jacob the blessing of the firstborn rather than Esau.[212]

Though admirably cunning, Jacob's actions toward his family are undeniably self-promoting. In unapologetically looking out for number one, Jacob leaves a wake of deception, bitterness and enemies. In an ironic twist, Jacob himself is tricked multiple times by his father in law, Laban. Yet Jacob's shrewdness and diplomatic skills, characteristic of his Catalyzer Base, continue to benefit him throughout his life; he eventually gets the wife he wants and leaves with some of

---

[211] Genesis 25:29-34, New International Version.
[212] See Genesis 27.

Laban's best flocks.

Jacob runs into a roadblock when he realizes he must again face his brother Esau, the very same twin whom he robbed of the birthright. In a midnight wrestling match, God redeems Jacob's story, restores his relationship with Esau, and gives Jacob a new name. Because of grace, Jacob the Supplanter receives a new chance to live out his design for God's purposes rather than for his own gain. Dallas Willard describes the deceived heart using strengths for its own gain as a corruption of God's original intent: "The question, 'What good can I bring about?' is replaced by 'How can I get my way?'"[213]

## IDENTITY CRISIS

When we begin twisting our Character Strengths for our own purposes, we feel an unnamed but swelling panic as our central identities—our understanding of who we are—become variable, in flux, and ultimately outside of right relationship to reality. For those who identify themselves as God's children, the deception that we must meet our own needs distorts our clear and accurate perception of Father God. We can no longer plainly see that our relationship to God rests upon the goodness of His character and under the umbrella of His constant and extravagant care. Thus we begin to question our position before God as *conditional*. If I am responsible for meeting my own needs and serving myself, I must also be responsible for earning, proving, or keeping my relationship with God based solely on my efforts and my performance. This is the process of Distress. It may occur from one moment to the next and also over a lifetime, not so much as a "shove" or "fall" but rather an underlying, often imperceptible, current that pulls us along further and further off course.

Consider this issue of identity in relationship to the metaphor of the Master and bondservant introduced in Chapter 1. The bondservant knows the Master's will is paramount, that obedience to the Master will also bring about his or her ultimate good, and that he or she can utterly depend upon the Master to provide all he or she needs.

---

[213] Willard, Dallas. (2002). *Renovation of the Heart* (pp. 145). Colorado Springs, CO: NavPress.

Thomas Merton describes this bondservant of pure intention:

> "The secret of pure intention is not to be sought in the renunciation of all advantages for ourselves. Our intentions are pure when we identify our advantage with God's glory, and see that our happiness consists in doing His will because His will is right and good. In order to make our intentions pure, we do not give up all idea of seeking our own good, we simply seek it where it can really be found: in a good that is beyond and above ourselves."[214]

Meaningful work and relationships (Psychological Needs) accompanied by a deepening sense of purpose and appreciation of the Master pervade this joy-filled, trusting bondservant's life. Gratitude is the mantra of the freely trusting, and this bondservant daily and abundantly comes alive in service.

But when we as bondservants and adopted, beloved children step outside of this home of provision and dependence, when we place meeting our own needs and accomplishing our own interests as the greatest aim, we again enslave ourselves to fear.[215] Rather than offering my strengths to the Master, I cling to them like a drowning man to a lifeboat. I see these strengths as the only means I have to define myself and temporarily lessen a deep ache within my soul. I willfully and blindly misuse my limited resources and distort my God-given design. It pervades my conversations and quietly poisons my attempts at relationship. It taints good works with false motives. As I step out of my place in the Master's household, I willingly reenter a slavery of "earning" and find that my worth and value feel conditional and fragile. I must prove myself in my "good" works at all costs. Or I must avoid service altogether because it now feels empty and unable to satisfy.

When I dig into the deception that my fulfillment and worth depend upon my efforts to successfully (if temporarily) meet my own needs, I am willfully living in the old reality that defined my life before I entered into the new covenant with my Master. I am just like God's chosen people Israel who longed for the slavery of Egypt while on the way to the

---

[214] Merton, Thomas. (2002). *No Man Is An Island* (pp. 54). New York, NY: Mariner Books.
[215] Romans 8:14-17.

Promised Land, willing to trade the ultimately rich and full inheritance of "then" for the immediacy of the familiar and comfortable "now".

Sin—in all of its warped and twisted separation from God—attempts to disconnect us from the source of life and leave us as orphans without roots, unsure of our true identities. Not only do we believe that God cannot meet our needs, we believe that we are not who God says we are—children of God, made worthy by Christ's death and resurrection, members of a royal priesthood.[216] Instead of loving and trusting Him, we might fear instead that He is displeased with what He has made and that the only way to regain His approval is to do wonderful things for Him. Or perhaps, in a glass half-empty kind of way, our life purpose becomes **not** doing lots of bad things and hoping to slide by without His notice on the rest. We may altogether lose sight of who He is and of our purpose in His plan and instead seek the momentary and inadequate counterfeit the world has to offer. Ultimately, the root belief that God is not trustworthy leads to a crisis of identity:

> MY ACCEPTANCE, SECURITY, AND LOVABILITY
> ARE CONDITIONAL AND SOMEHOW UP TO ME.

Do any of the following questions resonate with you?

// "Does God find me lovable just as I am, or must I change myself to gain His affection?"

// "Do I think that God attends to all the details and makes order out of the chaotic and seemingly haphazard circumstances of my life? Or must I take control?"

// "Does God value who I am and what I am doing in His Kingdom, or should I distrust Him and fear His judgment?"

// "Can God really protect me, or do I need to withdraw from fully experiencing life in order to avoid feeling unsafe?"

// "Will God actually stick with me through thick and thin, or must I be out for myself to have the life I desire?"

// "Can God enjoy me for all of who I am—my strengths and my failures alike—or do I have to try really hard to be acceptable to him, knowing that I will fail?"

---

[216] 1 John 3:1-3; Romans 3:21-26; 1 Peter 2:9.

When we believe that God's love for us is dependent on *who we are* rather than on *His perfect character*, we are deceived. When we believe that we must change ourselves into who we are **not** in order to be loved, we are unable to live into our unique, God-given designs. Our distorted self-perception and God-perception colors our actions. We are stuck in unproductive cycles we know do not work; yet, we see no alternative to the lonely path of prideful yet failing self-sufficiency.

If we do end up serving God or others from this place of deception, it is out of rising panic, simmering resentment, or a sense of hopelessness—for we are serving to earn, to prove ourselves, to try and gain God's approval. And this view of ourselves before God—as burdensome, or despicable, or insignificant—bleeds into how we perceive others and how we believe others must perceive us as well. We will be drowning in guilt or delusional pride, because none of our best attempts are good enough. From the most "holy" to the least, the prophet Isaiah tells it to us straight: "All our righteous acts are like filthy rags."[217]

Do you grasp how dire this situation is apart from God? Apart from the reality of a life transformative redemption and rescue, we have no choice but to operate out of our false beliefs, which then show up in unproductive and even hurtful behaviors. Apart from God, each of the six personality floors is *driven* (often unconsciously) to meet its own needs—making it on our own, answering our own existential questions, and trying to fool others (God included) into loving us or thinking we are worthwhile. The word *driven* implies that though we might be exercising some choice, we are not operating out of true freedom. We are **reacting**—sometimes subconsciously, unconsciously, habitually—out of a hunger or a lack rather than **responding** from an overflow of gratitude and provision enabled by trust.

## DECEPTIONS AND DRIVERS

In the *Process Communication Model*®, Dr. Kahler's research isolated six primary "Driver" Behaviors, sometimes referred to as "Doorways of Distress" which are associated

---

[217] Isaiah 64:6, New International Version.

with the six personality floors.[218] Dr. Kahler's six Doorways (Drivers) are: "I must please you to be OK" (Harmonizer); "I must be perfect for you" (Achiever); "You must be perfect for me" (Persister); "I must be strong for you" (Dreamer); "You must be strong for me" (Catalyzer); and "I must try hard for you" (Energizer). [219] The *Process Spiritual Model*™ conceptualizes these "Doorways" as the false beliefs, lies, or **Deceptions** that are at the root of Kahler's observable Driver behaviors. [220] These Deceptions begin as thoughts, false beliefs, and distortions of the truth. They are subtle, unconscious shifts in our thinking, open "Doorways" that issue an invitation into deeper distress. These Deceptions manifest differently in each of the six floors of our personality, practically arising from our particular distortion of Character Strengths, Perceptions, and misguided attempts to meet our particular Psychological Needs.[221]

If, while standing at this Doorway, we are able to remember and claim the truth that our significance, identity, and worth are found in God, we can trust Him to provide for our Needs. Stepping away from the belief that I must be my own god, I shut this Doorway of Deception. If, however, I instead act as though my particular Deception is true, I will begin to demonstrate Dr. Kahler's observable "Drivers" associated with my distressed personality floor. [222] These "Drivers" are the behavioral proof, the outward clue that I am momentarily accepting the "Deception" about my identity and security. Dr. Kahler refers to these behaviors as Drivers because when we are believing a Deception, we are DRIVEN to get our Needs met. These Driver behaviors may not even feel like a choice but rather like a necessity; we are driven to do whatever we can to feel "okay." In instances of mild to moderate distress, you will generally experience the Deception and Drivers of your Phase personality floor.[223]

---

[218] From Kahler, T. (1988, 1992, 2000, 2004). *The Mastery of Management*. Little Rock, AR: Kahler Communications, Inc.; adapted by permission. From Kahler, T. (1996, 2012). *The Process Communication Model® Seminar—Seminar One: Core Topics*. (pp. 59). Little Rock, AR: Kahler Communications, Inc.
[219] From Kahler, T. (1988, 1992, 2000, 2004). *The Mastery of Management*. Little Rock, AR: Kahler Communications, Inc.; adapted by permission. Kahler, T. (1996, 2012). *The Process Communication Model® Seminar—Seminar One: Core Topics*. Little Rock, AR: Kahler Communications, Inc.
[220] From Maris, R. (1996). *Your Great Design*. Little Rock, AR: Transpersonal Technologies, L.L.C
[221] From Kahler, T. and Capers, H. (1974, Jan). The Miniscript. *Transactional Analysis Journal, 4(1)*, 26-42; adapted by permission.
[222] From Kahler, T. (1996, 2012). The Process Communication Model® Seminar—Seminar One: Core Topics. Little Rock, AR: Kahler Communications, Inc.
[223] Kahler, T. (1996, 2012). *The Process Communication Model® Seminar—Seminar One: Core Topics*. (pp. 59). Little Rock, AR: Kahler Communications, Inc.

This is because your Distress is directly linked to your belief about whether God can meet your needs, and your Phase floor is the source of your immediate and pressing Psychological Needs. If you do not have a Phase personality floor, you will experience the Deception and Drivers of your Base personality floor. We will spend time unpacking the false beliefs fueling these Deceptions, believing that if we target the root of belief we will take great strides in eliminating the weeds of behavior. Remember: this picture of Distress is not meant to be a representation of who you truly are or of how you act on a regular basis—it is simply a glimpse of who you can be when living outside of a secure identity in Christ.

### The Harmonizer Deception—Please You[224]

THE DISTORTION:

The Harmonizer, seeing the world through the Perception of emotions, is gifted with the God-given strength of a warm, compassionate, and sensitive heart. Recall that one of the Harmonizer floor's main Psychological Needs is recognition of person —a deep desire to be loved and liked simply for who one is. When someone operating out of his Harmonizer floor moves away from the tender and all-encompassing care of the Master to meet this need, he becomes more susceptible to believing the lie that it is up to him to grasp this Psychological Need on his own apart from God. Seeing life and self through this distorted lens or Deception, he or she then misuses an empathetic heart to feel loved at all costs. Outside of God-reality, the Harmonizer is in danger of believing the Deception that love is conditional:

THE DECEPTION: I'm only okay/worthy/loved *if I am pleasing you.*[225]

THE BELIEF: When operating out of a false belief about your worth and resorting to **Please You** behaviors, you are not just hungry for relationship. You are craving affirmation

---

[224] Kahler, T. (1996, 2012). *The Process Communication Model® Seminar—Seminar One: Core Topics.* (pp. 61). Little Rock, AR: Kahler Communications, Inc.
[225] Kahler, T. (1996, 2012). *The Process Communication Model® Seminar—Seminar One: Core Topics.* Little Rock, AR: Kahler Communications, Inc.

about your self-worth from others, as if their feedback were the sustenance that you *must* have to feel good about yourself and feel loved. When not genuinely feeling and accepting that you are *already* loved by God, you may be *driven* rather than gently led to use your God-given sensitivity and ability to read and empathize with others to assure that they will like and affirm you. Yet any love you do receive through these pleasing efforts has been "paid for in advance" and thus cannot fill or satisfy you.

WARNING SIGNS/DRIVERS: According to *PCM®*, the Harmonizer floor believing this Deception begins to internally over-adapt to others in order to please everyone.[226] Driven by the Deception that our worth is conditional upon pleasing, Harmonizers exhibit particular behavioral clues or Drivers. Their language becomes unassertive and lacks confidence, using words such as "kinda," "maybe," and "you know?" Sentences meant to be statements often sound like questions, with the tone of the voice rising uncertainly at the end in a search for constant feedback.

This lack of confidence in a secure identity betrays itself tellingly in non-verbal ways as well. The Deception shows up in body posture as the shoulders roll inward and the head creeps forward. The Harmonizer nods with her chin tucked under in conciliatory agreement, avoiding conflict at all costs.[227] All of these verbal and non-verbal signs are clues that the individual, at a conscious or unconscious level, believes the specific Deception that "I am only okay if I am pleasing you."

## *The Achiever Deception—Be Perfect*[228]

THE DISTORTION:

The Achiever, seeing the world through the Perception of thoughts, has a unique, God-given ability to be logical, organized, and responsible. The analytical Achiever floor of our personalities finds the recognition of hard work and some control over

---

[226] Kahler, T. (1996, 2012). *The Process Communication Model® Seminar—Seminar One: Core Topics.* (pp. 61). Little Rock, AR: Kahler Communications, Inc.
[227] From Kahler, T. (1997). *The Advanced PCM Seminar.* Little Rock, AR: Kahler Communications, Inc.
[228] Kahler, T. (1996, 2012). *The Process Communication Model® Seminar—Seminar One: Core Topics.* (pp. 61). Little Rock, AR: Kahler Communications, Inc.

time schedule to be motivating. When someone operating out of the Achiever floor of his or her personality doubts the ability of God to care for all the details and restore order to chaos, he or she falls prey to a Deception which results in a harried grasping for a sense of self-precision:

THE DECEPTION: I'm only worthy/okay *if I am perfect*.[229]

THE BELIEF: When living into the Deception that you must **Be Perfect**, you not only desire accomplishment and excellence—you crave it like an addiction. You judge that anything short of perfection is unworthy and unacceptable. This may include your work, yourself, and your family and friends. While Being Perfect, you are misusing your God-given ability to organize, evaluate, and accomplish things as a means of self-justification. In the shadow of this Deception, you think that if you are perfect, you can control your life—avoiding losses and tightly managing emotions—and thus avoid hurt.

WARNING SIGNS/DRIVERS: According to *PCM®*, distressed Achievers believing the Deception that they must be perfect give themselves no room for mistakes and little to no permission to be incorrect, misunderstood, or unsure.[230] Those believing the specific Deception that "I must be perfect" begin to show Driver behaviors, *overdoing* in an attempt to prove competence and have control.

This false belief shows up in language that is overly descriptive and peppered with unneeded qualifications such as "to me" or "personally" (as well as numerous parenthetical notes). The Achiever will speak in measured, calculated, or slightly wooden tones, gesturing with abrupt and specific motions to ensure being understood perfectly. While operating out of this Deception, they may also appear stiff or unnatural with strained posture and facial expression, aware of the ever-looming possibility of imperfection.[231]

---

[229] Kahler, T. (1996, 2012). *The Process Communication Model® Seminar—Seminar One: Core Topics.* Little Rock, AR: Kahler Communications, Inc.
[230] Kahler, T. (1996, 2012). *The Process Communication Model® Seminar—Seminar One: Core Topics.* (pp. 61). Little Rock, AR: Kahler Communications, Inc.
[231] From Kahler, T. (1997). *The Advanced PCM Seminar.* Little Rock, AR: Kahler Communications, Inc.

## The Persister Deception—You Be Perfect[232]

THE DISTORTION:
The Persister, seeing the world through the Perception of opinions, brings unparalleled dedication, conscientiousness, and observation to each and every situation. Because of the depth of dedication, those with strong Persister floors have a Psychological Need to be recognized for their work as well as their convictions. When someone operating out of the Persister floor loses trust in God's commitment to justice, righteousness, and His promise of purposeful life, he or she takes on that job to protect or fix the world, clinging fearfully to the Deception that:

THE DECEPTION: I'm only okay/secure *if you are perfect*.[233]

THE BELIEF: While operating out of the Deception that **Others Must Be Perfect** in order for you to be okay, you run the risk of not only desiring and inspiring excellence in those around you, but actually demanding it as a condition for your love or, more precisely, your approval. You judge that anything short of perfection is unworthy and unacceptable. This may include people at your work, yourself, and your family and friends. Thus you might feel simultaneously responsible for the behaviors of others and yet unable to control their actions and choices, leading to underlying fear, discontentment, and a sense of constant disappointment both in yourself and those you want to be perfect.

When correcting or controlling others, your Persister floor is actually avoiding its own insecurity and fear of judgment by trying to assure that everyone else is acceptable, believing "If everyone else is acceptable, then maybe God will accept me as well." This is a twisting of your God-given ability to evaluate and discern what is right and wrong as a means of Self-justification. In this Deception, you are living by the Law, not by God's grace.

---

[232] Kahler, T. (1996, 2012). *The Process Communication Model® Seminar—Seminar One: Core Topics.* (pp. 61). Little Rock, AR: Kahler Communications, Inc.
[233] Kahler, T. (1996, 2012). *The Process Communication Model® Seminar—Seminar One: Core Topics.* Little Rock, AR: Kahler Communications, Inc.

**WARNING SIGNS/DRIVERS:** According to *PCM®*, Persisters in Distress begin to exhibit particular Driver behaviors, noticing and harping upon anything that is wrong or out of place with increasingly high expectations of others and innately keen observation.[234] Their posture and physical being communicates this internal judging, as they appear stiff, aloof, or rigid. When communicating, the Persister believing the Deception that others must be perfect tends to over-question, over-qualify, and over-speak with big words. They might be intimidating to converse with as they watch others with piercing eyes, a raised head, and clipped tones, making internal calculations and judgments.[235]

## *The Dreamer Deception—Be Strong*[236]

**THE DISTORTION:**

The Dreamer personality floor, seeing the world through the Perception of inactions (reflections), offers the strength of an unusually imaginative, calm, and reflective nature. In their internal world of abstraction and thought, those with a strong Dreamer personality floor need solitude. When someone operating out of the Dreamer floor of his or her personality loses touch with the reality of ultimate security and safety in God's care, he or she retreats from the world and burrows in the Deception that:

**THE DECEPTION:** I'm only okay/secure *if I am strong.*[237]

**THE BELIEF:** When believing the Deception that you are helpless and thus must constantly **Be Strong**, you might be tempted to twist your ability to accept the immaterial, abstract, and spiritual world into a self-protective impassivity, numbing yourself from the world around you so as not to feel unsafe or hurt. From this safe zone of apathy and distant

---

[234] Kahler, T. (1996, 2012). *The Process Communication Model® Seminar—Seminar One: Core Topics.* (pp. 61). Little Rock, AR: Kahler Communications, Inc.
[235] From Kahler, T. (1997). *The Advanced PCM Seminar.* Little Rock, AR: Kahler Communications, Inc.
[236] Kahler, T. (1996, 2012). *The Process Communication Model® Seminar—Seminar One: Core Topics.* (pp. 61). Little Rock, AR: Kahler Communications, Inc.
[237] Kahler, T. (1996, 2012). *The Process Communication Model® Seminar—Seminar One: Core Topics.* Little Rock, AR: Kahler Communications, Inc.

remove, you are likely to experience the events of the world as happening to you—further reinforcing your fears of perceived helplessness. You might play into this Deception by pulling away, being uninvolved, unaffected, or even unaware, sometimes to the point of failing to notice people, things or the raw data from your own senses.

If leaning into yourself to meet your need for protection, you can misuse your gift for reflection to pull completely into yourself and become perpetually internally absorbed. Others will find it difficult to engage you in intimate relationships, and you will be tempted to passively wait around for someone or something to "make things better."

WARNING SIGNS/DRIVERS: According to *PCM®*, Being Strong can look simply like being unaffected by external reality—whether people, events, or your own senses.[238] If Dreamers moving into distress appear weak or vulnerable by feeling or showing their feelings to others, their safety and security feels threatened. The deceived Dreamer's language demonstrates a growing passivity and unwillingness to see oneself as powerful, using phrases such as "it came to me," "it occurred to me," or "that **makes** me feel." Their physical body resembles a statue, frozen in posture and in facial expression—unaffected, unchanging, and unreadable.[239]

## *The Catalyzer Deception—You Be Strong*[240]

### THE DISTORTION:

Seeing the world through the Perception of actions, the Catalyzer floor is remarkably adaptable, persuasive, and charming. A lightning bolt of energy, the Catalyzer floor in our Personality Structure needs incidence or excitement and opportunities in order to feel energized and alive. When the Catalyzer doubts whether or not God will actually

---

[238] Kahler, T. (1996, 2012). *The Process Communication Model® Seminar—Seminar One: Core Topics.* (pp. 61). Little Rock, AR: Kahler Communications, Inc.
[239] From Kahler, T. (1997). *The Advanced PCM Seminar.* Little Rock, AR: Kahler Communications, Inc.
[240] Kahler, T. (1996, 2012). *The Process Communication Model® Seminar—Seminar One: Core Topics.* (pp. 61). Little Rock, AR: Kahler Communications, Inc.

stick around rather than leaving when the going gets tough, he or she becomes addicted to the adrenaline of a quick thrill, seeking out immediate and often reckless self-gratification fed by the Deception:

THE DECEPTION: I'm only okay *if others are strong*.[241]

THE BELIEF: When living in the Deception that **Others Must Be Strong**, you are vulnerable to a cynical perspective that everyone is secretly out for himself or herself. Thus you (and everyone else) must toughen up quickly and learn how to get by without depending on anyone else, because they will only abandon you when times get hard.

Since intimate relationships are impossible without trust and vulnerability, you turn your attention to making life exciting and enjoyable, even at the expense of others. In the midst of this Deception, seeking pleasure, stimulation, or excitement becomes twisted from the natural enjoyment of God-given sensations to a reckless craving for immediate gratification. Orienting life around the pursuit of temporary pleasures or excitement ultimately leads to emptiness rather than satisfaction. All the while, you are avoiding the fear of being abandoned by people upon whom you thought you could depend.

WARNING SIGNS: According to *PCM®*, distressed Catalyzers think they must look out for themselves and expect others to do the same.[242] Catalyzers cover up their tenuous life position with bravado. Their posture is often imposing and commanding, and their gestures are exaggerated and large.

When operating out of their Driver behavior, Catalyzers' facial expressions may be stone-like and difficult to read, conveying their expectation that others be strong and not depend upon them for support. The Catalyzer's language, when believing the Deception that others must be strong, invites others into a place of self-defense rather than vulnerability: "What made you think…?" and "How did he make you feel?". They often use the word "you" when they really mean "I".[243]

---

[241] Kahler, T. (1996, 2012). *The Process Communication Model® Seminar—Seminar One: Core Topics.* Little Rock, AR: Kahler Communications, Inc.
[242] Kahler, T. (1996, 2012). *The Process Communication Model® Seminar—Seminar One: Core Topics.* (pp. 61). Little Rock, AR: Kahler Communications, Inc.
[243] From Kahler, T. (1997). *The Advanced PCM Seminar.* Little Rock, AR: Kahler Communications, Inc.

## The Energizer Deception: Try Hard[244]

THE DISTORTION:
Energizers, seeing the world through the Perception of reactions, radiate creativity, spontaneity, and playfulness. With their childlike enthusiasm, those with strong Energizer floors desire contact—whether physical or verbal. When an individual operating out of his or her Energizer floor doubts that God's abounding forgiveness applies to him or her, he or she believes in a lie and therefore runs from responsibility and consequences:

THE DECEPTION: I'm only okay/accepted *if I try hard.*[245]

THE BELIEF: Believing the Deception that you must **Try Hard** to be acceptable is rooted in a deep fear that you are irredeemably guilty. Thus you might be driven to convince God, yourself, and others that you are blameless and thus not responsible, all the while experiencing the gnawing sense that you cannot keep up the act forever.

The Deception that you must try hard to be accepted is also the external sign of an internal struggle—indicating that while you might be taking reluctant responsibility on the outside, you are likely not taking responsibility for your inner attitude of half-hearted submission. The difference between genuine effort (even if unsuccessful) and "trying" (even if superficially successful) is a matter of the heart. When overshadowed by deceptive or false beliefs, the Energizer's greatest strengths can be twisted into symptoms of rebellion, irresponsibility, complaining, and superficial compliance.

WARNING SIGNS/DRIVERS: According to *PCM®*, an Energizer at the Doorway of Distress will avoid answering questions directly in order to withhold commitment.[246] Their posture communicates their belief that they must "try hard," leaning forward with head up and torso bent over in effort.

---

[244] Kahler, T. (1996, 2012). *The Process Communication Model® Seminar—Seminar One: Core Topics.* (pp. 61). Little Rock, AR: Kahler Communications, Inc.
[245] Kahler, T. (1996, 2012). *The Process Communication Model® Seminar—Seminar One: Core Topics.* Little Rock, AR: Kahler Communications, Inc.
[246] Kahler, T. (1996, 2012). *The Process Communication Model® Seminar—Seminar One: Core Topics.* (pp. 61). Little Rock, AR: Kahler Communications, Inc.

Phrases such as "I can't" and "I don't know" indicate an unwillingness to commit even verbally when something is asked of them.

The deceived Energizer exhibits Driver behaviors such as delegating inappropriately and making helpless gestures such as shrugging one's shoulders or throwing up the hands in confusion or defeat. Their expressive faces struggle with the effort of "trying," and the same internal pressure can be heard in their tone of voice.[247]

**Table 6:** Clues/"Drivers" Advertising Distress

| Personality Floor | Verbal Language | Body Language |
|---|---|---|
| **Harmonizer:** "I must **please you**." | Unassertive; lacks confidence; statements sound like questions | Shoulders and head rolled forward; head nods in agreement; submissive |
| **Achiever:** "I must **be perfect**." | Overly descriptive; "to me, …personally;" measured or robotic tones | Abrupt gestures with hands or fingers; stiff or strained posture |
| **Persister:** "**You** must **be perfect**." | Over-questioning; uses big words; intimidating | Piercing, calculating eyes; raised head; clipped tones; stiff or rigid posture |
| **Dreamer:** "I must **be strong**." | Passive phrases such as "It came to me" or "That made me feel…;" unaffected | Statue—frozen posture; neutral or unreadable facial expressions |
| **Catalyzer:** "**You** must **be strong**." | Accusatory; "What made you think…?;" inviting others into self-defense | Imposing or commanding posture; large gestures; face portrays absolute confidence |
| **Energizer:** "I must **try hard**." | Unwilling to commit; "I can't" or "I don't know;" struggling tones | Leaning forward with head up in effort; shrugging shoulders; helpless gestures |

From Kahler, T. (1996, 2012). *The Process Communication Model® Seminar—Seminar One: Core Topics.* Little Rock, AR: Kahler Communications, Inc.

## THE HEART OF THE MATTER

No matter which Deception an individual struggles with at the Doorway of Distress, it is important to remember that healing does not look like repression, avoidance, or a temporary behavioral fix. Healing requires a right relationship to reality—an understanding of ourselves in connection to

---

[247] From Kahler, T. (1997). *The Advanced PCM Seminar.* Little Rock, AR: Kahler Communications, Inc.

God's character, care, provision, and purpose. It is, like all things, a matter of Truth, a matter of the heart.

Any time we are operating out of one of these Deceptions about our worth, significance, and identity, we are not living in the truth of God's assessment of who we are. Here is the truth: Because of Jesus—His life, His sinless death, His resurrection—you are already loved. Already fully accepted.[248] Already safe and held and protected. Already invited into a life that is "far more than you could ever imagine or guess or request in your wildest dreams."[249] Already delighted in.[250] "A healthy response to the question, Who am I? is, 'I am a person *already* deeply pleasing to God."[251]

---

[248] Romans 8:1, New International Version.
[249] Ephesians 3:20, The Message.
[250] Zephaniah 3:17, New International Version.
[251] Thrall, B., McNicol, B., & Lynch, J.S. (2004). *TrueFaced* (pp. 63). Colorado Springs, CO: NavPress.

# 10 | Redeemed Designs

No matter how deep the distress, we as human beings simply cannot be stripped of our fundamental identities as individuals who were fearfully and wonderfully made by a good and loving Creator. Fearfully, wonderfully made individuals with a deep thirst for God. We were made to exist under the loving care of the Master, and yet at times we instead attempt to meet our own needs—seeking fulfillment apart from God and coming up empty. We are light-infused Image-Bearers who are tricked by subtle Deceptions, only to find ourselves trapped in darkness and longing for light.

Reflecting on our lives thus far with bold honesty and transparency, many of us can identify with the familiar taunts of our particular Deceptions. We too have daily trudged to shallow wells of self-sufficiency, feeling the heat of the day and the hopelessness of ever being fully satisfied. When you have never experienced a different reality, it is hard to even consider the possibility for change in and restoration of the darkest places in your story. At our core, we understand that we were created for more and feel the weight of settling for less.

Perpetual mild or moderate distress on a day to day basis drains your life of the fullness that God intended, and severe distress has the potential to impair your ability to function in daily life. Most of all, distress indicates you are living in the shadows of a deception rather than in the light of the truth that God has freed you to experience. Yet distress is never hopeless. Just as God is faithful to uncover our false beliefs, He is faithful to heal the havoc and hurt in our lives. He does far more than patch over our mess-ups or pain; He takes what sin (ours and others) has done and infuses it with deeper purpose, richness, and hope. He makes all things new.

From wherever you are, hear this: There is hope, for we serve a God of newness, of impossibilities, of breaking the most entrenched paths of destruction, of creating something good from nothing. The same God who said: "Forget the former things; do not dwell on the past. See, I am doing a new thing! Now it springs up; do you not perceive it? I am making a way in the wilderness and streams in the wasteland."[252]

What would it look like for God to touch the wastelands of your life? To pour water into the thirsty cracks of your heart? To point out a new pathway in the wilderness of despair, distress, and broken relationships? To lead you out of entrenched ruts of belief and behavior, no matter how deep or crooked or habitual? To literally transform the way you see everything, the way you have *always* seen it?

## MAINTENANCE AND RENOVATION

True transformation in your life always begins with a renovation of belief at the level of the heart. As Christian author Gary Smalley says, "the seeds that grow in your heart...will depend upon which ones you water and nurture the most."[253] It takes significant grace and effort both to discern underlying Deceptions and replace those falsehoods with beliefs rooted in and fed on truth. In this chapter, you will find suggestions for Maintenance (daily choices that you can make in light of your design) and also for Renovation (acknowledging that God's grace is transforming your life at the level of your heart). As Dallas Willard suggested, grace is never a matter of earning, but it does require effort.[254] God does not give us a five-step formula for a full life; neither does He shrug His shoulders and leave us clueless as to how to proceed.

---

[252] Isaiah 43:18-19, New International Version.
[253] Smalley, Gary. (2012). *Change Your Heart, Change Your Life* (pp. 130). Nashville, TN: Thomas Nelson, Inc.
[254] Willard, Dallas. (2002). *Renovation of the Heart* (pp. 25). Colorado Springs, CO: NavPress.

THERE IS A DELICATE DANCE HERE BETWEEN EFFORT AND
ACCEPTANCE, BETWEEN DOING AND BEING.

Nurture the truth about who God is and who He says you are. It is a gift of God that we have *needs*, because they remind us of our humanity and humble us to receive love. While our ultimate choice is whether or not to trust God with our needs, we can also make informed life decisions that honor our unique designs as individuals with different Character Strengths, Perceptions, Psychological Needs, etc.

By taking daily responsibility for meeting some of your needs as you can—receiving Psychological Needs in healthy ways and in full dependence on God—you are helping to maintain an internal equilibrium and stay in a place of health and freedom rather than slipping into Distress.[255] It's a form of soul "maintenance," a regular checking in and making contact with the heart and its core beliefs. The following suggestions for **maintenance**[256]—adapted from Dr. Kahler's Action Plans for each personality floor— contain everything from ways to decorate your office/work environment to taking relational risks.[257] Start small and accept God's empowerment, support, and grace; never lose sight that it is He who renovates and transforms your heart.

As you soak your Spirit with the Living Water, as you depend on grace to transform your heart, truth takes root in your heart and overflows into your actions. As you integrate the truth of who you were created to be, you can live into your unique design and serve out of gratitude and freedom. You can overflow with living water, becoming a stream in the desert.

## HARMONIZER: ALREADY LOVED

*The Truth to Counter Your Deception:*

Although we as Image-Bearers are often the vessels

---

[255] Kahler, T. (1996, 2012). *The Process Communication Model® Seminar—Seminar One: Core Topics.* (pp. 58). Little Rock, AR: Kahler Communications, Inc.

[256] Many of these suggestions are taken from Dr. Kahler's Action Plan. The term "maintenance" was coined as part of the *Process Spiritual Model*™ from Maris, R. (1996). *Your Great Design.* Little Rock, AR: Transpersonal Technologies, L.L.C..

[257] Dr. Kahler originally introduced the idea of an "Action Plan" to help individuals meet their Phase and/or Base Psychological Needs on a regular basis. The following suggestions for Maintenance are adapted with permission. From Kahler, T. (1996, 2012). *The Process Communication Model® Seminar— Seminar One: Core Topics.* Little Rock, AR: Kahler Communications, Inc.; Kahler, T. (1997). *The Advanced PCM Seminar.* Little Rock, AR: Kahler Communications, Inc.

through which God shows His love and compassion,[258] He never intended that your sense of worth as a person or of value in His eyes should depend on feedback exclusively from fellow humans. His love and your value are not based on any condition or thing that you may or may not do. The reality is that God's love for you is complete, perfect, and soul-sustaining. You were given an understanding heart and desire for relationship in order to love and serve God and others. Only He is capable of the unconditional love for which you long and which you cannot lose. And when you are living in the light of this Love, you are fulfilled in a way that invites you to spill over into the lives of others with divinely empowered compassion.

## Maintenance

If you have a strong Harmonizer floor, here are a few practical suggestions[259] for ways to take initiative in honoring and *living into* your design.

*In your daily relationships* [260]

Ask your family and friends to say "I love you" or "I like you" often.
Make weekly lunch dates with a close friend who enjoys your company and share life together.
Ask those close to you to show their love of you through appropriate physical affection—giving and receiving hugs, holding another's arm, etc.
Be "risky" in initiating deep and intimate sharing amongst friends, support groups, family, romantic partners, etc.

*In your home and work environments* [261]

Put notes/reminders around your house that say: "I am a special and precious child of God" or "God is especially fond of me."
Take time to make your home and office personal and comfortable—keep fresh flowers, pictures of loved ones, scented candles, soft blankets, favorite music on hand.

---

[258] Ephesians 4:32.
[259] By no means are these suggestions part of a conclusive or static list; rather, they are just a few hints to help you start thinking of ways to honor your God-given design.
[260] From Kahler, T. (1997). *The Advanced PCM Seminar*. Little Rock, AR: Kahler Communications, Inc.; adapted by permission.
[261] From Kahler, T. (1997). *The Advanced PCM Seminar*. Little Rock, AR: Kahler Communications, Inc.; adapted by permission.

Nurture your capacity for sensory and aesthetic enjoyment and share this appreciation with others—wear soft and comfortable clothes, take a good friend with you to enjoy beautiful works of art, spend time in the beauty of nature with someone you care about, get or give a massage.

*In your service*

Use your gifts of mercy and service to build others up through hospitality, thoughtful attention to others' practical and emotional needs, verbal affirmation, and encouragement.
Volunteer to cuddle babies in the church nursery.
Volunteer at an animal shelter.
Serve as a greeter or on a hospitality committee.
Make eye contact with strangers and smile! Your warmth goes a long way in the world.

## Renovation

As you co-labor with Christ to maintain and reinforce life choices that accurately reflect truth, God is uncovering and uprooting false perceptions of reality and ineffective or destructive ways of looking at the world. At the level of your heart, God is graciously making **renovations**[262] so that you might receive and reflect His love without condition. In order to nurture this kind of soul gardening, you can make grace-propelled choices to intentionally replace old false beliefs with the light of the Truth:

Pray for God's Spirit to reveal His unconditional love.
Confess and repent to God how you have spent your effort on pleasing men rather than trusting Him. Share this with a friend!
Practice the spiritual discipline of solitude and learn to be "alone" with God.
Study the Scriptures for an accurate perception of "love" as what is ultimately best for another. See how Jesus interacted with others through this lens.
Daily, hourly, moment by moment—meditate on Scriptures about the sufficient, unconditional, everlasting, longsuffering love of God.

---

[262] From Maris, R. (1996). *Your Great Design*. Little Rock, AR: Transpersonal Technologies, L.L.C..

As you are released from striving after the approval of others and demanding that they love you in the way that *you* want, you can feel content with the knowledge that their love, as well as yours, is imperfect but nonetheless precious. With tender care, God can reveal to you that your real self-worth lies in His truly unconditional love for you and His personal affection for you as His unique and precious child. You may fulfill the design and desire of your own heart as you fill it with God's love and share it with the world. After all, "we love because He first loved us."[263]

## ACHIEVER—ALREADY GOOD ENOUGH

### *The Truth to Counter Your Deception:*

Although God directs you to do your work diligently, He never intended that you expect perfection from yourself and base your value and assumed acceptability to Him on your own flawless performance. Neither His love nor His acceptance of you is based on anything that you do or don't do, no matter how well or how poorly. Your security and your significance are not in your hands. You were given these abilities to serve God by doing the work in His kingdom, not to assure your acceptability to yourself and to Him. The freeing truth is that He has already paid the price for your imperfection.

### *Maintenance*

If you have a strong Achiever floor in your personality, here are a few practical suggestions for ways to take initiative in honoring and *living into* your design.

*In your daily relationships* [264]

Ask your family and friends for verbal praise and acknowledgement of your accomplishments (and let yourself receive it).
Share your ideas with those close to you and give yourself permission to enjoy their positive feedback.
Schedule time weekly to meet with a friend or colleague

---

[263] 1 John 4:19, New International Version.
[264] From Kahler, T. (1997). *The Advanced PCM Seminar.* Little Rock, AR: Kahler Communications, Inc.; adapted by permission.

to talk about new insights, information, and discoveries from what you are studying, reading, or learning.

*In the way in which you approach work* [265]

Take time each day to recognize and appreciate what you have already accomplished before setting goals for the next day.
Practice saying, "That is good enough."
Make lists and cross off items as you complete them. In fact, add unexpected accomplishments onto the list and cross them off too!
Set short, medium, and long range goals; track your progress regularly.
Put exercise, recreation, and family time on your "to do" list as legitimate elements of your life and schedule.
Take a Sabbath day on which you do no work and *still* experience God's pleasure.
Take up a hobby with tangible results and visible progress, like painting, writing, planting a flower garden, or doing a carpentry project.

*In your service*

Volunteer to teach a class or workshop on some kind of research or information that interests you.
Serve on a church "steering" or planning committee where your gifts will be useful and appreciated.
Donate your valuable time and gifts to help someone else sort out their finances or make a budget.

## Renovation

At the level of your heart, God is graciously making renovations so that you might rest in His care and trust His sovereign control. In order to nurture this kind of soul gardening, you can make grace-propelled choices to replace old false beliefs with the light of the Truth:

Ask for the Spirit's help in remembering/believing that God is in sovereign and perfect control.
Meditate on the truth that it is safe to trust God's promise to perfect you in His timing and to trust His love of you

---

[265] From Kahler, T. (1997). *The Advanced PCM Seminar*. Little Rock, AR: Kahler Communications, Inc.; adapted by permission.

*right now.*
Confess and repent to God for arrogance regarding your accomplishments or misplaced trust in your own abilities. Share this with a friend or colleague.
Pray for God's discernment in seeking balance and not perfection. Search out the Scripture's view of perfection and grace.
Learn the discipline of rest. Structure your life so that you make rest a priority, and practice gratitude for God's gift of refreshment.

Moving from a need to be perfect to an appreciation for grace, rest, and enjoyment frees you from the destructive cycle of perpetually proving your worth through never-ending, never fully satisfying, task completion. You can enjoy what you achieve and freely proclaim that it is God's grace that enables you, not your own perfection. When you are not overly responsible and asking for control, you can accept that Jesus Christ's perfection enables you to live into your design and serve from gratitude rather than desperation. You will be able to offer your gifted intellect and keen mind to the praise and glory of God rather than your own importance. And you can also rest that intellect and humbly receive God's care and comfort.

## Persister—Already Valued

*The Truth to Counter Your Deception:*

Though God directs you to seek excellence in your life and maintain high standards and values, He never intended that you judge and expect perfection from others. Neither your security nor your significance depends on your leading others to perfection. You do not have to carry the heavy burden of judgment, discerning who or what is or is not acceptable. Fortunately, your security rests in God's grace and love. Your security is not dependent on anything that you, your neighbors, family, or co-workers do or don't do, no matter how well or how poorly. Trust this.

*Maintenance*

If you have a strong Persister floor in your personality,

here are a few practical suggestions for ways to take initiative in honoring and *living into* your design.

*In your relationships* [266]

Ask family and friends to express their admiration or respect for you on a regular basis.

Share with a respected friend the importance of your beliefs.

Meet regularly with a group of individuals to encourage and be encouraged by one another in living lives of purity, purpose, and integrity.

*In your work and at home* [267]

Show your work to others whom you respect and enjoy their feedback on the quality of your labors.

Reaffirm daily the value of your accomplishments even before you review your "to-do" lists for that day.

Create a display of your favorite verses, slogans, mottoes, and creeds to be prominently displayed at work or at home.

*In your service*

Find a cause about which you are passionate and find ways to stand up as an advocate—through writing, speaking, giving, etc.

Mentor a younger man or woman in your faith.

Volunteer to tutor underprivileged youth or an underserved group within your community.

Teach a class or workshop on something you find valuable—spiritual disciplines, advocacy, social justice, doctrine, Biblical interpretation, etc.

Take time and care to prioritize what you believe will be the best investment of your time to ensure wise expenditure of your efforts.

Review "your" personal mission statement to make sure that you are consistently and intentionally moving in that direction.

Keep a journal of insights that you believe are important—your own and those of people you respect.

---

[266] From Kahler, T. (1997). *The Advanced PCM Seminar*. Little Rock, AR: Kahler Communications, Inc.; adapted by permission.
[267] From Kahler, T. (1997). *The Advanced PCM Seminar*. Little Rock, AR: Kahler Communications, Inc.; adapted by permission.

## *Renovation*

At the level of your heart, God is graciously making renovations so that you might replace fear of judgment with a humble acceptance of grace. In order to nurture this kind of soul gardening, you can make grace-propelled choices to replace old false beliefs with the light of the Truth:

> Pray for God's help in giving you the ability to gratefully accept grace.
> Confess to God and to trusted friends the ways in which you may have been trying to justify yourself by works rather than trusting in God's provision.
> Study individuals in God's word who were used mightily in the Kingdom despite their imperfections.
> Study (and rejoice in) God's faithfulness and dependability to fulfill His every promise.
> Examine your beliefs about the heart of the Gospel.

The Truth is that no degree of adherence or enforcement will make you or your loved ones more secure in God's eyes. It is through His grace, not your vigilance or righteousness, that you and those for whom you take responsibility are eternally secure. Paul said, "I do not set aside the grace of God; for if righteousness comes through the law, then Christ died in vain."[268] But by His abundant and overflowing grace, you and those you love are truly safe in Him. You can gratefully and fully hold on to this grace as the means through which God is continually and lovingly refining His image in us. We are invited into a Kingdom of incredible purpose *right now*; we do not have to wait for perfection to be included in God's glorious design. Setting your fears aside and thus letting the "perfecting" be done to, for, and through, but not *by* you, you may literally "rest assured" in the One in whom you can fully put your trust.

## DREAMER—ALREADY SAFE

### *The Truth to Counter Your Deception:*

Although all of Scripture confirms a spiritual reality that transcends this material world, God does not direct you to

---

[268] Galatians 2:21, New International Version.

ignore, avoid, or be disconnected from the world in which you currently live. It takes immense faith to trust in God's protection and provision for you. It requires a willingness to live in and experience the world as God has made it, and it asks us to be willing to participate in all aspects of the fullness of life—from deep joy to intense suffering. A truly spiritual experience of life **adds** a welcome dimension of experience and an ever-deepening awareness; it takes nothing away.

## Maintenance

If you have a strong Dreamer floor in your personality, here are a few practical suggestions for ways to take initiative in honoring and *living into* your design.

*In your relationships* [269]

Give yourself a few moments at the beginning and end of each day to be alone; practice the discipline of solitude in prayer, meditation, and silence.

Ask a friend or someone close to you to occasionally be near you as you do what you enjoy, without requiring conversation or engagement.

Take morning or evening walks, alone or with a friend who is comfortable with being quiet.

Go to the movies, opera, theater, etc., alone.

Simply tell a friend that you are shy or unlikely to initiate; ask that friend to help you by occasionally calling you, inviting you out, or otherwise inviting you to join in.

*At home or at work* [270]

Schedule regular alone time for creative planning and dreaming.

Set aside time to read and reflect.

Work at home or elsewhere "out of the flow of traffic" on those occasions when you need uninterrupted work time.

Start (or continue giving time to) a solitary hobby—stamp collecting, bird watching, needlework, sewing, fishing, painting, writing poetry or stargazing.

Take time to lie down comfortably on the floor, put on

---

[269] From Kahler, T. (1997). *The Advanced PCM Seminar*. Little Rock, AR: Kahler Communications, Inc.; adapted by permission.
[270] From Kahler, T. (1997). *The Advanced PCM Seminar*. Little Rock, AR: Kahler Communications, Inc.; adapted by permission.

your favorite music, and just enjoy being alone.

*In your service*

Work with your hands in a quiet or restful way—in a garden, laying brick, knitting, kneading dough, making model airplanes, fixing up old bicycles, etc.
Ask for explicit directions.
Volunteer for tasks that lend themselves to solitude or that others might find monotonous.

## Renovation

At the level of your heart, God is graciously making renovations so that you might trust God to keep you secure as you experience all of life. In order to nurture this kind of soul gardening, you can make grace-propelled choices to replace old false beliefs with the light of the Truth:

Picture Jesus as your advocate, helper, and friend.
Pray earnestly for God's Spirit to reveal ways in which you have distorted reality to make it feel more secure for you.
Mediate on Scriptures that affirm that you have received the power of the Holy Spirit and that it is available to you right now.
Confess to God and a trusted friend the ways that you have relied on yourself and let your fears isolate you from others.
Study the mysteries of Christ's life as well as the nitty-gritty, day-in, day-out details of living with others.
Intentionally involve yourself in a community, asking for God's wisdom in balancing solitude and the pursuit of meaningful relationships.

As you move from habits of self-protective avoidance or withdrawal toward a deeper trust in God, you will gain confidence and initiative. Your questions about your ability to be empowered or take initiative will be replaced by a genuine and trustworthy assurance and confidence in Him. While retaining your gifts of imagination and your unique perspective, you may move from living in your own world into dwelling in His kingdom, using your special gifts to accomplish His transcendent purpose.

## CATALYZERS—ALREADY BELONGING

*The Truth to Counter Your Deception:*

God never intended that you would seek the gifts of excitement and stimulation at the expense of others or even at the expense of fulfilling His long-range plans for your life. When placed in proper perspective and submitted to God's care, these can be gifts to be enjoyed, intended to enrich and motivate your life. True meaning, excitement, and fulfillment, however, overflow solely in the act of offering your strengths to love God and love others. Shifting your focus from serving self to lovingly serving God and others will lead to incredible freedom in your relationships. A transformed perspective of serving others releases you from the deception that others will inevitably abandon you when you need them most and instead allows you to enjoy and contribute to loving communities where each member gives up his or her life for one another. In the light of God's sacrifice for you, there is no fear of abandonment. You belong to God, bought with an incredible and risky love that cost Him everything. You can now risk intimacy with God and with others.

*Maintenance*

If you have a strong Catalyzer floor, here are a few practical suggestions for ways to take initiative in honoring and *living into* your design.

*In your relationships* [271]

Invite friends and those you love to do something exciting with you—go camping, play sports together, sky dive, travel to new places.
Intentionally bring new people into different ways of seeing and doing things.
Allow yourself to lean into or receive help from a trusted friend.

*In your work, home, or recreation* [272]

Join a class or group that allows you to be physically

---

[271] From Kahler, T. (1997). The Advanced PCM Seminar. Little Rock, AR: Kahler Communications, Inc.; adapted by permission.
[272] From Kahler, T. (1997). *The Advanced PCM Seminar.* Little Rock, AR: Kahler Communications, Inc.; adapted by permission.

active and/or competitive such as intramural sports, martial arts, etc.

Get your pilot's license. Or climb Mt. Everest.

Read (or even write) adventure novels, travel diaries, stories of risky faith.

Change your focus to your current life context, looking for new opportunities to develop in your areas of work, ministry or home duties.

Train for something that provides you with a challenge, like a triathlon.

Travel and make your own way as you go!

*In your service*

Initiate the start of a new, exciting ministry or project, or jump into one that is already going, offering your fresh ideas and connections.

Use your ability to network with others to bring about something only God could accomplish that requires great risk, vision, and faith.

Organize a fundraiser for a worthy cause.

Freely offer your resources to others who cannot pay you back.

## *Renovation*

At the level of your heart, God is graciously making renovations so that you might trust His steadfastness and risk intimacy. In order to nurture this kind of soul gardening, you can make grace-propelled choices to replace old false beliefs with the light of the Truth:

Ask God to give you opportunities to serve others rather than yourself.

Confess to God and a trusted friend the ways in which you have relied on your own sense of sufficiency and adaptability to get what you want rather than relying on God.

Make sacrifices for which you will not necessarily be acknowledged; give anonymously.

Meditate on God's words about belonging to His family, and ask Him to replace your fear of being abandoned with a grateful awareness of belonging.

Practice spiritual disciplines that do not provide

immediate gratification and experience, over time, the reward of knowing God more.

As you move from your expectation that all must watch out for themselves to a realization of self-sacrifice and service, you may feel genuinely significant, secure, and excited about using your special gifts to serve God and your fellow man. Genuine repentance redirects your life focus to the real freedom flowing from a life of love, rather than in the façade of freedom found in ignoring rules altogether. With God's comforting hand on your shoulder, the pain of early abandonment may come to Light. Healing will take place as healthy grief replaces blame, and hope fills the void that cynicism has left. Assured by a loving God that He will not desert you, no matter what, you may open your own heart to genuinely caring for and leaning on others as indispensable and uniquely precious brothers and sisters.

## ENERGIZER—ALREADY FORGIVEN

### *The Truth to Counter Your Deception:*

God never intended for you to make atonement for your sin with blamelessness; He provided full forgiveness in the death of His Son, Jesus. Replacing deception with the truth that you are guilty can open the floodgates of reconciliation and redemption. You may "try hard," but in fact, you fail. We all do. We are all guilty; yet God's forgiveness is infinitely stronger, more resilient, and longer lasting than our sin. Through accepting responsibility and genuine guilt, you are released to openly receive God's full forgiveness and grace. Stubborn avoidance is transformed into an exuberant embrace of unimaginable renewal and joy that is gloriously contagious.

### *Maintenance*

If you have a strong Energizer floor in your personality, here are a few practical suggestions for ways to take initiative in honoring and *living into* your design.

### In your relationships [273]

Invite those you love to join you in activities that you think are fun. Take a ballroom dancing class with your spouse. Learn to juggle with your roommates.

Initiate parties, get togethers, etc.; throw a theme party!

Use your breaks, lunch hours, and "dead" times to visit with friends.

Strike up conversations with strangers.

### In your play and your work [274]

Do something fun **before** settling down to work.

Keep a music player with you wherever you go; enjoy dancing or lip-syncing to the music.

Decorate your office, house, or get-away place with lights, colors, gadgets, posters, knick-knacks that are distinctly "you."

Join or start a church league sports team or an aerobics or exercise group. Physical activity + relationship + external stimulation = feeling good!

Attend professional conferences or retreats; take a friend or make one there.

Doodle when things get boring…

Change your internal language from "making" yourself do something to "allowing" yourself.

Play around with a new form of artistic expression: pottery, drawing, painting, dancing, slam-poetry.

### In your service

Be a greeter at church. Seek out new members and invite them into a friend group.

Use your childlike spirit to connect with, enjoy, and play with children! Chaperone the youth ski trip. Play basketball downtown. Run around in the fountain with toddlers.

Find creative ways to invite others into experiencing God by reconnecting with a childlike faith and enjoying the fullness of life—put on plays, physically express yourself, introduce humor and hope in dark situations.

---

[273] From Kahler, T. (1997). *The Advanced PCM Seminar*. Little Rock, AR: Kahler Communications, Inc.; adapted by permission.

[274] From Kahler, T. (1997). *The Advanced PCM Seminar*. Little Rock, AR: Kahler Communications, Inc.; adapted by permission.

*Renovation*

At the level of your heart, God is graciously making renovations so that you might trust that you are fully forgiven and accepted. In order to nurture this kind of soul gardening, you can make grace-propelled choices to replace old false beliefs with the light of the Truth:

> Pray for God's Spirit to reveal ways in which you have been avoiding responsibility and misplacing blame when you are truly at fault.
> Confess to God that you have not trusted in His full forgiveness and chosen blamelessness or self-punishment for all of your mistakes.
> Apologize to those you have wrongly blamed, and allow yourself to experience both fault and forgiveness; find humble joy in reconciliation.
> Enjoy and express delight in your uniqueness!
> Offer forgiveness to others when they have wronged you.

When submitted to God's service, the Energizer's incredible childlike enthusiasm, creativity, and sense of fun can encourage, energize, and enliven friends and strangers alike. Living in the light of truth, you can move from trying to justify yourself on the basis of being blameless (not responsible and not guilty) to accepting both fault and forgiveness. Accepting God's payment, justification, and forgiveness for anything you have done or ever will do, you may finally lay down your burden of past guilt and your fear of future failures. You are free to accept both responsibility and forgiveness, trusting God to remove your sins as far as the east is from the west. His grace washes you, clothes you in new garments, and makes you acceptable.[275] In fact, you are more than acceptable; you are delighted in, enjoyed, and even liked by God!

## LIVING WATER

In the wasteland of our empty, aching places, God promises to bring streams of living water. During his earthly ministry, Jesus shouted to a crowd of thirsty, broken people: "Let anyone who is thirsty come to me and drink. Whoever

---

[275] Isaiah 1:18.

believes in me, as the Scripture has said, rivers of living water will flow from within them."[276] We all experience thirst—physical and spiritual. How we seek to quench that thirst can invite us into gratitude or into distress. God takes care of our thirst at a depth of satisfaction that makes our self-serving attempts to be our own gods look like drinking from a mud puddle when a waterfall is nearby. He takes our brokenness, bitterness, and hurt and lovingly redeems and restores us. Yet He does even more than give us Living Water for our desperately thirsty souls. He invites His children into a story more glorious, more global, and more generous than we could fathom.

---

[276] John 7:37-38, New International Version.

## 11 | *Many Members, One Body*

*"Instead, speaking the truth in love, we will in all things grow up into Him who is the Head, that is, Christ. From him the whole body, joined and held together by every supporting ligament, grows and builds itself up in love, as each part does its work."*[277]

*"He had been beckoned by an unknown Beauty that called to him in the night, urging him not to find himself in the lesser, but to lose himself in the greater."* -Safely Home, Randy Alcorn [278]

Within the sure and certain promises of God's Word, we discover our places in a larger story, graciously encompassing our individual narratives but also integrating these disparate threads into a grand tale of abundant redemption. As a masterful Author, God is constantly in the process of gathering up the loose ends, the unraveling story lines, and the seemingly unrelated characters and weaving all of the elements into a continuously unfolding tapestry of restoration. We have spent the last ten chapters exploring the marvelous individual designs, Character Strengths, Perceptions, and Psychological Needs God has given to each one of us. And we explored what can happen when we try to meet our own needs with these gifts rather than trusting our good and loving Master to give us "every spiritual blessing."[279] We are meant to live out these designs in connected community!

---

[277] Ephesians 4:15-16, New International Version.
[278] Alcorn, Randy. (2001). *Safely Home* (pp. 137). Carol Stream, Illinois: Tyndale House Publishers.
[279] Ephesians 1:3, New International Version.

## A Community of Believers

As participants in a grand redemption and bearers of a brilliant design, we are *more than* a grouping of individuals with different strengths. There is an old saying from Gestalt theorists: "The whole is greater than the sum of its parts." Christ's Church—the community of His followers and friends throughout the ages—is not merely a conglomeration of random individuals but something wholly *other*. There is a divine mathematics that occurs when diverse individuals are joined together and connected to the Source of Life itself, Jesus Christ.

Jesus uses a brilliant metaphor to describe His followers and the delicate dance of their inter-dependence and uniqueness. He calls this hodgepodge collective of individuals the **Body** of Christ. The more we learn about the intricate, detailed operation of the human body, the more we are utterly awed at its complexity and design. Every human body (regardless of race, personality, intelligence, etc.) is made up of the same material. Yet within the human body itself, there are many diverse parts with different functions. The elbow cannot and will not exhibit the same function as the nose (Imagine smelling someone's recently shampooed hair with your elbow. Or trying to break the fall off of your bike with your nose. Some of us have perhaps tried this latter approach with little success and intense pain!). Each part of our physical structure is uniquely designed with specific characteristics intended for particular uses, and it is the unified functioning of all these different parts together that makes the human body capable of incredible and vibrant life.

## "For the Common Good…"

In his letter to the church at Corinth, Paul says, "A spiritual gift is given to each of us so we can help each other."[280] Peter expands this thought in his first letter: "Each of you should use whatever gift you have received to serve others, as faithful stewards of God's grace in its various forms."[281] God's word says each individual is given a "specific gift" or a unique

---

[280] 1 Corinthians 12:7, New Living Translation.
[281] 1 Peter 4:10, New Living Translation.

manifestation of the Spirit, and that our calling is to graciously use these gifts in service to God, to the world, and to one another. The particularities of this calling might be unique, but the call to use these gifts in grace and truth is common to all.

If we as members of Christ's Church function like a Body, doesn't it make sense that certain members will be more naturally equipped for specific tasks? That each person has been entrusted to employ his or her special gift in serving one another, as Peter says above? Should the knee feel guilty or inadequate for not allowing the human body to see? It seems the body would benefit infinitely more if the knee engaged in bending the leg and rejoiced in making locomotion possible. And so it is with the Strengths of our personalities!

How glorious is the Harmonizer who loves with the tenderest compassion! How inspiring and alive the Catalyzers who take incredible risks! How precious to the Body of Christ is the Achiever who uses his or her mind to build up brothers and sisters in what is true. How valuable the Persister who upholds a righteous cause! How mystical and marvelous the Dreamer who quietly embodies peace and acceptance! How inspiring the Energizers who soak up life in each moment and invite others in the Body to do the same!

Paul mentions the idea of diverse gifts in the Body of Christ in multiple letters to his friends at various churches in Ephesus, Corinth, and Rome. To the church at Rome, Paul said:

> "Just as each of us has one body with many members, and these members do not all have the same function, so in Christ we who are many form one body, and each member belongs to all the others. We have different gifts according to the grace given us. If a man's gift is prophesying, let him use it in proportion to his faith. If it is serving, let him serve; if it is teaching, let him teach; if it is encouraging, let him encourage; if it is contributing to the needs of others, let him give generously; if it is leadership, let him govern diligently; if it is showing mercy, let him do it cheerfully."[282]

---

[282] Romans 12:4-8, New International Version.

Do you notice a trend in the last three of the list above? As Paul continues expounding upon these gifts of grace given to each of us, he seems caught up in increasing enthusiasm about utilizing these gifts! Give generously, extravagantly, abundantly! Lead with diligence—with steadfastness of character, with intention, with perseverance. Show mercy cheerfully...with the joyous gratitude of one who is fulfilling his or her purpose to the utmost. The works God has prepared for us are *good*! The work is fulfilling and nourishing, because it is born out of obedience and seasoned with the intimacy of knowing God and being known. What an incredible gift God has given us, to invite us into His good and purposeful work that we might know and love Him increasingly well!

## I'd Rather Be An Eyeball...

Somewhere along the way, these uniquely gifted members of the Body can fall into the trap of attributing greater importance to the more visible, glamorous, or "godly" types of contributions. We fashion man-made hierarchies, valuing certain roles over others. It's a toxic lie that paralyzes and devalues parts of the Body that equally desire to serve one another through the Spirit in a unique way. And it is a deception that threatens those possessing these much coveted or "more valuable" gifts with overwork, unrealistic expectations, and either feelings of utter inadequacy or pride.

These ideals might be personally formed based on our own expectations or experiences, while others can be perpetuated within the culture of the church. Perhaps the roles of some are simply more visible, and thus their contributions (as well as their failures) draw greater attention. Most church attendees could name their teaching pastor (except for those with a good deal of energy in the Dreamer floor, who might not have paid attention to that kind of detail). Members of the congregation can generally comment on whether or not Sunday's sermon was beneficial and echoed powerfully throughout their week or whether their husbands or wives interrupted their mid-sermon naps with an elbow to the ribs.

But few people are aware of the diligent work of the man

who manages the funds for all of the international and local mission work of the church. Or perhaps no one notices one woman's compassionate heart and unfailing commitment to the children in the church with special needs. Certainly few people are conscious of one widow's selfless financial contributions in the midst of crisis as well as her near constant prayers of intercession on behalf of her brothers and sisters.

Think about the ways we live in our physical bodies on a day-to-day basis. We might give great attention to the function of our eyes—their role in unveiling the world before us, casting shadows and revealing light, defining shapes. The eyes are the visible lens through which we experience our environment in all its radiance; they give color to life.

But rarely do we stop and think: "You know what I really appreciate? My sacrum. Thank goodness for that part of my body—what a gift!" Yet this fusion of vertebrae at the base of your spine plays an essential role in integrating the top half of your body with the lower half. Without the sacrum and its articulation with the pelvis, you could not stand upright because of the sacrum's essential role in weight distribution. Locomotion would be equally impossible.

And so it is with the Body of Christ. When we fail to function with an awareness of the importance of each member of the Body of Christ (including yourself!), we fall into two potential traps: mask-wearing and exhaustion.

## *Mask-Wearing vs. Acceptance*

When we get caught up in playing the role of "who we would like to be" rather than being fully who we were created to be, the Body becomes crippled. We feel the need to wear masks around one another in order to hide our true selves. In the *Process Communication Model*®, Dr. Kahler uses the term "masks" to refer to the distressed behavior of an individual.[283] Once these telltale masks are donned, authenticity is sacrificed on the altar of saving face. Conversations cannot delve into the deeper levels of the soul for fear of being "found out" for who we are underneath the masks.

How far this mask-wearing, role-playing approach to belonging to Christ strays from His true desire for us—to live

---

[283] From Kahler, T. (1982, 1996). *Process Communication Management Seminar.* Little Rock, AR: Taibi Kahler Associates, Inc.

into our unique designs and serve joyfully out of who He has created us to be! For if we try to be someone else, who will be us? Living out of this truth-filled identity requires a brave claiming that each member (including me!) truly is important, valued, and uniquely contributing to the greater whole of His Body, the Church.

## Exhaustion vs. Efficiency

In the accomplishment of physical tasks, bodily efficiency is crucial. World class athletes, professional ballet dancers, skilled craftsmen who use their hands like fine-tuned machines all understand the importance of utilizing the correct muscles (and only those muscles) to complete an action. Demanding each muscle of the body to work for the same length of time and in the exact same way diminishes and sabotages the physical body's natural way of functioning. Conversely, discovering which muscles are necessary for a task and firing those specific muscles into action enables the body to accomplish incredible feats of strength, grace, and athleticism.

In terms of "efficiency," we might think of the Body of Christ as functioning similarly to a well-trained athlete, ballet dancer, or Olympian. If each member of the Body responds to every need or call for every task, we will live—collectively as well as individually—at the perpetual edge of exhaustion. And ultimately we will be inefficient—a collection of worn-out fingers, ears, and toes rather than an integrated, growing, interdependent being relying on one another.

Yet how many of us go throughout life suffocated by the guilt of *not doing enough*? We falsely believe that if we're not juggling fourteen balls in the air at one time, we're not worthy to be in the circus. So we serve as a church usher. And take that tutoring job on the side. And pray a little and feel guilty about not praying more. And say yes and yes and yes until we feel exhaustion and frustration seeping through our very pores.[284]

What if we instead trusted in the nature of the Body as interdependent and fueled by the strength and grace of the

---

[284] It is important to note here that this kind of "yes" mentality can also be tied to a deep seated belief that we must *do more* in order to *please God*. This was discussed in the first chapter. Our focus here is more interpersonal—*doing more* because we do not trust/realize that we are called to serve in interdependence with one another.

Spirit? Perhaps we could release the weight of needing to do everything and live in the joyous freedom of doing what we are specifically gifted to do.

> "Instead, speaking the truth in love, we will in all things grow up into Him who is the Head, that is, Christ. From him the whole body, joined and held together by every supporting ligament, grows and builds itself up in love, as each part does its work."[285]

Operating out of grace and with a deep awareness of our ultimate source, Jesus, the Body of Christ is divinely gifted to love, to serve, to embody and engage in creation-healing redemption. I have seen this kind of Spirit-empowered Body of Christ in action, and it is a beautiful organism to behold!

## THE BODY THROUGHOUT THE AGES

### The Body at Work—Cite Lespwa

One of my daughter Anna's dearest friends Britney was working in Les Cayes, Haiti on the afternoon of the earthquake of January 12, 2010. Within 48 hours, the nation of Haiti had lost at least 300,000 people, and Britney had passed through bloody, chaotic streets in Port-au-Prince to be evacuated from the country. Haunted by the faces of Haitian brothers and sisters in deep need and grief, Britney came up with a grand (dare I say impractical) vision for raising money in her city to aid in earthquake relief.

It was called Cite Lespwa, a tent city of hope set up on a college campus. For one week, residents of Shreveport, Louisiana slept outside, gave generously, created art and beauty, built relationships around bonfires, and expressed solidarity with the people of Haiti. Though this was one small extension of the Body of Christ around the world, many members—each with his or her own function—came together for the work of the Kingdom.

Using the Character Strengths of her Catalyzer floor, Britney engaged in bold, risky vision and used her ability to connect with others to pool resources, raise support, and give leadership to the endeavor. Another friend, using the Dreamer Character Strengths of introspection and reflection,

---

[285] Ephesians 4:15-16, New International Version.

made a blog—giving voice and reflection to the events, weaving metaphors, and making abstract concepts and connections come alive in the written word. Another individual with energy in her Energizer floor responded out of her creativity and self-expression to write music that was shared and shaped by those involved. One friend used his strengths as an Achiever to tend to all the behind-the-scenes details of the event regarding finances, management, and organization. And still another friend listened and gave relational and emotional support from her strong Harmonizer floor as others processed their grief and their hope.

Without any one of these individuals, this expression of God's heart and manifestation of the Kingdom of God would have looked different and been incomplete. From the public faces on the news to the calm, steady presence of a listening friend, no one was expendable in this Kingdom expanding work.

Cite Lespwa was a living manifestation of the Body connected to the Head, Jesus Christ—allowing each individual to operate out of his or her gifting. Each member had a purpose that was recognized, utilized, and surrendered for the furthering of the Kingdom. As a community, as individuals, they felt alive and *on purpose, with purpose.*

### Moses and Bezalel...Bezawho?

God has been specifically calling His people throughout the ages. Consider this scenario from ancient Israel. God very specifically called Moses—an Israelite raised in Egypt and one "slow of speech and tongue"[286]—to lead the Israelites out of slavery and into the land of promise. Moses' role was a highly visible one; his failures and successes were splashed about for the whole nation to see. He acted as a mediator between God and the people, on several occasions intervening in what could have been Israel's destruction.[287] Called by the voice of God through a burning bush, Moses' role was undeniably and unquestionably crucial to the nation of Israel.

Have you ever heard of Bezalel? Unlikely. Yet Bezalel was also specifically called and equipped for a work that God highly valued. Just like Moses, Bezalel was indispensable to

---

[286] Exodus 4:10, New International Version.
[287] See Exodus 32, 33.

God's revelation of Himself to the nation of Israel.

> "Then the Lord said to Moses, 'See, I have chosen Bezalel son of Uri, the son of Hur, of the tribe of Judah, and I have filled him with the Spirit of God, with skill, ability and knowledge in all kinds of crafts—to make artistic designs for work in gold, silver, and bronze, to cut and set stones, to work in wood, and to engage in all kinds of craftsmanship.'"[288]

Bezalel was individually purposed, designed, and gifted—with skillful hands—to craft elements of the Tent of Meeting and the ark of the Testimony with the excellence and artistry befitting a holy and glorious God. The Tent of Meeting, the ark, the Holy Place—these were the very spaces where God dwelt, the sites of sacrifice and atonement, the places of individual and communal worship. Not just anyone could haphazardly carry out the intricate and artistic details of construction. Moses mediated and led. Bezalel built. Both were uniquely designed and equipped. Both were essential to God's revelation of Himself to the people of Israel.

## A Time for Stretching?

So are we always meant to operate within our specific strengths? Or are there times when we are called as individuals to be stretched beyond what feels like our natural gifting?

Throughout Scripture, there are times when God endows an individual with a particular gift or strength for a specified task and period of time. In the Old Testament, there were certain instances where the "Spirit of God" came upon an individual, such as when Saul rescued the city of Jabesh or Balaam prophesied in Israel's favor.[289] In the time of the early church following Jesus' resurrection, the apostles performed miraculous signs and supernatural acts, carrying out divine instances of God's power working through them. After the descending of the Holy Spirit at Pentecost, the believers were speaking in languages and native tongues that were not their own. Peter healed a paralytic named Aeneas and raised a woman named Tabitha from the dead; Paul was bitten by a

---
[288] Exodus 31:1-5, New International Version.
[289] 1 Samuel 11:6; Numbers 24:2.

viper and experienced no harmful effects. Certainly even now there are times when we are supernaturally enabled to work outside of our natural giftings or capacities to complete that to which God has called us.[290] These instances, however, seem to be the exception rather than the rule. Whether we are using our natural strengths or being faithful to complete a task that feels very "unnatural," we are always gratefully dependent upon God's grace as the One who empowers and sustains us.

## "Where would the Body be?"

Paul says that each member of this miraculous Body of Christ "belongs to all the others." We *need* one another; our healthy functioning as a living, growing Body depends upon our distinctiveness as individuals as well as our interdependence upon Christ as our Head.

> "If the whole body were an eye, where would the sense of hearing be? If the whole body were an ear, where would the sense of smell be? But in fact God arranged the parts of the body, every one of them, just as he wanted them to be. If they were all one part, where would the body be? As it is, there are many parts, but one body."[291]

The work of the Kingdom is of the broadest spectrum imaginable—and the need is great. There are children who ache for the nourishment of touch and food, longing to be held and fed. Slaves around the world stuck in cycles of debt and oppression need bold adventurers who are willing to enter risky situations for the sake of human life. Impoverished nations benefit from economists who turn the power of their detailed, data-gathering minds to breaking the cycle of poverty. The imprisoned need someone to sing to them of hope. The forgotten need advocates. The despondent, disillusioned, and cynical are desperate for bright souls who create liberating, healing art in the midst of destruction and brokenness. The illiterate need teachers of truth. Elderly neighbors need someone to listen, to anticipate

---

[290] See Acts 2:5-11, 9:32-43, 28:3-6.
[291] 1 Corinthians 12:17-20, New International Version.

simple needs, and to serve quietly and consistently. Forgotten buildings need to be restored by the steady hands of those who find contentment in solitude and honest manual labor. The sick and dying depend upon the healing of a God who manifests Himself in the minds and hearts of analytical, compassionate physicians.

WITHOUT ANY ONE OF THESE,<br>"WHERE WOULD THE BODY BE?"

But even greater than this—even more central to the bringing of God's Kingdom to earth than recognizing individual purpose and function—is the awareness of the One to whom we all belong and through whom we are connected.

> "He [Jesus] existed before anything else, and he holds all creation together. Christ is also the head of the church, which is His body. He is the beginning, supreme over all those who rise from the dead. So he is first in everything. For God in all His fullness was pleased to live in Christ, and through Him God reconciled everything to Himself. He made peace with everything in heaven and on earth by means of Christ's blood on the cross."[292]

*That* is what makes the Kingdom come together and move forward.

## Redeemed Body

Not only does God redeem individual designs for His greater purposes, He also integrates all of these individual reflections of His image into a beautiful, imperfect Body. Is this Body made up only of the unscarred, the aesthetically pleasing, or the emotionally whole? What about those of us who are broken? The once-glorious designs obscured by regret, blurred by hatred, smothered by insecurity? What about the jagged reality that the elbow has a gash that currently prevents it from fully bending, or that this eye's vision is impaired by a cloud of self-doubt and shame? What about members of the Body—ourselves included—who have been bruised, beaten, self-destructive, hurtful, cruel, or

---

[292] Colossians 1:17-20, New Living Translation.

violated by another? Is there still a place for these broken members within the Body of Christ? Is there still a *purpose* for us?

Yes. Yes. Yes.

"THANKS BE TO GOD, WHO DELIVERS ME
THROUGH CHRIST JESUS OUR LORD!"[293]

Gary Smalley described God's invitation to us—all of us—in this way:

> "God designed you and created you to be filled with love from him and love for him. He intended to fill you with so much of his love that it would overflow into love for others and abound in reciprocal relationships resulting in a life utterly swimming in oceans of love."[294]

God does not just use your individual gifts and strengths for the good of the Kingdom; He is creative enough to redeem *every* element of your story for ultimate good. He welcomes each Image-Bearer—no matter how distorted or broken—to individually and communally live out His glorious redemption.

God is not particularly concerned with your history. He is interested in your *destiny*, in your becoming who He always intended you to be, in doing the work he set aside for you—from the beginning of all creation, when something glorious came out of nothing. It is through co-laboring with God that we experience His loving presence, and this presence transforms us into people who are fully known and fully loved.[295] You may truly feel His pleasure as you come to love who you are and embrace your true identity—a Servant by Design.

---

[293] Romans 7:25, New International Version.
[294] Smalley, Gary. (2012). *Change Your Heart, Change Your Life* (pp. 171). Nashville, TN: Thomas Nelson, Inc.
[295] For more on this idea of experiencing God's presence, check out Henry Blackaby and Claude V. King's fantastic book, *Experiencing God: Knowing and Doing the Will of God.*

## ABOUT THE AUTHORS

**Dr. Robert S. Maris** is a clinical psychologist who has divided his time between teaching, private practice, and writing in the areas of personality and "gifting" for over 40 years. Dr. Maris is the originator of the *Process Spiritual Model*™, an interpretation of Dr. Taibi Kahler's original work, the *Process Communication Model*® through a Christian world view. He lives in Little Rock, Arkansas with his wife Laura. He has three grown daughters, Shannon, Wendy, and Anna—the latter of which is the co-author of this work—and one grandson, Jack. He lives each day thankfully, in absolute wonder of God's goodness to him.

**Anna Maris Kirkes** began collaborating with her father in 2009 while pursuing her MFA in Dance Performance at the University of Iowa. After dancing professionally, Anna and her fantastic husband Justin moved to Shreveport, LA with their dog Gypsy, where they live and work on Centenary College of Louisiana's campus. In addition to writing, Anna also currently works as a freelance choreographer and dance teacher in various settings with people of all ages. She loves Jesus, coffee dates with friends, laughing, and cheesecake.

## APPENDICES

APPENDIX A: THE GOOD NEWS
APPENDIX B: PCM® KEY TERMS

# Harmonizer

*The Good News:*

### You are already unconditionally loved.

"See what great love the Father has lavished on us, that we should be called children of God!"

*1 John 3:1 (NIV)*

"My dear children, let's not just talk about love; let's practice real love. This is the only way we'll know we're living truly, living in God's reality. It's also the way to shut down debilitating self-criticism, even when there is something to it. For God is greater than our worried hearts and knows more about us than we do ourselves. And friends, once that's taken care of and we're no longer accusing and condemning ourselves, we're bold and free before God! We're able to stretch our hands out and receive what we asked for because we're doing what he said, doing what pleases Him!"

*1 John 3:18-22 (The Message)*

"Since God chose you to be the holy people he loves, you must clothe yourselves with tenderhearted mercy, kindness, humility, gentleness, and patience. Make allowance for each other's faults, and forgive anyone who offends you. Remember, the Lord forgave you, so you must forgive others. Above all, clothe yourselves with love, which binds us all together in perfect harmony. And let the peace that comes from Christ rule in your hearts. For as members of one body you are called to live in peace. And always be thankful."

*Colossians 3: 12-15 (NLT)*

"You're blessed when you can show people how to cooperate instead of compete or fight. That's when you discover who you really are, and your place in God's family."

*Matthew 5:9 (The Message)*

# ACHIEVER

*The Good News:*

YOU ARE IN THE CARE OF A GOD WHO IS SOVEREIGN, PERFECT, AND IN CONTROL.

"Trust God from the bottom of your heart; don't try to figure out everything on your own. Listen for God's voice in everything you do, everywhere you go; he's the one who will keep you on track. Don't assume that you know it all…Dear Friend, guard Clear Thinking and Common Sense with your life; don't for a minute lose sight of them. They'll keep your soul alive and well; they'll keep you fit and attractive. You'll travel safely; you'll neither tire nor trip. You'll take afternoon naps without a worry; you'll enjoy a good night's sleep. No need to panic over alarms or surprises, or predictions that doomsday's just around the corner, because God will be right there with you; he'll keep you safe and sound."

*Proverbs 3:5-6, 21-26 (The Message)*

"For God is not a God of disorder but of peace…"

*1 Corinthians 14:33 (NLT)*

"Work willingly at whatever you do, as though you were working for the Lord rather than for people. Remember that the Lord will give you an inheritance as your reward, and that the Master you are serving is Christ."

*Colossians 3:23-24 (NLT)*

"Be diligent to present yourself approved to God as a workman who does not need to be ashamed, accurately handling the word of truth."

*2 Timothy 2:15 (NASB)*

# Persister

*The Good News:*

GOD IS BOTH PERFECTLY JUST AND INFINITELY MERCIFUL; YOU ARE UNCONDITIONALLY VALUABLE TO HIM!

"You took over and set everything right; when I needed you, you were there, taking charge…God holds the high center, He sees and sets the world's mess right. He decides what is right for us earthlings; gives people their just deserts. God's a safe-house for the battered, a sanctuary during bad times. The moment you arrive, you relax; you're never sorry you knocked."

*Psalm 9:4, 7-10 (The Message)*

"There is joy for those who deal justly with others and always do what is right."

*Psalm 106:3 (NLT)*

"Love does no wrong to others, so love fulfills the requirements of God's law."

*Romans 13:10 (NLT)*

"Religion that God our Father accepts as pure and faultless is this: to look after orphans and widows in their distress and to keep oneself from being polluted by the world."

*James 1:27 (NIV)*

"God saved you by his grace when you believed. And you can't take credit for this; it is a gift from God. Salvation is not a reward for the good things we have done, so none of us can boast about it. For we are God's masterpiece. He has created us anew in Christ Jesus, so we can do the good things he planned for us long ago."

*Ephesians 2:8-10 (NLT)*

# Dreamer

*The Good News:*

YOU ARE PROTECTED UNDER THE SHADOW OF THE ALMIGHTY GOD'S WINGS. HE WILL BE YOUR STRENGTH.

"Light, space, zest—that's God! So, with Him on my side I'm fearless, afraid of no one and nothing…When besieged, I'm calm as a baby. When all hell breaks loose, I'm collected and cool. I'm asking God for one thing, only one thing: to live with him in his house my whole life long. I'll contemplate his beauty; I'll study at his feet. That's the only quiet, secure place in a noisy world, the perfect getaway, far from the buzz of traffic."

*Psalm 27:1-5 (The Message)*

"The Lord is my shepherd; I shall not want. He makes me lie down in green pastures; he leads me beside quiet waters. He restores my soul; He guides me in the paths of righteousness for His name's sake."

*Psalm 23:1-3 (NASB)*

"Make it your goal to live a quiet life, minding your own business and working with your hands, just as we instructed you before. Then people who are not Christians will respect the way you live, and you will not need to depend on others."

*1 Thessalonians 4:11-12 (NLT)*

"… there are many whose conduct shows they are really enemies of the cross of Christ…they think only about this life here on earth. But we are citizens of heaven, where the Lord Jesus Christ lives. And we are eagerly waiting for him to return as our Savior. He will take our weak mortal bodies and change them into glorious bodies like his own, using the same power with which he will bring everything under his control."

*Philippians 3: 18-21 (NLT)*

# CATALYZER

*The Good News:*

> YOU WILL NEVER BE ABANDONED BY GOD.
> YOU'VE BEEN INVITED INTO HIS FAMILY.

"Don't be obsessed with getting more material things. Be relaxed with what you have. Since God assured us, 'I'll never let you down, never walk off and leave you,' we can boldly quote, 'God is there, ready to help; I'm fearless no matter what. Who or what can get to me?'"

*Hebrews 13:5 (The Message)*

"Be strong. Take courage. Don't be intimidated. Don't give them a second thought, because God, your God, is striding ahead of you. He's right there with you. He won't let you down; he won't leave you."

*Deuteronomy 31:6 (The Message)*

"But don't just listen to God's word. You must **do** what it says. Otherwise, you are only fooling yourselves. For if you listen to the word and don't obey, it is like glancing at your face in a mirror. You see yourself, walk away, and forget what you look like. But if you look carefully into the perfect law that sets you free, and if you **do** what it says and don't forget what you heard, then God will bless you for **doing** it."

*James 1:22-25 (NLT)*

"For the Kingdom of God is not a matter of talk, but of power."

*1 Corinthians 4:20 (NIV)*

# Energizer

*The Good News:*

> NO MATTER HOW "UNACCEPTABLE" YOU ARE,
> YOU ARE FULLY FORGIVEN BY GOD.

"If you, O Lord, kept a record of sins, O Lord, who could stand?"

*Psalm 130:3 (NIV)*

"So now there is no condemnation for those who belong to Christ Jesus."

*Romans 8:1 (NLT)*

"So what do you think? With God on our side like this, how can we lose? If God didn't hesitate to put everything on the line for us, embracing our condition and exposing himself to the worst by sending His own Son, is there anything else he wouldn't gladly and freely do for us? And who would dare tangle with God by messing with one of God's chosen? Who would dare even to point a finger? The One who died for us—who was raised to life for us!—is in the presence of God at this very moment sticking up for us. Do you think anyone is going to be able to drive a wedge between us and Christ's love for us? There is no way!"

*Romans 8: 33-34 (The Message)*

"Count yourself lucky, how happy you must be—you get a fresh start, your slate's wiped clean. Count yourself lucky—GOD holds nothing against you and you're holding nothing back from him... Celebrate GOD. Sing together—everyone! All you honest hearts, raise the roof!"

*Psalm 32: 1-2, 11 (The Message)*

# PCM ® Key Terms:

*Personality Structure:*

the particular order of the six floors in my personality and how much energy I have available for each floor.

*Base:*

the core of "who I am;" the source of my greatest Character Strengths as well as the natural way I see the world, what needs I have, and how I respond in distress.

*Phase:*

the floor where I am currently experiencing my strongest Psychological Needs; identifiable in my Personality Structure as the first floor with less than 100%. I might also experience new patterns of distress in my Phase as I try to meet these new Needs.

*Stage:*

a floor in my personality that I have "phased through;" an experienced phase. My Stage floor is identifiable as any floor above my Base in which I have 100% energy. I no longer experience my immediate Needs here, but I can draw on these Character Strengths and still appreciate the Psychological Needs of this floor.

*Attic:*

a floor in my personality where I have very little energy (less than 25%). Staying on this floor and being asked to operate out of this floor's Strengths for very long will make me feel tired, stressed, frustrated, etc. It might also be hard for me to "see the world" through the eyes of my Attic.

*Six personality floors:*

Harmonizer, Achiever, Persister, Dreamer, Catalyzer, Energizer

*Character Strengths:*

Each personality floor has God-given qualities and gifts.

*Harmonizer*—sensitive, compassionate, warm
*Achiever*—logical, responsible, organized
*Persister*—dedicated, observant, conscientious
*Dreamer*—calm, reflective, imaginative
*Catalyzer*—adaptable, persuasive, charming
*Energizer*—spontaneous, creative, playful

From Kahler, T. (1996, 2012). The Process Communication Model® Seminar—Seminar One: Core Topics. Little Rock, AR: Kahler Communications, Inc.

## *Perceptions:*

Each personality floor has a God-given "Perception," the glasses through which we see the world. This is part of how we were created and also affects how we communicate with other people.

*Harmonizer*—emotions
*Achiever*—thoughts
*Persister*—opinions
*Dreamer*—inactions (reflections)
*Catalyzer*—actions
*Energizer*—reactions (likes/dislikes)

From Kahler, T. (1996, 2012). The Process Communication Model® Seminar—Seminar One: Core Topics. Little Rock, AR: Kahler Communications, Inc.

## *Psychological Needs:*

Each personality floor experiences satisfaction and energy in specific ways; Psychological Needs are the activities, relationships, and things that we crave and which give us energy. Relying on God to meet these Psychological Needs encourages and deepens our trust in Him.

*Harmonizer*—recognition of person and sensory
*Achiever*—recognition of work and time structure
*Persister*—recognition of work and conviction
*Dreamer*—solitude
*Catalyzer*—incidence
*Energizer*—contact

From Kahler, T. (1996, 2012). The Process Communication Model® Seminar—Seminar One: Core Topics. Little Rock, AR: Kahler Communications, Inc.

*Phase Change:*

change in site of current Psychological Needs into the next floor up in the Personality Structure; generally initiated by a period of long term, severe distress.

From Kahler, T. (1996, 2012). The Process Communication Model® Seminar—Seminar One: Core Topics. Little Rock, AR: Kahler Communications, Inc.

*Phasing:*

the period of distressed behavior that occurs when an individual is faced with the unresolved issue associated with his or her phase.

From Kahler, T. (1996, 2012). The Process Communication Model® Seminar—Seminar One: Core Topics. Little Rock, AR: Kahler Communications, Inc.

*Phase Issues:*

underlying issues associated with each phase floor; facing this issue authentically from the start will not result in a phase change. If the issue is not faced authentically, the individual then enters a period of distress until the issue is resolved and a phase change occurs.

*Harmonizer*— Anger
*Achiever*— Loss
*Persister*— Fear
*Dreamer*— Autonomy
*Catalyzer*— Abandonment
*Energizer*— Responsibility

From Kahler, T. (1996, 2012). The Process Communication Model® Seminar—Seminar One: Core Topics. Little Rock, AR: Kahler Communications, Inc.

*Deceptions:*

the belief that precedes the observable distress behavior; each personality floor is prone to believe a particular lie, assuming that I am only okay if...

*Harmonizer*—I am pleasing you.
*Achiever*—I am being perfect.
*Persister*—You are being perfect.
*Dreamer*—I am being strong.
*Catalyzer*—You are being strong.
*Energizer*—I am trying hard.

From Kahler, T. (1996, 2012). The Process Communication Model® Seminar—Seminar One: Core Topics. Little Rock, AR: Kahler Communications, Inc.

*Drivers:*

the behavioral clues that follow from the Deception, evident in verbal and non-verbal communications.

From Kahler, T. (1996, 2012). The Process Communication Model® Seminar—Seminar One: Core Topics. Little Rock, AR: Kahler Communications, Inc